BRANDING

IN FIVE
AND A HALF
STEPS

THE DEFINITIVE GUIDE TO THE STRATEGY AND DESIGN OF BRAND IDENTITIES

1 Investigate

2 Strategy and Narrative

2.5 Bridging the Gap

3 Design

4 Implement

5 Engage or Revive

MICHAEL JOHNSON

BRANDING

IN FIVE
AND A HALF
STEPS

900+ illustrations

Thames & Hudson

CONTENTS

Design 168

This is where the design work starts. Designers need to be briefed thoroughly and the creative process itself needs to be handled carefully. But what's the best way to do this? Should there be as many designers as possible working flat out in search of the answer? Or should we allow time for good ideas to percolate through (and the bad ones to fall away)? When should clients get involved, and how do you get all parties 'onside'? How do design decisions interface with strategic ones, and how do you know when you've got to the end of the design journey?

Engage or Revive 268

The importance of our last stage is only really starting to be understood: brands can be nurtured and cultured, but, once launched, there is another task that must be on-going. This is the job of ensuring a new idea is fully understood deep within an organization or culture, and creating ways to revitalize and refresh ideas that are out-of-date and in need of rejuvenation.

Implement 220

The key to this stage is the understanding that, while the hard graft of Step 1 and the verbal and visual creativity of Steps 2 and 3 are vital, without solid and consistent implementation, an idea can quickly fall apart. It could be the greatest strategic idea or the world's finest symbol, but if it isn't seen, heard or understood, then it will fail. Step 4 depends on a mixture of single-minded application and rule-making, and a willingness to be flexible and adapt if circumstances or budgets become a constraint.

INTRODUCTION

From humble beginnings as a mark on cattle to today's all-encompassing global ideas, the notion of something 'being branded' has moved a long, long way in a short space of time. Let's examine how we got to where we are, agree on a few ground rules and explode some myths...

tand in almost any airport or train station in the world and your senses are attacked by branding, from the 'go-faster' font chosen by the rail operator to the post-modern, manga-style logo of the sushi bar on the concourse. While one coffee bar tries to persuade you that it is offering the only truly 'authentic' hot drink to represent a bridge between your home life and your work life, another is offering you a taste of something knowingly 'European'. Meanwhile, a sandwich shop offers you a written manifesto on the freshness of its products, while a shirt shop tries very hard to look as though it has been there forever.

This is now our life: one surrounded by products, services and organizations whose wares have been carefully 'branded'. We encounter branding from the moment we get up, decide which shirt to wear, which breakfast cereal to eat, which paper to read, which browser to use, which museum to visit at the weekend. All our decisions are driven, whether we like it or not, by branding.

Those who create and control brands often keep the 'process' close to their chest. It's a specialized industry, with its own unique language and methods. But it's actually an industry split in two. On one side, strategists and planners wield impenetrable charts, proprietary methods and PowerPoint decks, and their job is to research, distil and provide insight. On the other are the designers and communicators who interpret the strategic ideas and bring a brand or a campaign to life.

Writing a coherent brand strategy and getting it agreed is one thing, while creating a visual identity to match is another. Very, very few people are involved throughout every step and truly understand each stage. So that's the purpose of this book: to unpick, lay bare and better understand this often baffling, sometimes banal, but occasionally beautiful business.

Next time you're in a station or an airport, consider what all these brands are saying to you and how they make you feel. Just a few colours and typefaces conjure up completely different responses and reactions.

BIT BY BIT, STAGE BY STAGE

The majority of this book – in its five and a half steps – concerns the stages that most branding (or re-branding) projects will go through.

12 2.5 3 4 5

The early steps of the branding process – research, strategy and narrative; traditionally the domain of strategists and planners (sometimes cruelly called 'suits' in the advertising business)

The bit in the middle when one side tries to talk to the other

The design and implementation stages, which are often owned by those prickly, unpredictable creative types wearing difficult glasses

The true point of the book, however, is that rather than assume that you are either interested in Steps 1 and 2 or Steps 3, 4 and 5, I am assuming that you are interested in all of it. The narrative side of things may not be your 'thing', today, right now, but one day it might be useful to know more. Conversely, the avid reader might intend to read only the first half, but might keep going and find something of interest. Importantly, to show that branding is a continuum, Step 2.5 deals with the 'blurring' between strategy and design, and Step 5 with the way an idea can be embedded within a company, revisited and revitalized.

WHY PUT IT ALL IN ONE BOOK?

Well, there are almost no books out there that look at the entire process. There are a ton of strategic books on Steps 1 and 2, which are fascinating, in that 'buy it at the airport and I'll be an expert when I land' way, but they're often dense, with few images, and almost always proffer their own *Perfect Brand Theory*™ rather than give a synthesis of what's already being used. Conversely, there are 3,000 books on logos, 4,000 on symbols and very few on the processes and pitfalls of designing them, getting them approved and making sure they're properly used. So, that's the gap this book is going to fill.[1]

It's your choice. You could devour a pile of books on brand strategy, and then another pile on design, communications and logos. They are all great books in their own right, but they are in two quite separate camps...

AS WIDE A SCOPE AS POSSIBLE

If you read some of these books then you'll start to form the erroneous impression that, from the strategy side at least, the only serious users of 'branding' theory are manufacturers of fizzy drinks and training shoes, i.e., mass-market, business-to-consumer marketers. From the creative side, you may think that the only things designers ever care about are cool little geometric logos for arts institutions. (And, of course, there's a little bit of truth in both of these generalizations.)

But the theory and practice of branding is now as applicable to a city or a country as it is to a charity or a corporation. So the 'church' of examples in this book is determinedly broad and determinedly global. I have included a few dozen of my own projects, but usually just to make a key point that would have been tricky to illustrate otherwise (and I'm hoping that certain clients are going to be fine about the 'reveal all' nature of some of this).

SO, HOW DID WE GET HERE?

For centuries, 'branding' was little more than the signature of proprietors on the corner of their packaging; the word 'branding' didn't mean what it has come to mean now. The business of designing or choosing a 'logo', or a trademark, preceded branding as we now know it. A hundred and fifty years ago, Bass couldn't rely entirely on a famous Impressionist painting to do all its advertising,[2] so they sent a young man to be first in line on 1 January 1876 as the Trade Mark Registration Act came into effect. Hence Bass became one of the first companies in the world to register a trademark: for Bass & Co's Pale Ale. This wasn't a decision driven by a month-long series of design workshops and focus groups; Bass just wanted to 'protect' its red triangle, so it was theirs and no one else's.[3]

▾ Ford symbol / The Partners / UK / 2003   ▾ Boots symbol / UK / Original 1883

WHEN DID IDENTITY STOP AND BRANDING START?

The real origins of what we now call branding started to develop not long after that young man stood in that queue. Companies around the world began to formalize the way they presented their symbols, corporate 'signatures' and 'brand names'. Many of those hand-written, signature-style logos still exist in some form today, from Ford, through Fender and Boots, to the 'Spencerian'[4] script of Coca-Cola.

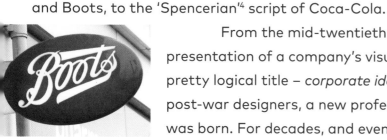

From the mid-twentieth century onwards, the consistent presentation of a company's visual 'identity' acquired a new and pretty logical title – *corporate identity* – and in the hands of the great post-war designers, a new profession and title, *graphic designer*, was born. For decades, and even in some circles now, the phrase 'corporate identity' held sway. Certain pioneering consultancies would attempt to broaden the phrase to incorporate the 'personality' of organizations[5] (as they dug deeper into a corporation's psyche), but for the most part it was a nascent profession concerned with logos, symbols and the basic applications thereof, carried out as well and as consistently as possible.

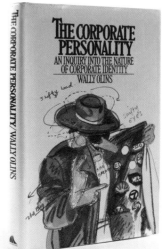

But as organizations started to ask more profound questions about what they stood for, what they valued and what their consumers thought of them, 'corporate identity' seemed to be too closely aligned to the visual and not closely enough to the verbal. If you wanted to talk about the reasons why someone chose your product or service, how they felt about that purchase, and whether you could begin to control or define that 'why' and 'how', there wasn't really a word available – not one that seemed to sum up all the tangible and intangible aspects, the functional *and* the emotional. So into this nomenclature vacuum fell the word 'brand'.

While branding (in its widest sense) and brand identity (in its visual sense) may not be perfect words, they are broad enough to encapsulate how an organization looks, how it 'feels' and how it wants others to feel about it. Many commentators will still use the word 'identity', but usually to mean the physical aspects of logos, symbols, colours, images and typefaces. To give you an example, if we talked about Virgin's 'brand identity', then most people would assume that we were talking about the scribbly signature logo and how it appears on planes, trains and credit cards.

▴ *The Corporate Personality* / Wally Olins / UK / 1978

A BRIEF TIMELINE OF BRANDING THEORY[6]

INDUSTRIAL ERA
1870s   The first trademarks are registered in the UK, USA and Germany

MODERN ERA
1905   Coca-Cola's 1905 slogan 'Coca-Cola Revives and Sustains'
1907   Peter Behrens appointed world's first 'industrial designer' at AEG Germany
1928   Edward Bernays pioneers public relations (PR)
1931   P&G's Neil McElroy invents the concept of 'brand managers'
1936   Dale Carnegie's *How to Win Friends and Influence People* published

POST-WAR: CONSUMER BOOM
Dominance of graphic design and design 'systems'
1940s   Lippincott and Margulies formed
1950s   Televisions become available
1955   Gardner and Levy coin the term 'brand image'
1956   Paul Rand designs the IBM logo
1964   Landor move to a ferryboat in San Francisco Bay
1965   Wolff Olins founded
1968   Social protests, revolution and baby boomers

POST-MODERN ERA: GLOBALIZATION
Dominance of advertising
1972   Al Ries and Jack Trout's article 'Positioning: The Battle for your Mind' published in *Advertising Age*
1978   Wally Olins' *The Corporate Personality* published
1981   Al Ries and Jack Trout's Positioning book becomes a bestseller
1984   Former McKinsey consultant Michael Lanning coins term 'value proposition'
1984   Apple Computer's iconic TV ad
1986   Jean-Noël Kapferer coins 'brand identity' phrase
1986   C. Whan Park, Bernard J. Jaworski and Deborah J. MacInnis's *Strategic Brand Concept-Image Management* published, coining the term 'Brand Concept Management' (BCM)
1988   First Interbrand brand valuation for Rank Hovis McDougall
1989   Wally Olins' *Corporate Identity* published

EARLY 1990s: SERVICES ECONOMY
Development of the internet, mobile phones and major global brands; branding matures as a discipline and 'science' of branding begins; era of the fast-moving consumer goods brand model – Unilever brand Key, McDonald's Ladder, Johnson & Johnson footprint
1990   Mergers and acquisitions triggered by prospect of single European market raises question of brand equity
1991   David A. Aaker's *Managing Brand Equity* published
1992   Jean-Noël Kapferer's *Strategic Brand Management* published
1994   Superbrands organization founded; first book published 1995
1994   Orange brand launch

LATE 1990s: HEIGHT OF CONSUMERISM, POST-MODERNISM
1993   Y&R BrandAsset Valuator introduced
1996   David A. Aaker's *Building Strong Brands* published
1996   Diesel opens flagship stores: retail as brand experience
1997   Apple Think Different campaign
1998/99   The movies *The Truman Show* and *The Matrix* both demonstrate awareness of a constructed reality
1999   Introduction of euro
1999   NikeTown opens in London
1999   Rita Clifton's *The Future of Brands* published

ANTI-CAPITALISM
1999   *The Blair Witch Project* movie – idea of home-made, authentic/lack of polish begins
1999   Naomi Klein's *No Logo* becomes a bestseller
1999   Launch of Innocent

POST-POST-MODERN ERA: DIGITAL
Branding takes over from advertising
2001   Keller's 'Customer-Based Brand Equity Pyramid'
2002   Marc Gobé's *Emotional Branding* published
2003   Wally Olins' *On Brand* published
2005   Seth Godin's *All Marketers Are Liars* published
2006   Marty Neumeier's *The Brand Gap* published
2006   John Grant's *The Brand Innovation Manifesto* published
2008   Financial crisis
2009   Simon Sinek's *Start With Why* published

2010–2015 INVERTING AUTHORITY
'Omnichannel' begins, agile methodology, collaboration, 'hipster' culture, social responsibility, start-up culture, social media
2010   Alexander Osterwalder's *Business Model Generation* published
2010   Ogilvy & Mather: 'The big ideaL'
2015   Wolff Olins' *Impossible and Now* published

2016   *Branding. In Five and a Half Steps: The Definitive Guide to the Strategy and Design of Brand Identities* published!

But if we asked 'what makes up Virgin's brand', we'd be balancing a whole basket of values, behaviours, the principle of 'challenging in markets', the irrepressible personality of its bearded founder – *and* the way the logo appears on planes, trains and credit cards... In essence, the whole kit and caboodle, of which the 'scribble' is just one part – the tip of a branding iceberg, if you like.

This broadening of what 'identity' once meant into what 'branding' now encompasses is, on one level, frustrating, as it takes hundreds of valuable words to explain the difference. But on another level, it is hugely liberating. Twenty years ago, my job started with a design brief and soon after that the commencement of the logo design. This was fine if those who wrote the brief were *completely clear* about what was needed, both then and in the future; were in complete agreement within their organization; and had some uncanny sixth sense about what was coming around the corner. Often, it was not fine. Twenty years later, the actual logo design might not start for six months, if ever, but when it does, and if the preliminary work has been done correctly, it will be a process starting in the *right place* and answering the *right questions* – rather than starting in the wrong place and offering solutions to wrongly identified problems.

HOW DO YOU DEFINE BRANDING? IT'S TRICKY

Nailing a definitive and irrefutable definition of branding is quite a challenge (a bit like defining what 'design' is).[7] Gathered here for you are just a few of the options, in seven broad groups. As you can see, each perspective is slightly different, and there is no agreed definition. Bewildering as this may seem, it reflects branding's relative youth as a discipline.[8]

Defined by visual identity, symbol or trademark

A trademark, whether made by burning or otherwise. (Applied to trademarks on casks of wines or liquors, timber, metals, and any description of goods except textile fabrics.)
Or
A particular sort or class of goods, as indicated by the trademarks on them.
Oxford English Dictionary

'A brand is a name, term, sign symbol (or a combination of these) that identifies the maker or seller of the product.'
Philip Kotler and Gary Armstrong

Defined by the tangible and intangible

'*The intangible sum of a product's attributes: its name, packaging, and price, its history, its reputation, and the way it's advertised.*'
David Ogilvy

'*A brand is an identifiable product, service, person or place, augmented in such a way that the buyer or user perceives relevant unique added values which match their needs most closely.*'
Leslie de Chernatony

'*In addition to our more formal textbook definitions, the most frequent themes to emerge are that a brand is a "relationship", a "reputation", a "set of expectations", a "promise".*'
Rita Clifton

Defined by customer perceptions

'Your brand, fundamentally, is the bundle of thoughts, feelings, actions and impulses about you that people have out there in the world – and that's why it's so powerful.'
Robert Jones

'A brand is a person's gut feeling about a product, service, or organization.'
Marty Neumeier

'Your brand is what other people say about you when you're not in the room.'
Jeff Bezos

Defined as a holistic system

'Brand is a delicate dance between intended meanings sent by the company and perceived meanings elicited through customer responses.'
Giep Franzen and Sandra E. Moriarty

'Brand is like film production: it's about bringing everything together with a purpose, knowing what you want to say, having a sense of the story, and finding an original and compelling way to get it across.'
Jane Wentworth

Defined by a promise or contract

'A brand is the contract between a company and consumers.'
Simon Clift

'A brand is the set of expectations, memories, stories and relationships that, taken together, account for a consumer's decision to choose one product or service over another. If the consumer (whether it's a business, a buyer, a voter or a donor) doesn't pay a premium, make a selection or spread the word, then no brand value exists for that consumer.'
Seth Godin

Defined by vision, values and actions

'[It's] about values. It's a complicated and noisy world, and we're not going to get a chance to get people to remember much about us. No company is. So we have to be really clear about what we want them to know about us.'
Steve Jobs (in reference to marketing)

'Authentic brands don't emerge from marketing cubicles or advertising agencies. They emanate from everything the company does. If enough people believe they share values with a company, they will stay loyal to the brand.'
Howard Schultz

Defined by a sense of social grouping

'It is about belonging: belonging to a tribe, to a religion, to a family. Branding demonstrates that sense of belonging. It has this function for both the people who are part of the same group and also for the people who don't belong.'
Wally Olins

WHY BRAND (OR RE-BRAND)?

There are many reasons to brand something new, or re-brand something old. Here's a starter list of the many factors affecting the decision.

Re-brand forced by corporate change

Increased tension throughout the 1990s between Andersen Consulting and Arthur Andersen led to a court settlement requiring the 'consulting' arm to pay owed fees and choose a new name (eventually based on the mixture of 'accent' and 'future').[9]

Re-branding to reflect structural realignment

Related to the above, branding can help with re-definition when organizations need to differentiate between one part of themselves and another. Google re-organized its structure under a newly created 'umbrella' brand called Alphabet, while the (PRODUCT)[RED] brand allows for multiple members of the (PRODUCT)[RED] brand family (see page 145).[10]

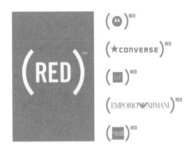

Re-brand forced by the competition

In highly competitive markets, re-branding can provide an extra edge – on the supermarket shelf, standing out can play a crucial role in sales. In the charity and NGO sector, to maintain or increase market share, many charities are now seeing re-branding as a strategic tool to drive awareness and to propel their commercial activities and fundraising.

Brands created from market insight and/or gaps in the market

Some of the greatest successes were created in response to a 'gap' in a market that the new product duly filled. Some innovations, of course, created markets for products people didn't even know they needed, such as the Walkman and the iPod (see page 72).

Re-branding to force a change of perception

There is a reason why countries and cities develop 'destination' and tourism brands. They hope that, by presenting themselves in a fresh and more coherent light, more visitors will be attracted (see page 205).

Re-branding forced by performance

Basic lack of consumer awareness can force a change of name or a wholesale brand identity change. For brands that are failing, starting again may help in the eyes of their customer (see page 287), or it may represent their final throw of the dice.

Re-branding forced by the product life cycle

Sometimes an idea or a product just reaches the end of its useful life. The decision must then come whether to abandon it or to create something new, seemingly out of thin air (see page 302).

Re-branding to seem more relevant and authentic

The days of organizations presenting themselves in the same way for decades have long gone. At its most basic level, a re-brand can, for a time, present a new approach. But if it's just wallpapering over cracks, 21st-century consumers and clients can often see straight through an inauthentic offer (see page 117).

The need to simplify

It is human nature to truncate people's names, so many brands are now doing the same with theirs. Federal Express simply became known by its nickname FedEx, Pan American Airways became Pan Am, The National Art Collections Fund eventually became Art Fund (see page 288). And what about PricewaterhouseCoopers? It bowed to the inevitable...

The need for clearer intellectual property

Even for brands as clearly identifiable as Habitat, by the early 2000s there was a need to better protect their name and

trademark. The addition of a symbol to the famous typographic mark did exactly that (see page 188).

The need to align brand with corporate strategy

Branding projects often come at a critical time for organizations and, carried out well, they can become a crucial catalyst for massive change. Therefore, the process of 'choosing the right route' can, itself, become a highly charged symbol of a new strategic direction (see page 128).

Reflecting mergers, de-mergers and internal politics

While Accenture's creation came as the result of a legal agreement between those sharing the 'Andersen' name, United Airlines wanted to reflect the acquisition of Continental Airlines. Having used variants of their 'tulip' symbol for 35 years, they switched in 2010 to a 'merger identity' based on Continental's typography and symbol. Later that same year, United Airlines adopted a typestyle more akin to their 2000s design approach, but retained Continental's globe symbol over the tulip.[11]

See the further credits on page 319 for design credits

'Santa', as we know and love him, is both the product of several historical myths merged into one and the clever colour-coding of a global soft drink.

WHAT BRANDING CAN DO

The direct corollary of the previous spread is that branding's power is now immense. In the right hands, and done well, branding can realign organizations and raise millions in donated funds or billions on the stockmarket. Re-branding can make us re-assess companies, countries and their citizens. It can transform the fate of ailing and failing services and make them relevant, wanted and understood again.

Even some of our most treasured cultural icons have undergone significant re-branding. The Santa Claus that children love and adults' bank balances loathe is himself a strange mash-up of Sinterklaas, a figure from French Flanders, Lorraine and Artois, and the pagan, mythical and also bearded figure of Odin. Export him to New Amsterdam (soon itself to be re-branded 'New York'), merge him with the Saint Nicolas tradition and mix in a Victorian revival of 'Father Christmas', and you have the basis of what we now see every late autumn.[12]

What solidified 'Santa' as we now know him was Haddon Sundblom's iconic Coca-Cola advertising of the 1930s, finally aligning our annual visitor to a suitably branded colour scheme (and his drink of choice in the process).[13]

If branding can effectively create Santa, what else can it do? In this book we will see how branding has enhanced the standing of footballers and presidents, turned little-known niche brands into world players and created multi-million-dollar businesses out of thin air. Take Abercrombie & Fitch. Who'd have thought that a sports goods manufacturer that closed for business in the mid-1970s[14] would be revived and emblazoning the shopping bags of teenage girls worldwide 30 years later? That, you'll have to agree, is the power of branding (and some carefully chosen male torsos).

We will also see that, in the wrong hands, the power of branding can work just as powerfully against us as for us. It can make us believe in things that we think are genuine and authentic, but are anything but. We'll also see that there's an underlying core of 'non-believers' who will have nothing to do with branding (even though their companies are, of course, impeccably 'branded').

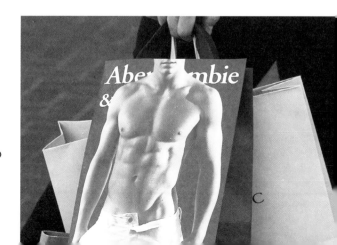

THE PARADOX OF 'BRANDED' GOODS

Brands have become so much part of our lives that we go to extraordinary lengths to bask in the status that certain classics seem to offer. Professional women regularly spend a month's salary on a handbag, replace it at the start of a new season, or seek good-quality fakes. Meanwhile, European and Japanese men regularly 'de-badge' their cars to remove any hint of which model they have purchased. This is either to gain credibility points among friends for owning a 'luxury' car marque (but not admitting that it is the cheapest, lowest-priced model) or to individualize what started as a factory product into their own customized property. In fact, most European manufacturers now offer a 'badge delete' option when a car is ordered, thus removing the need to carry out the tricky process of removing the chromium letters and scratching off the glue.

Owners of Leica cameras have long been taping over the distinctive red 'dot' logo on the body of the camera. Having saved up a significant amount of money to buy one, many new owners 'de-badge' them with humble gaffer tape.[15] Partly this behaviour is partly driven by pure economics and the hope that by removing the red roundel they will deter thieves, and partly it is for practical reasons – a street

photographer may hope it will help them merge further into the background. Perhaps there's also some inverse snobbery at play here: 'If you can spot the meaning of the black tape, then you can join the club.' You could, of course, opt to buy a version direct from Leica, without the distinctive dot.[16] Unfortunately, that will increase the price.

▸ Fake Prada handbag / Turkey / 2015 ▸ De-badged BMW 3 series

▸ De-badged Leica M series

• Enron logo / Paul Rand USA / 1995

▸ Yahoo logo development / In-house / USA / 2013

CAN GREAT BRANDING GUARANTEE SUCCESS?

The truth is you can have the greatest logo by the greatest living brand designer, but there is no guarantee of success. American gas and oil powerhouse Enron was a 70-billion-dollar company at its height. As befitted a company of that status, it turned to Paul Rand (who had designed the IBM and UPS symbols) for its angled 'E' monogram. Certain aspects of the new logo didn't bode well – colours dropped out when photocopied, and the mark could be interpreted as an obscene hand gesture by Italians. But as soon as Enron's dubious accounting practices began to come to light (the company filed for bankruptcy in late 2001), the 'crooked E' became an unfortunately apt symbol of a crooked company.[17]

Rand had forewarned others 10 years previously in an essay that 'a well-designed logo is a reflection of the business it symbolizes. It connotes a thoughtful and purposeful enterprise, and mirrors the quality of its products and services.' In Enron's case, perhaps only too well.[18]

Failure isn't restricted to the traditional corporate brand – we will see how Myspace stumbled (page 287) and how the digital pioneers of the 'portal' have found themselves turning to re-brands to revitalize their offering.

Yahoo confidently trumpeted its own re-brand by rolling out multiple versions over a 30-day period before settling on one, actually quite conservative, option.[19] AOL (see page 176) chose a more flexible identity, at least for re-launch. But for both pioneers it's still not clear if their re-brands will have truly and successfully repositioned them in the eyes of their consumers and, critically, their investors.

THE POWER OF POLITICAL SYMBOLISM

For centuries, generals and politicians have known the rallying power of a single unifying image behind which armies and eventually countries can unite. Legion banners were held aloft as the Romans marched into battle, serving to rally troops and intimidate enemies.

The Nazis knowingly adopted the 'Roman' approach to symbolism (as shown above) when they took an Indian fertility symbol,[20] turned it 45 degrees and made it the centrepiece of enormous red, black and white banners. A predilection for beheading and remorseless intimidation might be ISIS's 'narrative', but their visual imagery is carefully constructed white-out-of-black typography, Hollywood-style videos and the SS-like choice of a gothic black uniform.

Even the anti-capitalist (and presumably anti-brand) Occupy movement eventually adopted a graphic 'style',[21] but its universal visual symbol of protest remains the consistent

use of plastic Guy Fawkes masks – guaranteed to supply a surreal and jarring image for the front pages of the world's newspapers. Meanwhile, the Hong Kong democracy protests of 2014

chose an umbrella as their visual device after a councillor intentionally opened a yellow umbrella inside a reception. At that moment the 'symbol' of the movement was born and the 'umbrella revolution' was branded.[22]

Sometimes these symbols are 'born again' when they are re-discovered by new generations. A French graphic designer turned to the 1950s Campaign for Nuclear Disarmament (CND) symbol[23] for his poignant graphic protest at the Paris attacks of 2015, simply replacing the downward diagonals of the original with the sturdy legs of Paris's most famous monument.[24]

▲ CND flag / Gerald Holtom / UK / 1958

▲ 'Peace for Paris' symbol / Jean Jullien / France / 2015

INTIMIDATION OR CELEBRATION?

The meanings of some visual devices have now become so loaded that they acquire visceral importance to their owners. If you're a resident of Lewes, near Brighton on the south coast of England, the procession of 17 burning crosses every November stems from an early 17th-century reminder to the then pope Paul V (and, presumably, every pope since) that the burning of 17 Protestant martyrs wasn't acceptable.[25]

Conversely, the planting of a burning cross outside someone's house was the ultimate form of intimidation that Ku Klux Klan members could summon up. If you go one stage further and turn the cross upside down, then you're either reflecting the historical stance of St Peter (who refused to be crucified in the same manner as Christ) or you're actually a closet satanist who reveres the reversed cross for its more sinister meanings. Choose your crosses (and your orientation) carefully...

Meanwhile, the annual Burning Man festival in the USA creates an annual variant on its humanistic theme and then sets it alight, apparently as a metaphor for inclusion, self-reliance and self-expression.[26] So that's pope-baiting, racism and self-expression, all in three paragraphs, and three pretty different definitions of the meaning of burning wooden structures. And each symbol's proponents would vigorously defend the uniqueness and relevance of its particular treatment.

▲ Lewes bonfire celebrations / UK / early 1600s onwards   ▲ Ku Klux Klan / USA / from 1920s onwards

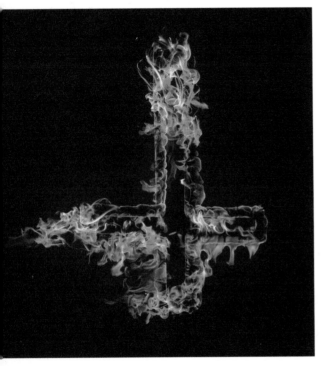 

◄ Upturned cross as a symbol of satanism   ▲ The Crucifixion of St Peter / Italy / 1st century AD

A Protestant protest or a statement of intimidation? It depends which side of the Atlantic you're on.

▲ Orange amplifiers / UK / from 1960s onwards
▲ Orange mobile telecommunications / UK, France / from 1990s onwards
▲ The Orange Revolution / Ukraine / 2004
◄ Orange Order / The Grand Orange Lodge of Scotland / Ireland / Scotland / from 1798 onwards

ONE MAN'S AMP, ANOTHER'S PHONE, MARCH OR REVOLUTION

A name can be appropriated by one organization to mean something completely different. To generations of guitar players, the name 'Orange' and an orange square represent a certain kind of guitar amplifier. Yet fast-forward to the 1990s and a graphic orange square was chosen to symbolize a groundbreaking brand in mobile telecommunications. Same name, same colour, same square, but a completely different 'bundle' of tangible and intangible emotions.[27]

Even the colour orange itself can mean completely different things to different people – to the Dutch the colour orange symbolizes William of Orange, who led a revolt against the French over 400 years ago.[28] So powerful is the colour to the Dutch that carrots were genetically mutated away from their purpley blue, and their sports teams long ago adopted the colour, virtually

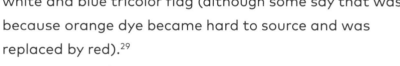

abandoning their much more predictable red, white and blue tricolor flag (although some say that was because orange dye became hard to source and was replaced by red).[29]

To a marcher in Northern Ireland, the colour is also synonymous with William of Orange, but in the form of the Orangemen who parade every year to commemorate the Protestant victory at the Battle of the Boyne.[30]

Whether embodied in symbols of protest, in the figure of the cross or in particular colours, the power of visual cues and their different histories is immense.

Increasingly, modern brands have been learning and borrowing from these historical sources of inspiration to create their own branding myths.

▸ KNVB shirt / The Netherlands / 1980s

BRANDING IN THE AGE OF UBIQUITY

Branding has been brought to the fore by the advent of product ubiquity. Once there was only one type of soda, a single mode of transport, solitary bars of soap, but, for at least the last hundred years, there has been choice, and with choice comes decision (and indecision). And, there to help, whether you want it or not, is branding.

The choice of which bottled water to buy can seem mind-boggling, but next time you're in a supermarket and you have to pick one out think about what you're consciously (or unconsciously) doing. Why are you selecting one bottle over another? Can you *really* taste the difference? So is it actually the bottle shape or the font that you are choosing? Probably not. What about the ad you drove past in your car, or skimmed in the paper, or the 'emotional' bond that may have developed between you and a particular type of water? Any one of these factors may have had an effect.

Consider cars: there's an aerodynamically driven reason why modern cars follow a similar streamlined shape. Trouble is, it means they tend to look the same. So the drive to establish a difference between cars, to make us form some type of connection to one brand over another, becomes hugely important. Often, it's only the 'brand' that helps us tell one car apart from another, because, as shown by the diagram opposite, their physical shapes aren't going to help us very much.[31]

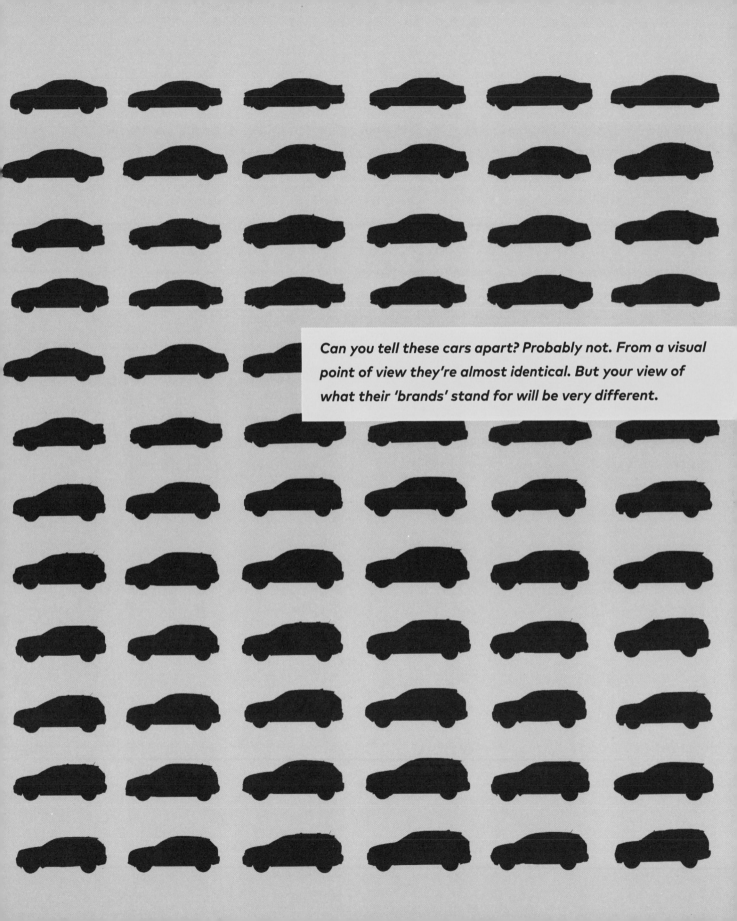

Can you tell these cars apart? Probably not. From a visual point of view they're almost identical. But your view of what their 'brands' stand for will be very different.

HOW BRANDING MAKES A DIFFERENCE

Branding can be a genuine game-changer. The discipline has come a long, long way, from starting out as the stamping of marks of ownership on the backsides of cattle, through the manufacture of identities for products competing on supermarket shelves, to the creation of complex marketing and communications glue for countless global organizations.

At a banal level, a slight tweak of pizza packaging can lead to an increase in sales. At another level, a world-famous airline can fight off predators by 're-positioning' itself in the minds of its customers. Meanwhile, an innate sense of brand ownership can make adults ride old-fashioned, massively vibrating motorcycles such as Harley-Davidsons purely because of the perceived 'cool' they give off.

Now, I'm the first to admit that branding has its downsides – and some organizations are more than capable of using and misusing the ideas discussed in this book. There's no doubt that in the hands of the dangerous or the eyes of the gullible (whether they be terrorists or clothes horses), branding works at a psychological level that can be downright scary.

But I'm going to stay positive. At a higher level, I'm going to show you how the re-branding of NGOs can transform their ability to raise funds, help millions of lives and fundamentally alter the way donors understand what they do, and how they do it.

We'll see a university start to raise funds and attract more graduate students, a school write down a set of 'beliefs' we would all love to sign up to. We'll see how corporations can use branding to help them merge and de-merge, see brands appear and disappear, and watch how brand and brand identity can translate flux into change made visible…and sometimes change that helps people's lives.

Branding has its naysayers and detractors. It has those who deny it even exists and, conversely, those who *know* it exists, yet fear its power.

So you can reject or deny what branding does. Or you can read on, find out how branding works and decide how best to use it to your advantage.

↑ *Easy Rider* / Featuring Peter Fonda and Dennis Hopper / Columbia Pictures / USA / 1969

For many, having a Harley is abo
a universal 'cool' that the brand
(not the bone-shattering ride tho

Finding out where a brand stands (or, more importantly, doesn't stand) in a market is a crucial first step. If you don't investigate, immerse yourself and carry out proper research, then you won't understand the issues. You'll end up creating fantastic solutions – for the wrong problems. Step 1 can help to identify the correct problems to solve...

1

INVESTIGATE

The biggest temptation at the start of any brand project is for someone to stand up and declare that they know exactly what the problem is and how it should be fixed.

Now, of course, that kind of certainty can be very appealing. If you're reading this as a client, there's something undeniably attractive about booking a meeting with a brand consultant who will declare they have the answer after just 20 minutes' conversation. Just think how much you could save on fees; you could just jump ahead to Step 3 and start designing...

The chance naturally of that assertion, or that hunch, being correct depends on a number of factors – the residual knowledge that people hold, a few well-informed guesses and a healthy dose of luck. The point of this first, investigative step, however, is not to rely much on hunches, or luck. You truly need to understand the market for an idea, product or service, and how the latter is perceived (and whether that perception is good, bad or indifferent). Without this, how are you going to create a brand idea that stands out? If there were already 47 books available on the entire branding process, would I have sat down and written this? Probably not – in other words, there was a significant 'gap' in a market that could be filled.

Organizational brands often forget to ask their own staff what they should do, and where they think they should go. Other companies assume they know their target market, yet swiftly discover they have spent so long on 'product' that they're not sure who that product is actually for any more. That's the point of this step. Before you go anywhere, *work out where you are first, where you could be, and whether you are strategically capable of getting there.*

If you were a Martian who had just landed on Earth, you could visit almost every major city and find the metro station – they all present themselves in strikingly similar ways.

SAME OLD, SAME OLD

It is remarkable just how much unanimity you find when you start examining many sectors. Rather than stand out and demonstrate difference, many markets exhibit a sheep-like herd mentality. For some reason, virtually every 'brand' that you encounter for mass transportation involves a geometric, often monogrammatic (i.e., based upon a letter), one- or two-colour mark designed to be back-lit on a tall pole somewhere.[1]

If you don't believe me, then look around at other sectors. Take universities and colleges: their logos are often blue, purple or red, featuring crests and semi-heraldic devices, with the names written in extra-large letters. Or logos for countries and tourism: they are almost always multi-coloured and feature paint-brushed, hand-drawn lettering.

So why do they do this? Mass transit has followed historical precedent and presents itself as clear and uncluttered. The education sector is saying 'trust me, I'm serious, that's why my NAME IS WRITTEN IN CAPS' (and 'my shield has a book in it, for goodness sake, I must be smart'). The tourism sector is saying 'our country is vibrant, exciting and multi-faceted, and this is where you should spend your well-earned tourist dollar'. From Chile to Croatia and Malta to the Maldives, the message seems to be the same...and yet Chile and Croatia could not be more different.

The same applies to the words that companies use as their straplines. 'Good things come to those who wait' works beautifully for dark beer that takes a while to pour (Guinness), but even a cursory glance at the straplines of countless other organizations reveals thousands of people *connecting to others*, *reaching higher*, *helping others feel good* and *seeing a better future*.

Ask Why? / Be Your Way / Distilled in Hell / High performance. Delivered / High performance. Amplified / Cutting through complexity / Live your life / Intelligence everywhere / Delivering on the promise / By knowledge, design and understanding / Tomorrow's answers today / For people who spit blood when they clean their teeth / We make it nice and easy / You can make it / Delighting you always / Make more happen / We turn on ideas / Your potential. Our passion / Imagine it. Done / Passion for the road / Your vision, our future / Here for you / What Business wants / The future of awesome...

TITLE
GOES
HERE
IN SUITABLY 'MUSEUMY' TYPE

...that the museum sector has a generic 'poster ...mplate on its computers, much like this one, ...ing to be re-used for each new exhibition.

Don't forget to tell them the full name of the show again (in case they forgot). The full name of the museum again (in case the logo doesn't tell them).

and then the dates of the show and how to get there and what time and what tube all in a few blocks of ranged left type and then the website address.

S
sponsor's name

O
other sponsor's name

M
MUSEUM NAME

Some sectors, such as the cultural sector, have become so pre-programmed in their approach that parody seems to be the only way forward (see opposite). Exhibition posters always feature large 'bleed' images from the show, the typography is in a particular font, the museum/gallery's logo (and sponsors' logos) nestle discreetly in pre-ordained spots. The irony of this is that if you pick up a 'what's on' magazine and lift your thumb to cover the logo, then you could be pretty much anywhere in the world, looking at any museum advert for a show in any global city.

The question I'm asking is: if standardization is everywhere, how do brands deal with it? How do they raise themselves from the crowd? More to the point, *do they want to raise themselves from the crowd?*

You could make a strategic point by demonstrating the level of commonality in a market – these 'thumb test' pictures could work in almost any sector. Techniques such as these help to illustrate that brand identity is so much more than just a logo in the corner and is as much concerned with a brand's 'toolkits', its tone of voice and its display of true points of difference. You have to look hard at what's out there, and if there are commonalities across a sector, recognize them. There may be a perfectly good reason why 'everything's the same', but it's the role of a good brand investigation to flag this early, as it will help frame the decisions that come next.

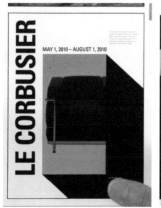

Exhibition advertisements ▴ Le Corbusier / Museum of Modern Art, New York / USA / 2010 ▴ **Velázquez** / Grand Palais, Paris / France / 2015 ▴ **Ming** / National Museum of Scotland, Edinburgh / UK / 2014 ▴ **Big Bang Data** / Somerset House, London / Design Morag Myerscough / UK / 2015

HOW RESEARCH CAN UNCOVER THE TRUTH

There are different ways of looking at the prevalence of the trend towards uniformity. We can either accept that deep down every bottled water, or airline flight, or cola is essentially the same and that our job as communications thinkers is to find, establish or even 'create' some form of difference. Cynical, perhaps, but sometimes true. Or we can seek clients, organizations and projects which, at their core, have something unique and genuinely different to say.

The latter is obviously easier to work with. But what about the former? Some say a true test of a strategic and creative mind is to have to find a new way to 'sell' a box of matches or a soap powder – to uncover uniqueness from ubiquity. It's the job of every team member – whether you're an intern, MBA, CEO, designer, or strategist – to look for what makes something special, what makes it different and to make that difference obvious and attractive.

For some products discovering a core point of difference can be based on simple measures. For example, this famous campaign for Parker pens was based almost entirely on facts gleaned from a factory visit, which then directly informed the campaign itself.[2]

But sometimes the real 'truth' is harder to acknowledge. In the early 1960s an agency team toiled over what the car rental company Avis *truly offered* to the world. Its researchers kept coming back with the same phrase: 'We try harder because we have to.' There was little else to differentiate Avis from Hertz, the market leader, or the other rental brands. This research insight led to one of the finest copy lines of the last 50 years: 'Avis is only No.2... We try harder', which over time was shortened to 'Avis. We try harder'. This honesty carried over into the headlines – 'Avis can't afford not to be nice', 'Avis can't afford dirty ashtrays', 'Avis can't afford to make you

• Parker Pens / Collett Dickenson Pearce / UK / 1977

Avis can't afford dirty ashtrays.

Or to start you out without a full gas tank, a new car like a lively, super-torque Ford, a smile.
Why?
When you're not the biggest in rent a cars, you have to try harder.
We do.
We're only No. 2.

Avis can't afford not to be nice.

Or not give you a new car like a lively, super-torque Ford, or not know a pastrami-on-rye place in Duluth.
Why?
When you're not the biggest in rent a cars, you have to try harder.
We do. We're only No. 2.

If you have a complaint, call the president of Avis. His number is CH 8-9150.

AREA CODE 516
CH 8-9150

If he doesn't answer after 3 rings, try later.

There isn't a single secretary to protect him. He answers the phone himself.

He's a nut about keeping in touch. He believes it's one of the big advantages of a small company.

You know who is responsible for what. There's nobody to pass the buck to.

One of the frustrations of complaining to a big company is finding someone to blame.

Well, our president feels responsible for the whole kit and caboodle. He has us working like crazy to keep our super-torque Fords super. But he knows there will be an occasional dirty ashtray or temperamental wiper.

If you find one, call our president collect.

He won't be thrilled to hear from you, but he'll get you some action.

© 1964 AVIS, INC.

wait'.[3] The durability of the insight and the quality of the work continued for decades. In 2012 Avis rolled out a new campaign aimed at business travellers headed with the line 'It's Your Space', but they soon returned to 'We try harder', with their first European TV campaign in 60 years.

So why is it that, even 60 years later, this example is so interesting. Because it **doesn't pretend** to be something it's not (Avis isn't pitching to be the world's biggest or best). It has **warmth, humility**, is based in a product '**truth**', it is '**defensible**' (i.e., hard for others to adopt) and helps Avis **stand out** in a tricky and competitive market. And it came directly from great and thorough research.

We try harder.

THE ROLE OF THE AUDIT

What the last few pages have illustrated is that before any useful branding discussions can start it is vital to open everyone's eyes to the position of the product in the market. This is where the role of research and audits becomes crucial, especially if key players and senior management aren't completely aware of the challenges they are facing.

Here's a starter list of the kind of audits that can really help.

A visual audit	Particularly for brands already in existence; it helps all parties to 'see' where they are and to appreciate and highlight issues
A verbal audit	The words and phrases a brand/company/organization uses; these can either act as a stepping stone to improve the language used or to trigger a complete change of tack
A behavioural audit	Useful for brands interfacing directly with their consumers; this looks at how employees speak and talk and interact, including the messages and signals they give off about a brand (consciously and unconsciously)
A competition audit	This would normally take all the factors above – visual, verbal and behavioural – across the key competition
A peer audit	Not an audit of direct competition, but a look at the kind of organization that a company might aspire to, or benchmark against, often across multiple sectors

There might be a bit of eye-rolling when these types of audit are suggested – and there may not be time for all of them – but they are incredibly important. Not only do they help with the strategic planning and potentially inform creative solutions, but 'client-side', however painful collecting the elements can be, they often serve to demonstrate the depth of key problems.

For example, a cultural quarter in a city might benefit greatly from looking at how other cities approach a problem – not because they are direct competitors, but because something can be learned from studying other cities. New York's Lincoln Center or London's Southbank might appear to embody coherent, 'umbrella' destination brands – 'what's on at the Lincoln Center/Southbank this weekend?' – but on paper, from a visual perspective, they have very different brand approaches.

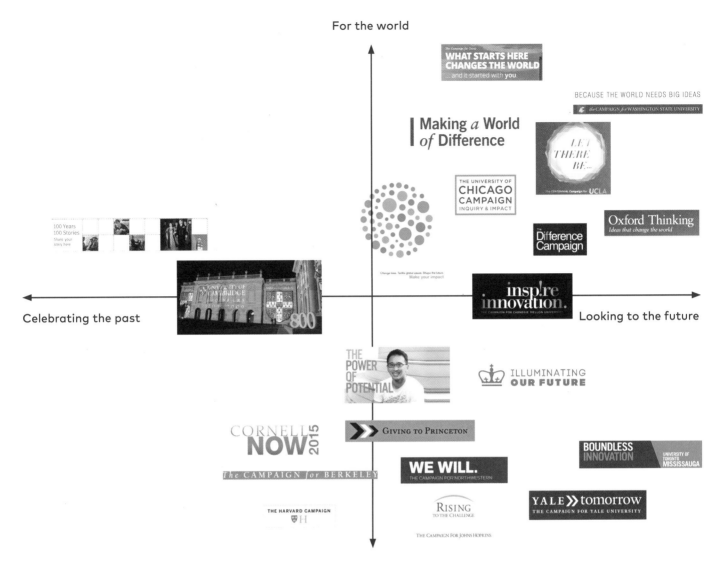

Looking at what others are doing is incredibly helpful. For example, a decade ago the world's major universities weren't spending that much time talking to alumni and philanthropists, but now if you plot their development campaigns on a two-by-two (see above) you'll see that this is a busy and competitive market.[4] If you pitch something new into this mix, then it has to be very carefully thought through if it's going to have any impact. Even examples outside a direct client area can provide inspiration at this stage of research. If a brand wants to share unique content, then it can look, for instance, at how TED does it (see page 91). If the time is right to publish a manifesto, it should consider what others have done, across different sectors. If a brand wants to be more product-led, then it should look hard at Apple and Dyson, and learn from Sony's mistakes. This is the time to 'sponge up' all types of input and all manner of influences.

SIMPLE EXERCISES, BIG OUTCOMES

There's no hard-and-fast rule about who undertakes the research outlined in this first step. It's true that direct consultation and interviews on thorny strategic questions are often best carried out by external parties – it's hard for internal employees to challenge a chief exec on her or his high horse and get them back on track.

However, some basic techniques that were once 'consultant-side' have moved 'client-side'. A classic is SWOT analysis, which stands for 'strengths, weaknesses, opportunities, threats'. Written up on a simple chart, with people chipping in, it's a really effective and easy way for all parties to 'have a say', and neatly encapsulates issues faced and the directions in which a company or brand can go. If contributors can be honest about the opportunities and threats, in particular, then it can also provide valuable strategic insight going forward.

A variant on this is simply to list three things: *the facts, the obstacles and the opportunities.* Try starting a meeting with an open notebook with those three areas delineated on the page. It will be invaluable source material for months to come.[5]

Another useful exercise is to ask groups to identify the 'functional' versus the 'emotional' benefits of the brand, going forward. This forces teams to separate out the 'what we do' from the 'why we do it' and lays the groundwork for the narrative stage that comes next.

Simple target market analysis can also be of great use, either when considering a re-brand or when creating a new brand in a market. It's amazing how many companies and organizations don't *really* know who their customers are and how to reach them – they have often been so obsessed with themselves, and what they do, that they forget to turn the frame around and look at it from the outside in. In some markets this might involve identifying clear customer archetypes or creating consumer 'personas', which can then be used to target marketing spend going forward.

Facts

Obstacles   Opportunities

Try making notes at the beginning of a project using this simple structure. It quickly begins to identify key issues, but keeps all the information on one page.

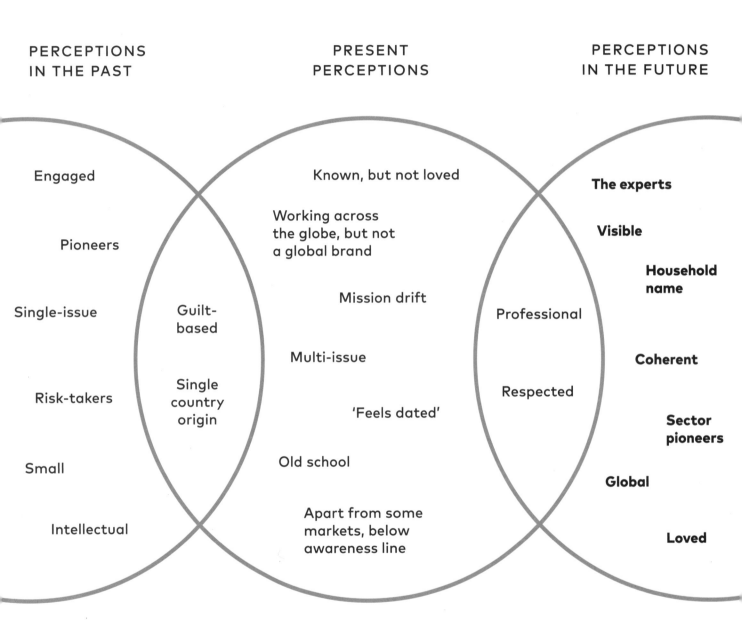

PERCEPTIONS
IN THE PAST

PRESENT
PERCEPTIONS

PERCEPTIONS
IN THE FUTURE

Engaged

Pioneers

Single-issue

Risk-takers

Small

Intellectual

Guilt-based

Single country origin

Known, but not loved

Working across the globe, but not a global brand

Mission drift

Multi-issue

'Feels dated'

Old school

Apart from some markets, below awareness line

Professional

Respected

The experts

Visible

Household name

Coherent

Sector pioneers

Global

Loved

This simple 'past, present, future' exercise seems to work well and gives staff teams 'their say'.

▾ Past, present, future model / johnson banks / UK / from 2012 onwards

Another valuable exercise, especially in a group workshop, is the 'past, present future' task. In this exercise, delegates are asked to plot what the core attributes of their company/organization are at present, how these have changed from before, and what their aspirations are for the future. This simple diagram seems to 'allow' employees to critique others without fear of retribution (although it's best to make it anonymous, just in case), while mapping their aspirations going forward. Shown opposite is a slightly anonymized set of results from a workshop with a global NGO.

It might only take 30 minutes to do, but when presented back to a boardroom – 'you say you want to do this, but look where your staff want you to go' – it can be an incredibly powerful tool.

ASKING THE RIGHT QUESTIONS.

One of the best ways to assess where an organization could, or should, go next is to interview key staff and ideally consumers in key target markets, peers and influencers, in order to get an internal and external perspective. This could take the form of a day's interviews at HQ, or a month-long series of meetings, plus online staff surveys.

Whichever end of the scale, asking the right questions results not only in priceless information; it also offers insurance against the future. Now that branding (and re-branding) has become fundamental to so many organizations, involving key troublemakers – as much as key decision-makers – early on has become critical.

Put it another way: would you rather have the argument about 'future direction' during Step 1 or at the end of Step 3 when the brand is about to be signed off? If a key director feels disenfranchised and/or not consulted, they will carefully choose their moment to plunge a stake through the project's heart (that's assuming that branding is seen as the devil's work, of course).

Further key aims of the interviewing stage are to ascertain whether the problem that has been identified is *really* the problem at hand, and whether an organization's real point of difference is truly what the company thinks it is.

It's amazing how many times – months into the process – everyone begins to see that where a project started is not where it's going to finish, as the findings of the investigation begin to reveal themselves.

What's the problem we're here to fix?	Why does that matter, now?
What are we doing about it?	What do we want others to do?

WHICH QUESTIONS SHOULD YOU ASK?

Through your research you're gathering key data to inform the strategic and narrative stage, so asking the right questions is crucial. Here are some suggestions:

1   Questions about the functional: the nuts and bolts stuff

You have to ask what can seem painfully obvious questions, such as 'what is it that you do', 'how do you do it', 'what is it about your approach that differs from that of others'? These are usually fairly simple for people to answer, but bear in mind that if the response to the 'difference' question is 'nothing', then, Houston, you may have a problem.

2   Questions about the more emotional aspects: personality and values

You have to dig a little deeper and ask questions such as 'are you clear what this organization/company/brand believes in', 'what does it value the most', 'what kind of personality does it have (and does that change for different audiences')? If people are struggling to answer these questions, then it is sometimes useful to couch them in future terms, e.g., 'if you currently stand for this, what should you stand for in the future'?

3   Questions about 'why we're here'

These are the trickiest questions of all. One option is to go directly to 'purpose', so 'what have you been put on this earth to do', 'what problem do you exist to solve', or 'what's your long-term ambition' (and 'why will it matter in the future')? If you follow this with questions such as 'what are you doing about it' and 'what do you want others to do', this should start to link you to target markets.[6] If you want, you can finish with something like 'what does success look like' and you'll start to unpick some long-range goals and ambitions.

If the answers to the third set of questions veer drastically away from the first, then there's some serious work to be done, i.e., 'what they do', 'how they do it' and 'what makes them stand apart' doesn't tally with their 'reason to be', purpose and ambition. Sometimes the responses to the last questions are great, yet the current product or service is humdrum at best and generic at worst. Sometimes people are clear about 'why it matters' and yet they aren't sure 'who it matters to', which becomes a targeting/audiences challenge. Very few people can answer all of the questions coherently. If you can, well, you probably don't need any more help, so I'd say 'go directly to Step 2.5'.

FOR EVERY CHILD IN DANGER

unicef
UNITED KINGDOM

One simple question: 'Why are you here?'
Answer: 'For every child in danger.'

THE ROLE OF TRADITIONAL RESEARCH

One of the confusing aspects of the word 'research' is that it means different things to different people. To me, it really means 'digging', visually and verbally, with audits and interviews with decision-makers, to find where a brand sits (or could sit) in a market.

My definition is pretty broad, and yet many of you reading this will associate the word 'research' with the qualitative and quantitative work done for decades by consumer goods manufacturers. You know, the ones who find out through research that by slightly changing the colour of the 'swoosh' on their packaging they can sell 6% more biscuits. I'm actually not trying to belittle this kind of research: it's saved my bacon several times and, for many, the idea of rapid researching and prototyping has become key.

There can be a kind of 'pride' in creative circles in ignoring the implications of research. There is an urban myth that Henry Ford said, 'If I'd have asked my customers what they wanted, they'd have said, "A faster horse".'[7] Steve Jobs also made the very fair point that 'customers don't know what they want until we've shown them',[8] which, from a product design perspective, is probably useful to bear in mind.

THERE ARE SOME ACRONYMS THAT JUST SHOULDN'T EXIST.
Help stop female genital mutilation for good
unicef.org.uk

FOR EVERY CHILD IN DANGER   unicef UNITED KINGDOM

The kind of research that can be invaluable at this stage is research that points out issues, gaps and frailties, and increases understanding. For example, in tracking research in the UK, Unicef discovered that only 38% of the British public actually knew that they supported children. The same studies revealed that people didn't feel very emotionally connected to what Unicef did.[9]

These were two pretty damning pieces of insight for what is the world's largest children's organization. From this admittedly low base, Unicef was then able to answer one key question, 'why are you here?', with one simple answer, 'for every child in danger'. Those five words could be used to prompt an entire scheme. The original research didn't really reveal anything *that* unusual or *that* insightful – but importantly it showed that Unicef had to take some drastic action.

SAFETY   FOR EVERY CHILD IN DANGER
unicef UNITED KINGDOM

For the example on the previous page, the research revealed a lack of brand clarity. Sometimes qualitative research can provide a real platform for some genuinely creative thinking. Entire brands have been based on exactly these kinds of consumer insights. The team behind the re-brand of BT Cellnet had noted in their research that consumers had said 'my mobile is as essential to me as my house keys or my wallet – I wouldn't leave home without it',[10] and from this one thought came the creative leap to the essentials of life, and hence to 'oxygen' and its chemical formula, O_2. Backed up by a series of dramatic photographs of bubbles in motion, a key visual property and an entire brand toolkit was born. It was so powerful that its launch adverts simply used this brand idea with the line 'a breath of fresh air' and very little else.[11] Through multiple campaigns, straplines and 'owners', the company's core 'idea' has remained intact for over a decade.

BALANCING INTERNAL DESIRE AND EXTERNAL REALITY

One of the recurring issues that Step 1 uncovers is an imbalance between how an organization feels about itself, where it feels it should be going and *how it is seen externally*. These 'perceptions' can be wildly different from one another. You can enter an organization that presents itself as a calm, steady ship and discover, just below the surface, that there is a highly disaffected group of people waiting for the chance to get their story out. The difficult bit is knowing quite how to deal with this information.

For example, mid-to-senior-level managers might want drastic, even radical, change, and yet senior management are often risk averse. Polarity in brand identity doesn't often translate into a successful outcome until the lack of clarity effectively forces the management to make a decision. The task during this first step (at least in my experience) is to hear the many views, air the disagreements, without naming names, and then take those polar views into the strategic and narrative work in Step 2.

In an ideal world, a brand, company or organization is already well thought of internally and its external audiences have a positive view of it, too, so the brand and identity process can just serve to clarify and improve what is already established. The truth, however, is that sometimes there's as much confusion externally as there is internally, and both views have to be balanced.

GETTING THE BALANCE RIGHT

Organizations that have grown more by word of mouth or power of personality may have established strong 'brand perceptions' in the minds of their audience, yet when audited the actual physical, visual and verbal branding can lag far behind. For example, Virgin Atlantic had traded successfully for 25 years on cult of personality and joie de vivre rather than the quality of its brand identity. When laid out on a table, the elements, logos and designs didn't really fit together at all. Visually, it was close to chaos.

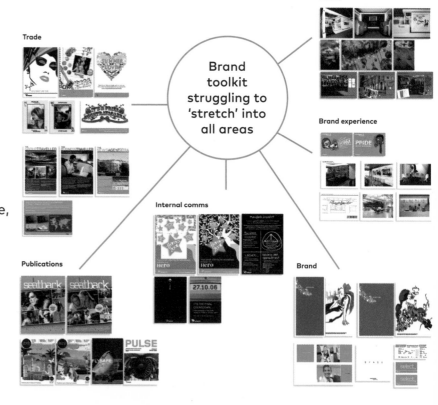

While the company promised a great brand 'experience', the reality didn't always live up to the promise, i.e., the brand identity and physical experiences and environments didn't always match up with customers' perceptions. So Virgin embarked on a wholesale re-orientation and re-design of its core brand, looking at how fare classes related to one another, and introduced more consistency and colour-coding. The brand 'grew up' a little and pulled itself up to match the very high perceptions and positive attributes that most customers attached to the brand in their minds.

THE ROLE OF MAPPING

In order to 'unpick' a market, one of the simplest approaches is to 'map' what's there already and then examine the gaps.

Here's a straightforward diagram of car brands placed onto a simple map with two axes: 'a brand I like/a brand I don't like' versus 'economy/premium'. It's not a diagram based on years of painstaking research, just informed hunches.[12]

If you 'read' the map, you'll realize no brand really wants to be in the bottom left quadrant (i.e., 'an economy brand I don't like'). Brands such as Skoda and Daewoo are desperate to move 'up' into the top left quadrant to 'an economy brand I do like'. Equally, many of the car manufacturers currently top left will probably be eyeing up the top right quadrant and furiously discussing whether their brand can really move there or whether that's just wishful thinking.

Some are probably perfectly happy where they are. Mass-market manufacturers such as Ford will be content to be placed bang in the middle and will be developing products that can extend into the two desirable quadrants. Toyota have already made the decision that to move 'right' isn't appropriate for their brand, but they created the Lexus marque to fill that luxury, premium space that they couldn't quite occupy.

BMW is a fairly mass-market brand in Germany, but marketed as 'luxury' around the world, so its brand perceptions would probably map quite differently in its home and international markets. The acquisition and re-development of the Mini brand has allowed them to market to an upwardly mobile, female-biased sector that their BMW-branded efforts weren't reaching.

What does a 'map' like this illustrate? In a diagrammatic form it reveals insights that would have taken several PowerPoint slides to unpick. And it does so in a highly visual and understandable way that can elicit discussion.

Economy

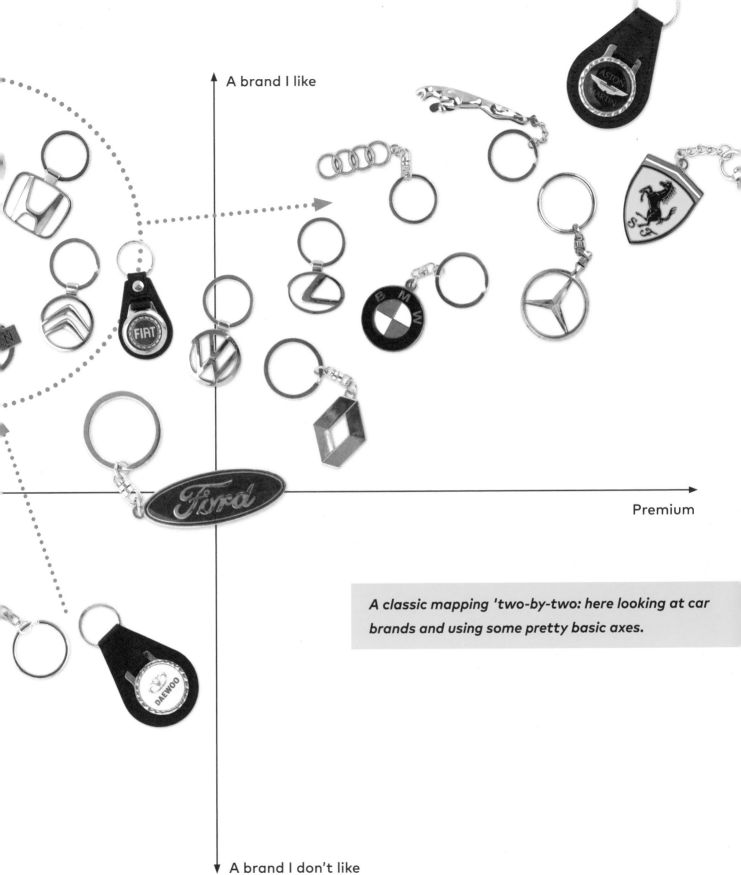

A brand I like

Premium

A brand I don't like

A classic mapping 'two-by-two: here looking at car brands and using some pretty basic axes.

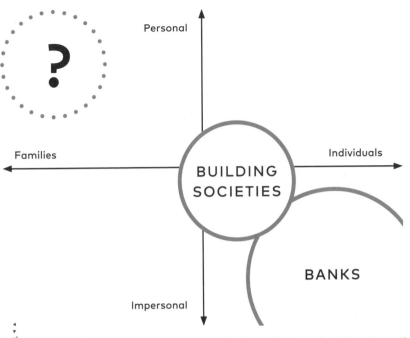

Personal

Families ← BUILDING SOCIETIES → Individuals

BANKS

Impersonal

An example of a brand idea based on market mapping, and looking for a gap, is the Family Building Society. The brand's core offer builds from the observation that banks and building societies (or mutuals) don't really cater for the personal, inter-generational giving and lending that families are increasingly doing between themselves. When grandparents lend a granddaughter cash to buy her first flat, or parents act as guarantors for first mortgages, there's no one 'official' to help. The Family Building Society caters entirely for this market, filling 'the gap' that no one else had chosen to enter. To emphasize its uniqueness even further, the design toolkit allows the brand identity itself to be customized, so that letters to the Atkinson family, for example, have their name overprinted onto the logo. This breaks about a hundred brand and identity rules, but in the process establishes unheard-of levels of personalization in a market dominated by large and impersonal behemoths.

Mr J Atkinson,
Ebbisham House,
30 Church Street,
Epsom, Surrey
KT17 4NL

10.07.14

Dear Mr Atkinson,

The Family Building Society is a financial organisation specifically designed to help families who can work together to use their money and their assets more successfully.

We believe many standard financial products and services are failing to meet the real needs of families who now face a very different set of circumstances to those faced in past generations.

The costs of buying a first home and education are having a major impact on younger family members, whilst older family members are seeking help in planning their finances in later life. Caught in the middle is a sandwich generation who want to help both but have their own retirement plans to address.

That is why we promise to deliver innovative products and services which meet the real and ever changing concerns of the family whatever its structure or composition. We treat you as an individual and deliver a service, tailored for your family, with a single point of contact.

We have partnered with specialists. Where we recognise that another provider has the expertise to and is better equipped to help a customer meet a financial need, we have researched the market to find trusted and capable partners to deliver that service to a high standard.

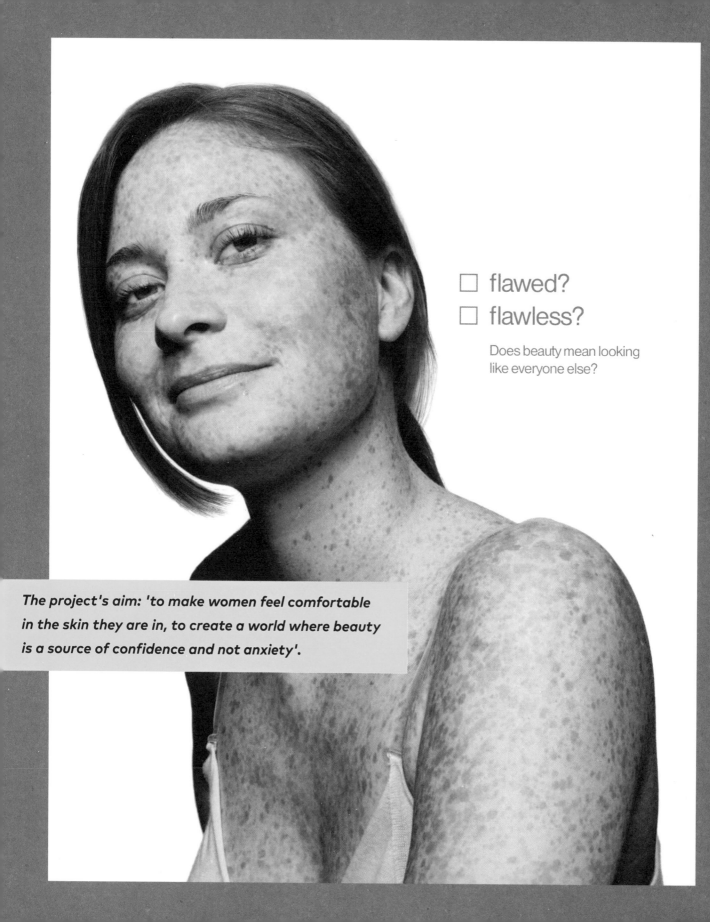

flawed?
flawless?

Does beauty mean looking
like everyone else?

The project's aim: 'to make women feel comfortable
in the skin they are in, to create a world where beauty
is a source of confidence and not anxiety'.

Dove Campaign for Real Beauty / Ogilvy & Mather / UK, Germany / from 2004 onwards

DARING TO GO WHERE OTHERS WON'T

Sometimes a combination of mapping, intuition and sheer bravery can open up entirely new approaches. Examine Dove's actual products and you'll see a predominance of white, fairly innocuous packaging, and a slightly vague claim to being 'creamy'. On paper, this is not a great deal to work with and not unique.

Yet, within a decade, Dove has re-orientated itself around the central concept of a 'campaign for real beauty'. By tapping into and rejecting the inauthentic and overly glossy approach of most 'beauty' communications, Dove has managed to become the brand of ordinary, everyday, normal-sized women – where freckles and wrinkles are celebrated, not criticized.

In developing the campaign over a number of treatments over many years, the brand has not only dramatically increased its sales but has also been at the forefront of the presentation of women in the media, forcing the examination of traditional prejudices and accepted communications techniques.[13]

☐ oversized?
☐ outstanding?

Does true beauty only
squeeze into a size 6?

▲ Dove Real Beauty Sketches / Ogilvy & Mather / USA / 2013

This 'why not?' style of thinking
has arguably paved the way for
campaigns such as 'This Girl Can',
which encourages women to get involved
in sport: 'a celebration of active women up
and down the country who are doing their
thing no matter how well they do it, how

they look or even how red their face gets' and the 'Like a Girl' project which takes the
classic verbal put-down and turns it into a phrase of empowerment, prompting a flood
of online activity. Two of the above three examples are, at the end of the day, flogging

product – beauty products and feminine hygiene.
But, at least in the principles that underlie the
thinking, they are reflecting a degree of societal
change. The 'gap', of course, for all of this is clear –
afford women some respect, 'sell' in an authentic
way and don't resort to advertising cliché. As is the
way with all gaps, once filled successfully they are
pretty obvious in retrospect.

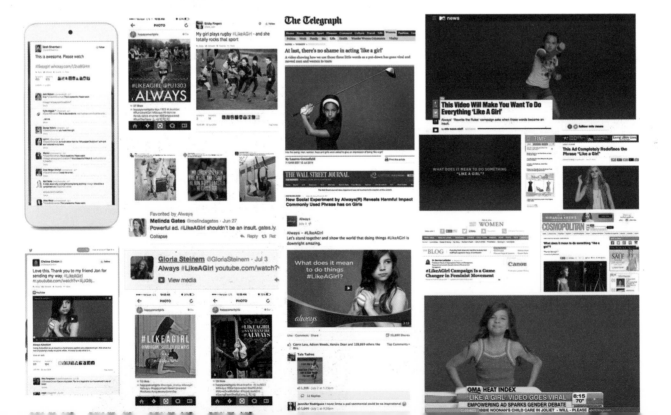

Finally, advertising has realized that its portrayal of women must change. It's taken a while...

The genius of the Dave re-brand is that very little of the channel content changed, but its true market was found.

Dave
the home of witty banter

Dave / Red Bee Media / UK / 2008 and 2014

ALIGNING BRAND AND TARGET MARKET

In the fiercely competitive world of multi-channel TV there once was a channel called UK Gold which featured comedy-based and popular factual shows, often re-running previously aired programmes. It attracted a younger, male audience, but only those willing and able to unpick its scheduling and discover the content for themselves.

An attempt to attract more of the same by shortening the name to UKG2 didn't seem to help much. Research showed that only 1% of pay-TV viewers could spontaneously recall it, and it languished at an unimpressive 32nd in the channel popularity tables. What happened next? Something quite radical, but entirely logical.

On the grounds that 'everyone knows a bloke like Dave', UK Gold went through a fundamental re-brand so that Dave – the channel's new name – became 'not just a place you visit but a mate you want to spend time with'. Following the re-brand, its recognition stats shot up to 32% and within a month of relaunch it had become the tenth largest channel in the UK.[14]

The 'blokey' language is carried across into multiple stings and the humour is knowingly self-referential. So a sting for a programme might be suffixed '... happened last week. Unless you're watching the repeat on Dave in which case it happened 3 years ago.'

Dave had seen and filled a gap, and had filled it with a product that already existed. Its target market just needed to be recognized, told that it was there, and told that it was 'OK' to watch it.

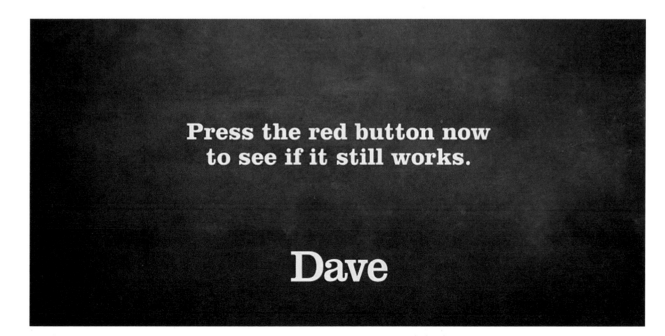

Press the red button now
to see if it still works.

Dave

DIGGING DEEPER TO FIND A STORY

Although it's currently a little unfashionable, digging deep into a brand's history can sometimes provide the inspiration for its future. For years, the insurance brand Prudential drove its communications through the personification of its brand, its door-to-door army of salesmen – each known as the 'Man from the Pru'. Unsurprisingly, the be-suited chap with ever-present trilby eventually seemed a little anachronistic, so the company went further back into its history and mined its 1848 company seal for 'Prudence', her arrow, serpent

and mirror representing 'traditional values yet looking forward to the future'.[15]

Paradoxically, the research that drives a brand's story – as with the Prudential – can also lead to a 'created' back-story. For 30 years, the Dutch paint and chemical company Akzo (now AkzoNobel) has used a man with outstretched arms as its identifier, having previously had an abstract 'A'. Is this based on a sculpture carved above their office doors? Is it their founder who was caught handing alms from the wealthy to the poor at the time of a great Dutch 18th-century famine? No, it's based on a Greek sculpture that resides in a museum in Britain and was chosen as an icon of both art and science to symbolize 'striving and achievement', and more recently carrying the slightly hammy strapline 'tomorrow's answers today'.[16] At this precise moment in time, an appropriated

history such as this seems a little odd – should the research step of a project always include a wander through Greek mythology? But, love it or loathe it, Akzo can at least present a human face, which its previous identity wasn't able to do.

◄ Prudential / Wolff Olins / UK / 1986 / amended early 2000s, WCRS ◄ Akzo logo / The Netherlands / 1969 ◄ Akzo redesign / Wolff Olins / UK / 1988 ◄ Akzo Nobel / Saffron / UK / 2008

▸ Agip/Eni dog / Luigi Broggini / Italy / 1952

Other symbols have an equally unusual provenance. Pass the symbol below on a European road and you get a fleeting sense of an extraordinary fire-breathing creature. But look closer and you'll see it's a six-legged dog. Is this a modern-day centaur, a reference to African mythology, or, as some suggest, the legend of Romulus and Remus?[17]

Well, the six legs of the imaginary animal were actually carefully designed as references to an automobile's four wheels and the driver's two legs, while the flame represents 'the energy itself'. This is coupled with bespoke typography designed to represent two lanes of a highway, divided by a simple white line. So across Italy and all over the world, first Agip and now Eni has one of the world's most powerful visual identities, summing up strength, energy and speed – a symbol that was 'created' and yet in half a century has managed to create a mythology all of its own.

▼ Fiat 500 / Italy / from 1957 and 2007 onwards

▼ Mini / UK, Germany / from 1959 and 2001 onwards

HOW NOSTALGIA CAN DRIVE PRODUCT INNOVATION

Despite the anti-research protestations of some product-driven companies, car manufacturers have increasingly tapped into a more basic form of research by studying what it was that was so liked about their successful models of yesteryear in an attempt to repeat previous successes.

While there is clearly a need for new, modern and aerodynamically efficient cars, there also seems to be a viable place in the market for 21st-century versions of the old, so now we have 'remixes' of Fiat's famous 500, Volkswagen's Beetle and the Mini. Each, in turn, was loved in its first iteration and was re-invented for the 21st century – now, more efficient, quicker and quite possibly more nimble; often also sleeker and a little larger (and, finally, the newly enlarged Fiat can carry normal-sized passengers).

Yet there's something unmistakably familiar and more authentic about these re-inventions, and the world seems happy to fall in love with each of them all over again (but this time around with added air conditioning). A little like Hollywood and its sequels, the market for the 're-invented classic car' seems unlikely to die soon.

▲ VW Beetle / Germany / from 1938 and 1997 onwards

HOW DISSATISFACTION AND NEED DRIVE PRODUCT AND BRAND

The essence of this first step in the branding process is to understand what exists in a sector, often in order to help inform how an existing brand can amend and modulate what it stands for and be clearer and better understood.

Yet research at a customer level poses issues for cutting-edge product innovation. How could Apple have researched the potential impact of the iPad on sales and come to any concrete conclusions (given that many others had tried and failed to make 'tablet-style' products work up until that point)? There were also several, largely unsuccessful attempts to introduce MP3 players before Apple re-invented the market for portable music with the iPod, taking largely existing technology but simplifying it, re-packaging the product and offering memorable design such as the famous spinning wheel to scroll through tracks.[18]

In the case of raw product innovation, the drive to create may not stem from a clear customer need (and is hence notoriously hard to research in advance); it usually comes from a key individual insight. Legend has it that the Sony Walkman was the result of the desire of its co-founder to listen to opera on his travels.[19] Equally legendary is the creation of early Nike trainers with the use of a waffle iron...and not focus groups.[20] Dyson's early work looked to re-invent the humble wheelbarrow. Then he followed an engineer's hunch about vacuum cleaners: that what existed simply wasn't good enough and that understanding the effect of cyclones could be the answer.[21]

This approach – taking issue with what's there, or the perceived injustice of what *isn't* there – often drives brands that could be classified as 'challengers'. By definition, these brands challenge the status quo. First Direct, the telephone and online banking brand, launched its 24-hour service in 1989 and positioned itself just about as far away from traditional banks as possible. Conceived soon after, the Orange telecoms brand challenged a market then seen as dominated by used-car salesmen clutching brick-like mobile phones to their heads.

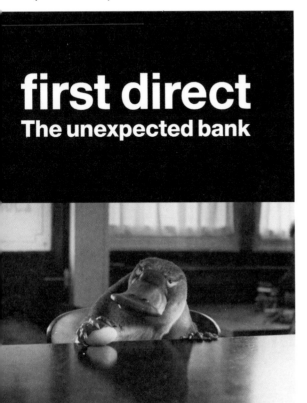

▸ Ballbarrow / Dyson / UK / 1974 ▸ Walkman / Sony / Japan / 1979 ▸ iPod / Apple / USA / 2001 ▸ Waffle trainer / Nike / USA / 1970s

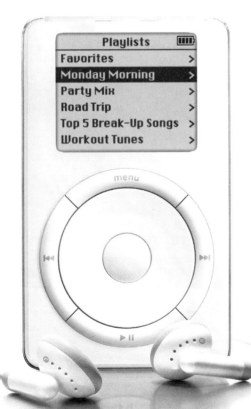

The ballbarrow. The Walkman.
The iPod. The first 'waffle' trainer.

Some brand innovations stem entirely from this principle of not taking what's offered at face value and searching for something better. The original principle of the Gap clothing brand was based on a simple need: to find a pair of jeans that fitted. Its founders wanted to 'make the process of buying jeans easier',[22] spotted a market opportunity and even took inspiration from 'the generation gap' when deciding on the name.

One of the founders of Warby Parker discovered the 'problem' that his future brand had to solve while squinting his way through the first semester of grad school, having smashed his only pair of glasses (he was too poor to replace them). The solution? Online prescription glasses and sunglasses 'founded with a rebellious spirit and a lofty objective: to offer designer eyewear at a revolutionary price'.

It doesn't mean, of course, that there will always be a space in a market. There

may be an overwhelmingly great reason why no one has filled it. Take the cola market, which has been dominated historically by two global giants, Coca-Cola and Pepsi, and then a smattering of 'own-brand' colas at a supermarket level. Even a globally recognized brand such as Virgin was unable to break this duopoly.[23] There may have been a gap in the market for a third cola but without distribution and enough coverage truly to attack the two great powers in it, Virgin Cola couldn't compete.

But the principle of forensically examining a market, just as the building society example on pages 60–61 showed us, and then searching for opportunities, can often lead to product innovation. The Uber taxi brand only went international in 2012, but three years later it was available in 58 countries and 300 cities. Although mired in controversy wherever it operates, Uber simply offers a very well-thought-through online experience, taking all the best bits of GPS tracking technology and creating a platform for its users and drivers to get on with it.

This is a prevailing trend with many 21st-century breakthrough brands. Bypass the need for thousands of employees and just become the conduit between the supplier of a spare bedroom and the tourist in search of a bargain (in the case of Airbnb), or cut

out the need for physical shops and move most of the brand and shopping experience online (in the case of mattress supplier Casper).

It's tempting to read about these kinds of examples and assume that 'online' is the only way to create cutting-edge brands, but finding an innovative 'offer' doesn't always have to involve searching for a signal and battling with a smartphone. We all know what McDonald's supplies, but it's at the fringes of the burger world that the more interesting ideas are found. For over half a century, In-N-Out Burgers has been offering what its name implies, but one of its most original ideas is what's known as its 'secret menu'. It's not on offer publicly in the stores, but should you want to sign up to a '4x4', which involves four beef patties, the same number of cheese slices and, yes, somewhere, some bread, then you could. However counter-intuitive the idea of a secret menu is, it seems to work.

Alternatively, you could search for a Five Guys restaurant that resolutely shuns advertising, relies on word of mouth and has walls covered in crisp red and white tiles, an open and viewable kitchen and a menu that doesn't change: an apparently authentic environment that – in the nicest way – suggests you should 'shut up, sit down and eat'.[24]

Art Not Oil Coalition / UK / 2011 ▾ Greenpeace logo competition / Laurent Hunziker / France / 2010

A DIFFERENT KIND OF DISSATISFACTION

Obviously what no brand wants is the equivalent of what has happened to the reputation of VW. An icon around the world and a powerhouse of the German economy, it has been critically damaged by the unveiling of a piece of computer software designed to 'trick' testers into registering emission values that are a fraction of the actual reading.

Long-term, what this will do to the VW brand is hard to quantify. If the software shenanigans have helped to pump an extra million tonnes of pollution into the atmosphere, then that places a series of question marks over the brand and its green credentials, and will simultaneously destroy the image of 'clean diesel' in one fell swoop.[25]

If there's any precedent here, it's Toyota's reaction to the discovery of safety defects in its cars, linking the company to the deaths of dozens of people since 2000. Toyota responded with an internal and external campaign, and went all out to re-gain customer trust.

And, eventually, customers and that critical trust will return – if companies, organizations and their CEOs behave responsibly. Having said that, in the case of BP, its attempts to return to the status quo after the Gulf of Mexico oil spill disaster have been continually hampered by targeted and visually unforgettable protests against its continued sponsorship of the arts world.

If such organizations are to recover and become 'positive' again (and not join the likes of Enron, Fannie Mae[26] and Northern Rock[27] in the pantheon of corporate disasters), it is as much to do with brand management and public relations as it is to do with brand definition.

LISTEN CAREFULLY: THAT MAY BE THE ANSWER

Here's one last example of why investigation can be so critical and so useful. In early discussions about the re-brand of a medical charity raising funds for cystic fibrosis, there was a constant need for clarification about what the condition actually 'is' and its effects. (It's a condition with no outward signs that slowly clogs up your lungs.) This led to a throwaway comment about the 'is' at the end of the word 'fibrosis' and how that might be used to explain it.

Cystic Fibrosis why we're here

Cystic Fibrosis a sticky, painful, suffocating condition

Cystic Fibrosis killing thousands and carried in the genes of millions – help us search for a cure

Cystic Fibrosis beatable

Cystic Fibrosis cutting lives in half

Cystic Fibrosis a fight we must win

An immediate discussion followed and the swapping of multiple emails – all months and months before the naming and design stage were due to commence. The idea had struck a chord, and it became the backbone of an entire scheme that used the 'is' and allowed the charity a free choice of 42 'logos' that acted as miniature, branded headlines.

The moral of this last story, and this entire step, is that, carefully carried out, and thoughtfully presented 'back', research and discussion can lay the groundwork for what is to come. It can make the case for change, concentrate minds on the true problem at hand (not an imaginary one) and, in some cases, provide the eventual answer itself.

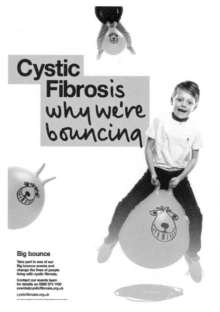

Cystic Fibrosis why we're bouncing

Big bounce
Take part in one of our Big bounce events and change the lives of people living with cystic fibrosis.
Contact our events team for details on 0300 373 1100 events@cysticfibrosis.org.uk
cysticfibrosis.org.uk

Summing up what we've covered in Step 1:
- *How to audit and research where a brand sits, or could sit, in a market*
- *How to use simple techniques such as 'obstacles/opportunities' and 'past/present/future'*
- *How to frame the questions you might ask internally...and externally*
- *How to use mapping to unpick and understand a market*
- *How mapping and gap analysis can lead directly to great ideas and insights*
- *How company myths and product history can be exploited, or even created*
- *How consumer dissatisfaction and the identification of key problems can drive solutions*

2

STRATEGY AND NARRATIVE

There is a lot of theory, bluff and bluster about this step. And some of it may leave you scratching your head at times. But understanding it is vital to a project's success. Brands across the world are discovering that their overall strategic and verbal approach is what glues them together and drives who, and what, they really are...

f this book had been written 40 years ago, then this chapter wouldn't have existed. What have words got to do with brands? Brands are visual, tangible 'things' or bits of hot metal pushed onto the rumps of cattle, aren't they? Well, no.

There has always been a sense that you could 'write down' an idea for a design or a piece of communication. One famous graphic designer said decades ago that 'if an idea was good enough it could be described over the phone'.[1] This has proved to be a prophetic statement in a way because a brand's verbal definition has now become paramount. This chapter is about demonstrating that great ideas and brands can be 'described' and planned way before they become 'visual'.

In some cases, the short-form phrases that are used to define brands become as powerful as the images that follow, and many of the greatest straplines ever written – 'Just do it', 'We try harder', 'Coke is it' – become central to those brands' very existence, even though they are just a collection of three-word statements.

I don't want you to start thinking that this section is all about writing snappy headlines and straplines. It's true that short versions of the idea that sum up a brand are useful. It helps if they are memorable. But the strapline is not everything – it's just the tip of an iceberg that involves careful thought, copywriting and the process of arriving at consensus.

DOES A BRAND'S STRATEGY AND NARRATIVE ALREADY EXIST?

Many brands could give you a list of what their brand means to them, as ascertained from customer data at least. There might be a lot of 'doing' phrases on the list ('they deliver on time'), or product attributes ('I like the way it tastes').

But, increasingly, customers can quite easily give you a separate list of traits and reflections, what we might call 'emotional' observations: 'drinking it makes me feel happier, I'm not sure why'. And it's this emotional reaction that brands seek to define and pre-define. Fly on one airline and observe the crew talking to customers, then fly on another and compare and contrast. Some airlines are officious, almost bossy. Some are so laid-back you might start to wonder if it's a flight or an all-night party in a highly pressurized white cylinder. But how much of this is pre-planned and how much is spontaneous?

JUST F**K IT

*Paul Smith: summed up by the words 'unmistakable
English-ness augmented by the unexpected'.*

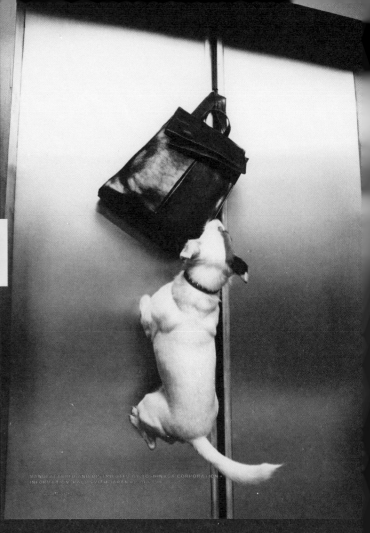

⁎ Paul Smith / Adoud Sodano / UK / 2000s

This is what Step 2 is really about. You can choose to have your brand defined by your customers or your clients, or you can choose to try and define it yourself. If you're smart, you can define and control the 'functional', 'doing' stuff and start to carefully define the emotional bits, too – not only *why people should use your product or service* but *why they should care.*

STARTING SOMEWHERE

Much of the language surrounding this step is dense and impenetrable, and, on behalf of my entire profession, I apologize.

I'm constantly being asked the difference between a *brand essence* and a *brand positioning*, or how to differentiate a *core truth* from a *core idea*. Some people value their *values* most of all and attach *behaviours* and *outcomes* to them; others use values as quick check points but are far more concerned about their *personality.*

Confused? I don't blame you.

The idea of defining what an organization is here to do, and what it wants from the world, stems from the old management principles of *mission* and *vision*, and many organizations cling to the principles of this famous duo.[2]

So what's wrong with them then?

Well, not that much, but they've often been written by a board of management who don't really know, or perhaps don't even care, what a brand is. Their mission tends to have a quasi-military aspect to it – 'our mission, should we choose to accept it, is to end the march of child mortality, gentlemen' – and their vision is sometimes highly laudable but often way out of reach.

The trouble with these 'high' statements is that they aren't often grounded in the day-to-day of what a brand/organization/company could and should stand for. They're sometimes useful on annual retreats, but not on a Monday morning.

If there are still organizations clinging onto mission and vision, then it is sometimes helpful to reconfigure these in some way – for example, if one thinks about them as long-term 'ambitions', then that allows them to be high-falutin' without getting in the way of the nuts and bolts of the everyday workings of the brand. Increasingly, as we will see, there has been a realization that the link between what a brand can do and its customers' 'needs' (both physically and emotionally) can be more clearly defined.

Abraham Maslow's well-known analysis of the 'hierarchy of needs'[3] is a slightly overused diagram, but his core point is still valid. At the top of the pyramid (and hence the most important) are 'self-actualization', personal fulfilment, esteem and status 'needs'. At the bottom are the basics of protection, shelter, sleep, etc.

So, in a nutshell, you could choose to build your brand around the basic needs of just existing, being secure and safe, and, as we'll see, there are still several brands doing exactly that. But the higher up the pyramid you can go, the more likely you are to strike an emotional connection with people.

Self-actualization — Morality, creativity, spontaneity, problem solving, lack of prejudice, acceptance of facts

Esteem — Self-esteem, confidence, achievement, respect of others, respect by others

Love/belonging — Friendship, family, sexual intimacy

Safety — Security of: body, employment, resources, morality, the family, health, property

Physiology — Breathing, food, water, sex, sleep, homeostasis, excretion

Maslow's Hierarchy of Needs / USA / 1943, 1954 ▲ Innocent / In-house / UK / 2011

FINDING A WAY FORWARD

So where shall we start? Let's start with the core. Most people in this business agree that a core, central 'idea' is critical. In order to define what this can be, it helps to think of it as the *core purpose* of a company, brand or organization. Start by answering the questions, 'why are we here?', 'what have we been put upon this earth to do?' If you

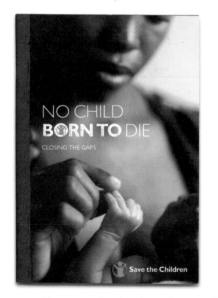

can clearly define why you're here, then it makes it a lot easier for people to 'get' what you stand for. For example, despite the name, potential donors weren't really clear what Save the Children stood for. So the charity made it unmistakable with the phrase 'No child born to die', which linked the charity umbilically to the cause of child mortality and provided a key platform for fundraising.

Here are some other examples of clear core purposes: take the Science Museum in London, which says it's 'the home of human ingenuity'. Paul Smith sums itself up with the words 'unmistakable English-ness augmented by the unexpected'. At the core of the Starbucks brand are the words: 'to inspire and nurture the human spirit – one person, one cup and one neighbourhood at a time'. And what is Innocent's stated purpose? To 'make natural, delicious and healthy drinks that help people live well and die old'. Even the quickest scan of that paragraph would make Maslow very happy. The key words here are *ingenuity*, *human spirit*, *live well* – all up at the top of his pyramid and not at the bottom.

▲ Save the Children – No Child Born to Die / Adam and Eve, johnson banks, in-house design / UK / 2011

Innocent's purpose: make natural, delicious and healthy drinks that help people live well and die old.

hungry grassy van

HUNGRY?

The innocent recipe book to help fill families with good stuff.

a book by innocent

innocent

This 'why', or 'core purpose', has a very prominent place in most modern brand theory because it forces those doing the defining to make hard choices about what they stand for. There is no room for obfuscation or waffle.

The way the rest of a brand can then be defined varies wildly. I've learned to navigate this (and now so will you) by removing as much jargon as I can and simplifying it to the following six questions and one statement:

Why are we here?	A simple statement that sums up your core purpose, usually relatively emotional in tone, and often simplified to just a few headline words.
What do we do and how do we do it?	These are usually descriptive, nuts and bolts, functional, 'doing' and 'process' statements.
What makes us different?	This helps to 'position' a brand away, in customers' minds, from what others offer, and to enhance any unique properties.
Who are we here for?	The key audiences/customers for the product, service or organization (linked to this are the 'messages' that fit with each audience).
What do we value the most?	The core beliefs and universal truths that are shared...which, in turn, affect how a brand, its founders, directors and employees behave.
What's our personality?	How we express ourselves to the outside world, our brand's character, the tone of voice we use and how we communicate.

- -

Our ambition	The long-term aim – either linked to legacy 'mission/vision' statements or written afresh.

Shown opposite are some core 'why are we here' statements for a range of brands.

▲ Various brands and core statements / see further credits on page 319 for logo design credits

ACUMEN
CHANGING
THE WAY
THE WORLD
TACKLES
POVERTY

Changing the way the world
tackles poverty.

Coca-Cola brings joy.
It's happiness in a bottle.

To embrace the human spirit
and let it fly.

The world on time.

To be Earth's most
customer-centric company.

Our knowledge inspires
your creativity.

Trustworthiness and creativity.

To beat cancer sooner.

Together we're stronger.

To give everyone the power
to create and share ideas
and information instantly,
without barriers.

To inspire and nurture the human
spirit – one person, one cup and
one neighbourhood at a time.

In a world rich in resources,
poverty isn't inevitable. It's an
injustice which can, and must,
be overcome.

The fascinating thing about these six simple questions (and one statement) is the amount of heartache and discussion that companies and organizations go through to answer them. Entire careers have been built around just one of the questions – for example, the theory of positioning,[4] essentially 'what makes us different', or how we go about deciding the 'why' of organizations.[5]

The six-question model has been designed to be as broad as possible and applicable across multiple sectors, but it may well need adapting for some brands. Companies that serve the general public, for instance, will often expand on the values section and dig deep into their character, the 'personality' they want to express, and how their brand or their employees should best behave. Alternatively, in highly competitive markets, 'what's different' unsurprisingly gets a lot of attention. In service environments, the what and how is extrapolated further into 'the offer', and so on.

But if you boil most brand models down to what they are really saying, then the list on the previous page gets to the heart of it.

If you're reading this and thinking 'there's no way we can boil our brand down to just a few words', then that's fair enough. But think about it for a moment: if you can't sum up your 'reason to be' in just a few words, then why should anyone listen to you (or, indeed, work for you). If you go to a dinner party and can't communicate clearly and succinctly with the person next to you, then they have a simple choice – to turn and talk to someone else.

And that's just what unengaged and uninterested customers do. There's a reason why Hollywood coined the phrase 'elevator pitch' – if an idea can't be summed up between the mezzanine and the eleventh floor, then it can't be that interesting, can it?

Example: TED

Founded in 1984, the original Technology, Entertainment and Design conference (TED) included presentations from Lucasfilm and the king of fractals, Benoit Mandelbrot.

TED lost money, though, and didn't restart until the 1990s when its popularity and remit slowly grew. When it changed ownership at the end of the 1990s it started to distribute its groundbreaking lectures online, under the banner 'Ideas Worth Spreading'. The TEDx format (a kind of 'TED in a box' franchise) allows locally organized events to spread these ideas and create more content.

TED is a perfect illustration of a product whose communications came together in a perfect marriage with the rapid surge of online availability. 'Ideas Worth Spreading' is an encapsulation of what the company stands for and is up there with the best core ideas. Its reason to be is not just to hold events, but to ensure that those events can be played back across the world, by millions.

Who we are

TED

What makes us different?

TED is a non-profit devoted to spreading ideas, usually in the form of short, powerful talks (18 minutes or less) that concentrate on using storytelling and speech, not slides.

Why we're here

Ideas worth spreading

We believe passionately in the power of ideas to change attitudes, lives and, ultimately, the world.

What do we do and how do we do it?

A conference that covers almost all topics – from science to business to global issues – in more than 100 languages. Independently run TEDx events help share ideas in communities around the world. On TED.com, we're building a clearing-house of free knowledge from the world's most inspired thinkers.

Who are we here for?

A global community, welcoming people from every discipline and culture who seek a deeper understanding of the world. A community of curious souls who engage with ideas and each other, both online and at events around the world, all year long.

x = independently organized TED event

Pictured: Hilary Cottam, Jacqueline Novogratz *Brand narrative extrapolated from TED's public domain definitions* [6]

WE HAVE A MODEL, SO WHERE DO WE START?

What we're going to do next is walk through the approach that I have found the most helpful, and then it's up to you to decide whether it will work for you. We'll refer back to our six questions as we go along.

These unassuming questions might at first seem easy to answer, but they're not. It's almost impossible for one client and one consultant to sit down at a table and fill in each box, on one piece of paper, and then email it to all concerned (subject heading: 'We've decided our brand strategy, hope you agree?').

Even if it was possible, it would rule out one of the most important reasons to do this: defining a brand's strategy and narrative should be a unifying process. It brings people, often teams of people, and sometimes entire organizations, together. It may be painful, it may take months (sometimes years), but, once agreed, those who help and co-author a brand's strategy and narrative are far more likely to adopt and use it.

WHAT ORDER SHOULD WE DO THINGS IN?

The precise order of which bit to do first is a little unpredictable. For companies and organizations that already exist, undergoing what most of us call a 're-branding', it seems to make sense to start with 'what we do' and slowly work toward the core.

So, start with **what we do and how we do it** and **who we are here for** (which helps to check that all are agreed on both of these), then move to **what we value the most, what's our personality** and **what makes us different**, and then end with **why we are here**. This gives the process a good 'arc' and helps it finish at the most important stage, coming to a logical discussion point at the end.

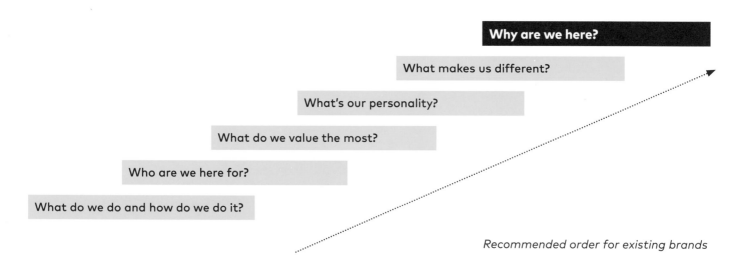

Why are we here?

What makes us different?

What's our personality?

What do we value the most?

Who are we here for?

What do we do and how do we do it?

Recommended order for existing brands

Conversely, for new brands it seems to make more sense to start at 'why' and then work from there. There's no point in agreeing a core reason to be and then not drafting supportive statements that reflect that core.

Recommended order for new brands

For the purposes of Step 2, and much of the rest of this book, we're going to put 'why are we here' in the centre of our model, so the final form of it is like this.

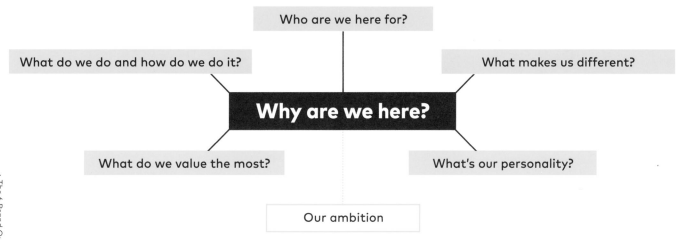

That's our working model. It may not be perfect and it certainly isn't a case of one size fits all, but it's a start. It contains no jargon and should make sense to most people.

We should give it a snappy name, though, so let's call it **the 6 brand questions** that any brand has to answer. Sorry, that should be **the 6 brand questions**™. Now I'm going to show you how to answer each of these questions.

WORKING OUT THE 'WHY' USING VARIOUS SCENARIOS

If we look at page 51 again and see the kind of questions we might ask in our investigation about purpose ('what problem do you exist to solve?', 'why will it matter in the future?') we should have some sense of what a brand has set out to do. It's rare, however, that it's *clear* which is the most appropriate route to take, and this is where writing narrative scenarios can be very helpful.

So, rather than presenting 'the final route', sketch out several, just with words. Here's an example of a series of initial verbal scenarios shared with a major airline brand.

Unforgettable travel	Love to fly	Spirit of adventure
Humanizing the business of travel	Celebrate the magic of human flight	Get more out of life and life's adventures

None of the above was actually selected in the end (we'll see what was a little later), but they offered options for discussion and workshops, and helped navigate the way towards a final answer.

Here's a version of a diagram shared with a major children's charity when it had become apparent that some kind of brand clarity was needed.[7]

1 Fight for their rights	2 Changing lives	3 The big breakthroughs	4 Through children's eyes
Righting wrongs Justice for children Tapping into a sense of moral outrage 'What's happening is a disgrace'	'Change' for children Making change tangible Change your world, and change your view of the world	Take the high ground Make the most of being 'the first' Be part of the next big breakthroughs and change the world	Entirely child-focused Big change of language Explore the 'child's voice' Explore the 'return to childhood' Grown-up 'lies'

Even though each project had already been through extensive research and consultation processes, scenarios became the backbone of very useful discussions on 'where next?' and helped get closer to the core.

It seems to chime with human nature that if you present a room full of people with one option they will pull it apart. But present them with three, or even five, and you will have a valuable discussion that *can* end with consensus (of course, it can also end in compromise, but that's a different story).

There is often a temptation to take a 'bit of scenario three and mix it with some of scenario four', but success at this stage seems to depend on the initial verbal proposals being clearly different from one another before the inevitable merging takes place. And when that merging does come, ask yourself, if we start with three clearly separate brand ideas, and merge them, won't that just create a woolly brand in people's eyes? (People will still try, just to warn you.)

Ideally, these types of scenarios become the catalyst for strategic and narrative decisions that can have a radical effect on brands. The options for the children's charity shown opposite eventually led to a powerful piece of narrative that helped move Save the Children to a more 'agit' point of difference.[8]

'We're outraged that millions of children are still denied proper healthcare, food, education and protection.

We're working flat out to get every child their basic rights and we don't let the usual excuses stand in our way.

So far, this bold, radical stance has helped us achieve dramatic breakthroughs for children. And we're determined to make further, faster changes.

How many? How fast? It's up to you.'

Examine this closely and it actually draws on parts of both scenarios one and three and then builds on both to create continuous, powerful prose that is angry ('we're outraged') and won't take no for an answer ('don't let the usual excuses stand in our way'). This 'boilerplate' text was printed on all of the charity's communications for many years.

Here's to the crazy ones. The misfits. The rebels. The troublemakers. The round pegs in the square holes. The ones who see things differently. They're not fond of rules. And they have no respect for the status quo. You can quote them, disagree with them, glorify or vilify them. About the only thing you can't do is ignore them. Because they change things. They push the human race forward. While some may see them as the crazy ones, we see genius. Because the people who are crazy enough to think they can change the world are the ones who do.

Think different.

WHEN 'WHY' BECOMES 'MANIFESTO'

The process of looking hard at an organization's 'core' inevitably leads to stronger and stronger statements, and has led to a revival of interest in the manifesto.

For decades, the principle of the manifesto seemed to be the preserve of artists: F. T. Marinetti's Futurist manifesto, first published in 1908, set the tone for the 20th century.

When reading this today some sections stand out (to say the least),[9] but the statement of artistic intent and the determination to 'stick a flag in the sand' made its mark. Now, decades later, brands are starting to recover the art of strident prose to help them re-define, with utmost clarity, what it is that they stand for.

When Steve Jobs returned to Apple in 1997, he felt that he had to re-assert their determination, credentials and reason to be. With the help of his ad agency, Apple began to craft, write and re-write a new campaign to re-position the brand in the eyes of the world's consumers. This eventually became the famous 'Think Different' campaign, accompanied by its own manifesto.[10]

The campaign – alongside, of course, newly designed Apple products that people actually wanted to buy – was hugely successful and placed Apple back on the map, as well as introducing the world to the concept of 'nouning' (Jobs felt that 'think differently' wouldn't be colloquial and would lose the power of 'think big' or 'think beauty').[11]

From Marinetti's 11-point list to Jobs' comeback manifesto, the idea of plainly stating who you are and what you do in an assertive way is incredibly persuasive (as long, of course, as you have something persuasive to say).

◄ Filippo Tommaso Marinetti / Italy / 1909 ▼ Apple's 'Think Different' manifesto and campaign / TBWA\Chiat\Day / USA / 1997

Marinetti's Manifesto

1.   We want to sing the love of danger, the habit of energy and rashness.

2.   The essential elements of our poetry will be courage, audacity and revolt.

3.   Literature has up to now magnified pensive immobility, ecstasy and slumber. We want to exalt movements of aggression, feverish sleeplessness, the double march, the perilous leap, the slap and the blow with the fist.

4.   We declare that the splendour of the world has been enriched by a new beauty: the beauty of speed. A racing automobile with its bonnet adorned with great tubes like serpents with explosive breath…a roaring motor car which seems to run on machine-gun fire, is more beautiful than the Victory of Samothrace.

5.   We want to sing the man at the wheel, the ideal axis of which crosses the earth, itself hurled along its orbit.

6.   The poet must spend himself with warmth, glamour and prodigality to increase the enthusiastic fervour of the primordial elements.

7.   Beauty exists only in struggle. There is no masterpiece that has not an aggressive character. Poetry must be a violent assault on the forces of the unknown, to force them to bow before man.

8.   We are on the extreme promontory of the centuries! What is the use of looking behind at the moment when we must open the mysterious shutters of the impossible? Time and Space died yesterday. We are already living in the absolute, since we have already created eternal, omnipresent speed.

9.   We want to glorify war – the only cure for the world – militarism, patriotism, the destructive gesture of the anarchists, the beautiful ideas which kill, and contempt for woman.

10.   We want to demolish museums and libraries, fight morality, feminism and all opportunist and utilitarian cowardice.

11.   We will sing of the great crowds agitated by work, pleasure and revolt; the multi-coloured and polyphonic surf of revolutions in modern capitals; the nocturnal vibration of the arsenals and the workshops beneath their violent electric moons; the gluttonous railway stations devouring smoking serpents; factories suspended from the clouds by the thread of their smoke; bridges with the leap of gymnasts flung across the diabolic cutlery of sunny rivers; adventurous steamers sniffing the horizon; great-breasted locomotives, puffing on the rails like enormous steel horses with long tubes for bridle, and the gliding flight of aeroplanes whose propeller sounds like the flapping of a flag and the applause of enthusiastic crowds.

ACUMEN
PATIENT CAPITAL
THAT DARES
TO GO WHERE
MARKETS
HAVE FAILED
AND AID HAS
FALLEN SHORT

ACUMEN
REJECTING
COMPLACENCY,
CHALLENGING
CORRUPTION,
BREAKING
THROUGH
BUREAUCRACY

ACUMEN
LEADERSHIP
THAT DOES
WHAT
IS RIGHT,
NOT WHAT
IS EASY

ACUMEN
THE HUMILITY
TO SEE THE
WORLD AS IT IS,
THE AUDACITY
TO IMAGINE
THE WORLD AS
IT COULD BE

ACUMEN
THE AMBITION
TO LEARN AT
THE EDGE, THE
WISDOM TO
ADMIT FAILURE,
THE COURAGE
TO START AGAIN

ACUMEN
THE RADICAL
IDEA OF
CREATING
HOPE IN
A CYNICAL
WORLD

ACUMEN
CHANGING
THE WAY
THE WORLD
TACKLES
POVERTY

**MADHU
GOPAL**
ONE OF
10 MILLION
BENEFITTING
WITH
POWER
FROM
D. LIGHT
DESIGN

Acumen / johnson banks / UK / 2013

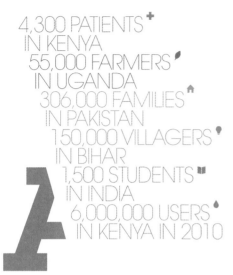

4,300 PATIENTS
IN KENYA
55,000 FARMERS
IN UGANDA
306,000 FAMILIES
IN PAKISTAN
150,000 VILLAGERS
IN BIHAR
1,500 STUDENTS
IN INDIA
6,000,000 USERS
IN KENYA IN 2010

The global 'impact investor' Acumen, when re-calibrating its brand in 2013, decided to introduce its own 148-word manifesto that clearly stated its reason to be and acted as its 'moral compass':

It starts by standing with the poor, listening to voices unheard, and recognizing potential where others see despair.

It demands investing as a means, not an end, daring to go where markets have failed and aid has fallen short. It makes capital work for us, not control us.

It thrives on moral imagination: the humility to see the world as it is, and the audacity to imagine the world as it could be. It's having the ambition to learn at the edge, the wisdom to admit failure, and the courage to start again.

It requires patience and kindness, resilience and grit: a hard-edged hope. It's leadership that rejects complacency, breaks through bureaucracy, challenges corruption. Doing what's right, not what's easy.

It's the radical idea of creating hope in a cynical world. Changing the way the world tackles poverty and building a world based on dignity.

▲ AIA manifesto / Pentagram / USA / 2013

This verbal 'call to action' became the glue for an entire brand identity, using mini-manifestos that became the linking devices for the brand. From the website header to a simple structure for the chief executive's keynote speeches, Acumen's new verbal stance cemented its thought-leadership in the emerging sector of impact investment.

Other organizations have found manifesto-writing key to the process of self-definition. Shown on the right is the AIA's clear and proud statement of what it is to be an architect and what drives them: 'We are America's architects. We are committed to building a better world. And we can only do it together.'[12]

What do we do and how do we do it?

THE WHAT AND THE HOW

The value of working out 'what we do and how we do it' is that then we can summarize all the functional, 'doing' stuff. So if, for instance, you and I, and the team from Samsung were filling out this box, we'd start with something like 'design and produce world-class technological solutions, from mobile phones to TVs and washing machines'. This is pretty straightforward stuff and, of course, many global users value what their Samsung products do and how they do it, but they don't always form an emotional bond with their supplier. Samsung are a bit cheaper than some of the alternatives, they produce many new models a year and they aren't Apple. They seem to sit in the middle of Maslow's pyramid, unable (or unwilling?) to clamber up into 'status' or 'self-esteem'. But perhaps that's entirely intentional.

Audi's use of 'Vorsprung durch Technik' (crudely translated as 'advancement through technology') puts the what and how of technology at the forefront. Meanwhile, Volvo would probably describe itself as making solid, dependable, workman-like vehicles (they did, after all, make tractors for decades[13]), yet they have found a way to take the corollary of this – safety – as their key emotional driver. The founders stated that, 'Cars are driven by people. The guiding principle behind everything we make at Volvo, therefore, is – and must remain – safety.' The intention is to persuade you that, yes, a Volvo estate may not be groovy, will not turn heads or attract admiring glances, but it will keep you and your loved ones safe. And, for some time, Volvo has used the strapline 'For Life'. More recently, they have taken this principle one step further and begun distributing a spray paint that makes surfaces glow when headlights shine on them, hence turning cyclist safety into part of *their* brand territory. Clever.

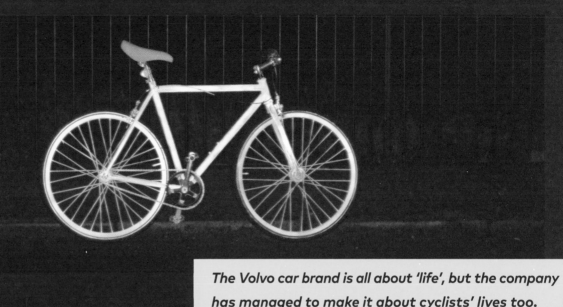

The Volvo car brand is all about 'life', but the company has managed to make it about cyclists' lives too.

WHEN 'WHAT AND HOW' BECOMES 'WHAT WE'RE NOT'

To me, at least, the core purpose of a brand is critical, but that doesn't mean the 'what and how' can't take the lead in the way a brand is communicated. Some brands take great pleasure in avoiding 'marketing speak' altogether, and they tend to be those who are led by – and hence stand or fall by – the quality of their product.

The technology company Dyson, which was founded on innovative engineering and design, has no marketing department. The idea is that the company is judged purely and simply on its latest products – 'I don't believe in brand at all', Sir James Dyson once said – and it remains committed to 'invention and improvement'.[14] Of course, the Dyson 'brand' does exist – in an existential way, brands always do – and a Dyson brand book is given to all employees on their first day, but the company chooses to be defined by what it does, with its products becoming the sole builders of the brand. Just the briefest look at the Dyson product range demonstrates many of the tics of modern marketing – catchy descriptions such as 'Doesn't lose suction, ever' and nattily named products such as Airblade™ – but the company is just as likely to talk about taking five years and 5,127 prototypes to get to the world's first functioning bagless vacuum cleaner.

Steve Jobs had similar views on the interface of marketing, seemingly permanently associating the principles of branding with the notion of 'selling'. That's why it's pretty hard to say how Apple officially defines its brand. We can all define the 'what and how' – Apple designs and produces the finest possible products for the digital age, but the 'why' is a little harder to define. Perhaps it's to do with ease and sheer enjoyment: *to transform and delight our daily lives with the finest technology, ideas, interfaces and solutions that man can imagine. And then the ones most people can't*. Perhaps.

The closest we can get to any formal statement of how and why Apple does what it does is by studying the words of its key designer, Jonathan Ive: 'Apple's goal isn't to make money. Our goal is to design and develop and bring to market good products... We try not to bring out another product that's just different. Different and "new" is relatively easy. Doing something that's genuinely better is very hard.'[15]

Tesla Motors, set up by PayPal co-founder Elon Musk, takes the 'product-first' approach to its logical conclusion by presenting itself as 'product-only', relying entirely on forums, videos and blogs and putting precisely zero dollars into advertising. As Musk himself points out: 'A lot of companies get confused – they spend money on things that don't actually make the company better.'[16] Clearly this places a huge onus on the product experience itself to be sensational in order for that 'buzz' to spread and for word of mouth to replace word of ad man. As it happens, travelling in a Tesla is a unique experience, and perhaps its zero-budget ad spend will become the new normal.

THE MUJI APPROACH: NO BRAND

Another distinct 'anti-brand' is the Japanese retailer Muji. Originally conceived as a reaction to 1980s consumer excesses, Muji (derived from 'Mujirushi', which is Japanese for 'no brand') adopts the stance of 'su', which means 'plain' or 'unadorned', so the products are merely a frame for its customers' individuality. Muji projects no names or logos, and the products are designed entirely around purchasers' needs. 'Mujirushi' overlaps with the key concept of 'ryohin' – the value of good items that may not try to be the very best but merely try to be 'enough'.[17]

Muji sticks carefully to anonymity. Unless you accidentally leave the label on, there is nothing about the products that will reveal where they were bought. The company also refuses to use strong colours, celebrity advertising or excess packaging, or to carry out discount marketing, or to use any demographics in target marketing. Muji won't do link-ups with famous designers or, critically, design products that wouldn't work in a small- to medium-sized apartment. Much as some fashion labels deliberately stop making clothes over a certain size ('36-inch waist, sir? Sorry, nothing for you here'), Muji's aesthetic is so minimal, so unadorned, that its target market is self-selecting.

▲ ▶ Muji packaging / Japan / from 1979 onwards

Research kills cancer.

cruk.org

Related to the 'no brand' concept is the idea of pure, unadulterated honesty. For decades, it seemed that telling the truth about what was *really* happening in a market, really telling it straight, was a complete no-no. This is perhaps why a generation of innovators such as Dyson and Jobs came to conflate 'marketing' with 'selling' – i.e., marketing could never really bring itself to tell the truth.

An interesting twist on this is the recent adopted stance of the charity Cancer Research. For decades, cancer charities had skirted nervously around the core truth of what they do: raise cash to invest into more research.

Paradoxically, the simple observation that 'if we raise more money we stand a greater chance of stopping cancer' was downplayed for fear of either offending those either affected or over-promising as regards solutions.

But, finally, Cancer Research took the bold step of simply stating the truth – *research kills cancer* – and this combative, almost belligerent, stance now supplies a key point of difference and positions them as the truth-tellers in a very competitive market.

THE KEY TO STANDING OUT

Many people use the word 'positioning' to describe this part of the brand model and, to those who understand the concept, that's fine. To those who don't, and to make things simpler, just ask – what makes us different? What makes us stand apart from others in our market? This forces people to concentrate hard on true differentials.

As we've already seen with Step 2's product-led examples, a precise design approach can *be* that difference. A Leica camera is clearly differentiated on performance and quality, but also trades on a unique history in the timeline of photography. Who wouldn't want to use the same brand of camera as Andreas Feininger or Henri Cartier-Bresson?

The Avis case study in the previous chapter remains another classic example of 'difference' – and in an undifferentiated market such as car hire, it was the masterstroke that put Avis in a different place in the minds of its consumers.

It is in generic markets that concentrating hard on the true difference can often be the key to unlocking a brand's potential: in our Dove example on page 63, it's the authenticity of the Campaign for Real Beauty that has helped create that critical point of difference. This can, of course, increasingly work from an employee and HR perspective. If you're considering working for or with an organization that has no perceivable point of difference, why do it? Increasingly, companies are realizing that just 'doing what they always did' may not be enough to guarantee that the next generation of recruits will share their homogeneous, default vision of the future – the old marketing principle of a 'me too' brand just isn't enough any more. Being aware of and trying to define your brand, and having a point of difference in customers' and potential employees' minds is the key, rather than just functional product differences.

THE VALUE OF A CLEAR TARGET

There's an old phrase – the target market – which sounds a little like being at a rifle range, but it does at least focus a brand's mind on who they are really here for, and it's remarkably easy for brands to lose sight of this. Clothing brands such as Gap in the USA and Billabong in Australia started with clear ideals (clothes for the generation gap, or cool surfwear) but decades later have lost their way – their audiences are so wide and diffuse that no one really knows what they stand for any more. How many teenage and twenty-something hipsters want to be seen buying clothes at the same place that dad buys his trousers? Not many.

No wonder that brands such as Supreme have far more traction with a teenage audience, coupled with canny marketing techniques that mum and dad are never going to understand – that's the whole point. Refusing to 'sell out' like other 'once-skate-now-mass' brands such as Stüssy and Skechers, Supreme cultivates its cult of hard-core skaters. It limits its brand to one store per city, and produces intentionally scarce editions of clothing, making a feature of their rarity and hence escalating the brand even higher.[18]

Who are we here for?

AlibaBaiduMaz DatSuzuKia HyunDawovo ShiNissAcuratsu FujubishiSubaruji Samkookult.

A recurring issue for Asian brands: how to successfully stop merging into their competition.

* Asian brand-mash / Nick Asbury / UK / 2015

FINDING NEW MARKETS, DISCOVERING THAT DIFFERENCE

One of the key challenges for emerging brands and developing economies is how to differentiate their products clearly in a global marketplace.

For example, while the fact that Samsung represents somewhere between a fifth and a quarter of South Korea's economy is undeniable, because the company itself produces everything from phones to washing machines it's hard for a North American or European consumer to get a *true fix* on what the brand really stands for. This has been a perennial issue for Asian brands for decades.

Japanese brands such as Sony, Canon and Nikon only decided to adopt 'Western' versions of their names relatively recently. In the 1930s Canon was actually called Kwanon, and Nikon Kogaku Tokyo was only shortened to Nikon in the 1950s, which is

also when Sony's current typestyle began to emerge. National/ Panasonic adopted 'English' lettering in the 1960s, but the now-prevalent Panasonic logo only emerged in the early 1970s.

Unfortunately, the choice of the Panasonic logo, set in a ubiquitous sans-serif bold typeface, presents virtually no personality to the world; nonetheless one of its brands, Technics, is loved the world over for its speakers and turntables. Perhaps 'no personality' is what the team at Panasonic is going for – but I doubt it.

This challenge for Asian brands to differentiate has been met by Uniqlo, which (as we will see on page 238) has embraced its Japanese-ness and made it key to its personality, and how it interacts with the world.

Emerging Chinese brands such as Lenovo, Huawei and Mi have serious 'positioning' questions to answer, as we will see on page 155, but as more Chinese brands begin to emerge and 'Made in China' morphs into 'Designed in China'[19] they, too, like Japanese brands half a century earlier, will have to decide how much of their heritage to leave behind. Just the briefest of scans of any list of 'valuable Chinese brands' reveals that many of them still have the word 'China' in their name: Bank of China, China Mobile, China Life, Air China, China Telecommunications, etc. Whether these locally focused brands can make the jump to global status without a name change is debatable, unless they simply see their national market as sufficient and stop there.

FRET CREATES

HANDMADE
NATURAL FOOD
avoiding the obscure,
CHEMICALS, ADDITIVES
& PRESERVATIVES
common to so much of the
'PREPARED' AND 'FAST'
FOOD ON THE M
TODAY

A BUSY KITCHEN, A BAKER'S OVEN
THE BEST INGREDIENTS
(WILTSHIRE-CURED HAM, FRESH
SMOKED SCOTTISH SALMON, FRESH
OD ORGANIC COFF

Don't be shy
Go for good, honest, natural food
(look and feel great).

Eat colourful
Enjoy fresh, vibrant food
in all its natural glory.

LOVINGLY HANDMADE USING AMAZING
NATURAL INGREDIENTS
IN OUR KITCHEN
IN THIS SHOP

THE VALUE OF VALUES

In certain circles, overly rigid 'brand values' can become little more than a tick-box or a rod with which to beat a project. 'You can't do this' (shouts an overly zealous brand manager) 'because it only satisfies 7 out of our 8 values! It must tick all 8!' I'm joking, but only just.

Let's widen the topic out a little. Even though on one level it seems bizarre to write down what someone values and believes in the most, and then debate their personality, character and behaviour, it's often incredibly helpful from an internal perspective to have a clear 'map' of what the company someone works for believes in.

For example, by consistently stating their brand mantra, 'never knowingly undersold', John Lewis is putting its values and 'honesty' to the fore (while, of course, cannily using 'never knowingly', just in case any product is actually more expensive in its stores).

The difficulty with brand values seems to come when many companies appear to share the same ones – indeed, there's a school of thought that maintains there is a universal set from which we could all choose those that apply to us. So when those values get trotted out the same way by different organizations, it's little wonder that people glaze over.

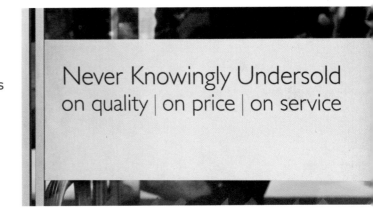

Never Knowingly Undersold
on quality | on price | on service

Done well and chosen carefully, however, values and beliefs can become critical in defining organizations. Gourmet food chain Pret A Manger is committed to making its food fresh, every day, and partners charities with their local Pret. At the end of each day, unsold food goes to a worthy cause rather than in the bin. It's part of what Pret believes in and has become a powerful way to define the brand. It makes consumers who hear the story admire them more and appreciate the commitment to freshness.

Here's how to make 'values' really mean something: let employees define their own and then display them in reception for all to see (and share).

The best definition of 'what we value the most' seems to be a judicious mix of what is currently true and what is aspired to. This is especially true for those re-branding, otherwise the values won't be adopted and consumers will see through them straightaway. There's absolutely no hard and fast way to proceed.

When Google originally sat down in the early 2000s and wrote its famous 'ten things we know to be true' list, it was identifying the universal truths at the core of what it does. Google called it a manifesto, but it's essentially a list of the things Google believed in, and valued most, and it became their driving force, in many different versions, for years to come.

Google's Ten Things

1. Focus on the user and all else will follow.
2. It's best to do one thing really, really well.
3. Fast is better than slow.
4. Democracy on the web works.
5. You don't need to be at your desk to need an answer.
6. You can make money without doing evil.
7. There's always more information out there.
8. The need for information crosses all borders.
9. You can be serious without a suit.
10. Great just isn't good enough.

US-based Uncommon Schools developed a compelling chart (below) to describe how it approaches its work, firmly throwing out the sector clichés and adopting something far stronger. No one can read this brief list of what it stands for and not be impressed.

Some choose to drive their entire organization with their agreed values at the very centre of what they do. By choosing a 'values-based model', the aim is that the organization and the employees become aligned and begin to share common beliefs.

As an example, the 90-year-old stone company, Luck Stone, has agreed its core values (*creativity, commitment, leadership and integrity*) and every single one of its 900-odd employees has also decided on and agreed their own personal set. Every morning all of the employees are involved in a discussion about company and personal values and how they overlap. In the project opposite, employees' own core values are shown in a vast sculpture in reception. It sends out a pretty powerful message to visitors about how values can be made to mean something real, personal and genuinely tangible.[20]

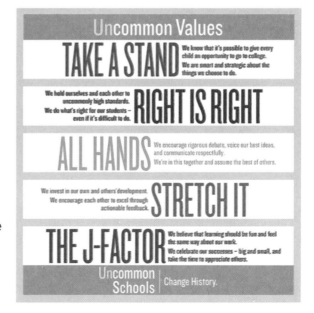

▲ Uncommon values / Uncommon Schools / USA / from 2005 onwards

HOW TO GET VALUES AGREED

There are various techniques that can be used to find brand values. The most direct is to stand with a flip-chart and pen and ask a room full of people, 'so what do you value the most?' and take it from there. Experience, however, suggests that this may not always be the most productive route. What seems to work better is to take interviewees' responses from the interviews in Step 1 and 'cluster' the values, in the manner of the diagram shown right.

This becomes a launch pad from which teams can rule out, add and re-write. Clustering provides a place from which to start, just as the idea of drafting brand scenarios provided a 'start'. Most teams aim to agree on three to five words that strike the right chord, and increasingly these are phrases or sentences. Some consultants drill further into the shortlisted values and sub-divide them into key groups, so for the Virgin Atlantic example we looked at on page 94, the final core idea became 'everyday pioneers', surrounded by groups of values, as shown below.

HOW SOME VALUES BECOME MORE VALUED

Sometimes certain values become points of difference in their own right. It is extremely fashionable at the moment for customer-facing brands to play up any perceived 'authenticity', primarily because this has been identified as a key driver for the generation of consumers who have followed on from Generation X, most commonly known as either 'Generation Y' or the 'millennials'. Another one of their nicknames neatly sums them up – 'Generation Next' – because this is the next big market for consumer brands.[21]

Commentators have suggested that millennials don't want to 'play the game' like their boomer parents whose divorces and poor work-life balance they view negatively, and can swiftly find out online if something is genuine, legit and honest.

So countless brands are chasing honesty and authenticity as key perceived values...but how good are they at doing this? One of the first to use authenticity was Nike when it defined its brand 'mantra' as 'Authentic Athletic Performance', famously

summed up by the strapline 'Just do it'. On the face of it, not a particularly meaningful strapline, but when backed up by relentless advertising campaigns leading with the gung-ho, 'get on with it' aspect of the line, it has become one of the world's most famous three-word phrases.

Superdry may look like a Japanese brand, but it isn't. It reaches the world from its headquarters on an industrial estate in Cheltenham, England.

Some brands have literally 'created' authenticity in order to present themselves in a particular way. The seemingly 'Japanese' brand Superdry, for example, isn't actually even Asian. Inspired by a trip to Asia by one of its founders in the early 2000s, Superdry has built a significant global presence by mashing together vintage Americana and Japanese references, and badging virtually every piece of clothing accordingly. This has all been done with a pretty astonishing amount of chutzpah and a lack of interest in any factual accuracy. Did they have anything to do with the 1954 Japanese ski squad? Or with Japanese athletics in 1961? Er, no.

But that doesn't stop them suggesting so on hoodies. Nor do they have any proven links to Japanese universities or Tokyo State Athletics. Even their 'translated' name makes no apparent sense, allegedly translating as 'Maximum dry – do'.[22]

In some ways, this is a bizarre reversal of the time when any visitor to Japan would be greeted with a sea of 'cool' T-shirts brandishing meaningless English phrases – the boot (and T-shirt, and fleece) is now on the other foot. And it seems that millions of people across the world either don't know or don't care – and they definitely don't search out the label hidden inside the clothes that quietly says 'British design. Spirit of Japan'. But, while the hoodies might declare that they are from 'London, Paris, New York, Tokyo', the closest shop to Japan itself is actually nearly 600 miles away – in South Korea.[23]

As it happens, this type of 'created' brand isn't a new idea. Cooking icon Betty Crocker was invented as a virtual entity to answer a flood of letters to General Mills, Inc.[24] Betty does, however, move with the times – her portrait gets updated every decade.

The back-story of Jack Daniel's seems almost too good to be true, but, yes, there was an actual Jack Daniel (albeit a very short chap standing just over five foot, who allegedly named the flagship brand, Number 7, after the number of his mistresses). While it took

Jug c. 1890   Glass Bottle c. 1895   Amber Glass c. 1905   Pre Prohibition

Pre Prohibition   Round c. 1947   c. 1964   2003

a while for the adverts to be based on the legend of 'Jack', the label itself has only undergone tiny amendments since before Prohibition. So, amazingly, that's about a century with a virtually untouched piece of packaging design. Now other liquor brands are looking at the Jack Daniel's example and beginning to understand that any perceived history and inherent brand 'legacy' can finally be exploited. Bacardi has shifted to selling itself as the living, breathing epitome of Hemingway-quoting Havana spirit of rampant revolutionary excess (or something like that).[25]

In a different category, yet steeped in heritage, Royal Enfield branched out from weapons and lawnmowers to motorcycles, and by the 1960s was building and marketing bikes in India. The Indian branch survived the demise of the original HQ and has become a local market leader in its mid-size sector. A recent brand re-invention is aimed at the global marketplace with exclusive stores across Europe, North and South America and South-East Asia, and a distinctive new swagger.[26] Also in India, Apollo tyres has looked hard at its brand, re-designed many of its elements, and taken the honest step of pointing out that these are tyres for 'where the Silk Road meets the Autobahn' and are 'engineered for the worst' – a wry observation about the fact that if they can survive Indian roads, they can survive anywhere.

The Royal Enfield brand has been reborn, but now it's exporting from *India* – not to.

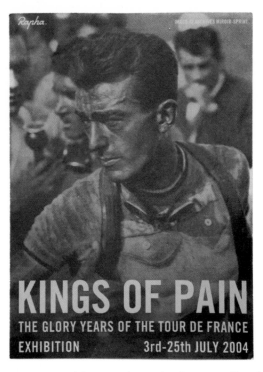

KINGS OF PAIN

THE GLORY YEARS OF THE TOUR DE FRANCE

EXHIBITION   3rd–25th JULY 2004

In a significant contrast to Superdry, the cycling brand Rapha, over virtually the same period, has also established itself, but in a very different way. While Superdry's 'Japanese' roots are, in effect, entirely artificial, Rapha's authentic commitment to and love of road racing drives everything it does. Propelled by a personal love of the sport and the spotting of a clear 'gap' in the market for cycling clothes that were both high-performance and stylish, its founder endured hundreds of meetings looking for backers, proving there was a market in that gap. On paper it must have seemed a risky venture: this was long before cycling had acquired any of the 'cool' it now exudes, and most cycling clothes only came in varying hues of fluorescent.[27]

Inspired by the physical travails that long-distance cyclists endure over hours in the saddle, this is a brand created by cyclists, for cyclists. The 'Rapha' name is itself a revival of a sub-brand of the legendary French Saint Raphaël team. The brand's launch wasn't celebrated with

a catwalk show but with an exhibition entitled 'Kings of Pain' about Rapha's cycling heroes. Since the dotcom wasn't available, they used the '.cc' suffix – technically the Cocos Islands in the Indian Ocean – but now thanks to Rapha, synonymous with 'cycling clubs'.

Odd though it may seem, especially to non-cyclists, the brand narrative is built around endurance and courage – personal gain despite prolonged pain and punishment. Rapha's motto is 'Ex duris gloria' ('glory through suffering') and the second of its four core values is to 'suffer'.

By recognizing a crucial symbiosis between the physical torture of the sport and the sheer personal achievement of climbing mountains or finishing 60-kilometre road rides, Rapha is simply saying to its core audience, 'we understand'.

And this understanding is delivered with the products. The first signature jersey replaced the fluoro with black, used state-of-the-art wool and concentrated on crucial details such as chin guards and easily reached O-ring pocket pulls – product innovations born not from focus groups or catwalks, but Wednesday morning rides and a deep understanding of the sport. Rapha products are made to be seen at 50 metres yet survive close inspection at 50 mm: impact and detail are equally paramount.

As the brand expands its reach into endorsement deals (Team Sky, Wiggins), holidays and skincare, eyes up the glasses and helmet markets, and leads the way in the expansion of

women's cycling, one thing remains paramount – that its employees believe in the company's first core value – 'love the sport'. That love comes across in every jersey they sell and every cappuccino they serve.[28]

PERSONALITY AND THE RISE OF POSSESSIVE BRANDING

Discovering and deciding their verbal definition can have a profound impact on some brands, bringing words right into the foreground. Rather than spending precious time defining core beliefs, and then leaving them in internal documents, some organizations are making these definitions the basis of their entire communications strategies.

One of the earliest examples of this was the Young Women's Christian Association's decision to subvert the norm by making their strapline twice as large as their actual acronym. They sought to re-define themselves by placing great emphasis on the words, and inspired a series of projects that turned unexpected norms upside down. The next logical step was to start sentences with 'we' and 'I' – the words you use when entering into genuine, first- and second-person conversations and dialogues.

Charities such as Macmillan Cancer Support also began to define themselves with a series of 'we' statements – 'we fund nurses, we climb mountains, we change lives, we are Macmillan...'. This was a radical opening up of the charity's reason to be and was hugely successful in gaining supporters. For organizations keen to re-define themselves in their audience's eyes, this showed a way to do it and to reassess. Other organizations are now seeing how their personality can be strongly expressed in a personal way – so for Invictus Games, a series of games for wounded, injured and sick servicemen and women, the 'I am' portion of the name becomes the beginning of a series of statements about both the competitors and the games.

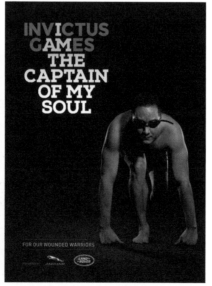

▲ Invictus Games / Lambie-Nairn / UK / 2014 ▲ YWCA / Landor / USA / 2003

▲ Macmillan Cancer Support / Wolff Olins, in-house creative team, Arthur London / UK / 2006 onwards

WE FUND NURSES
WE FIGHT INEQUALITY
WE MAKE COFFEE
WE RUN MARATHONS
WE SUPPORT FAMILIES
WE PROVIDE GRANTS
WE GIVE OUR TIME
WE CHANGE LIVES

We're all affected by cancer.
We can all do something to help.
www.macmillan.org.uk

Supported by JCDecaux

WE ARE MACMILLAN.
CANCER SUPPORT

If you're living with cancer
visit **macmillan.org.uk** for
emotional support

**WE ARE
MACMILLAN.
CANCER SUPPORT**

TIRED
OF
PUTTING
ON A
BRAVE
FACE?

This re-branding showed just how powerfully a verbal repositioning of a major charity could change perceptions, clarify...and also differentiat

---

Talking about cancer toolkit

MAKING A
BIG SUBJECT
EASY
TO TALK
ABOUT

WE ARE
MACMILLAN.
CANCER SUPPORT

Bring and buy sale

WE
LOVE A
BARGAIN

WE ARE
MACMILLAN.
CANCER SUPPORT

WE ARE
MACMILLAN.
CANCER SUPPORT

WHAT
TO SAY
TO
CHILDREN
WHEN AN
ADULT
HAS CANCER

We've got a new visual language

If a picture can paint a thousand words it's important
we get those pictures right. Our brand identity refresh
will help us make our images more personal, more
engaging and more inspiring. In fact – as our alphabet
spells out – we can do and say so much more. Find out
more on the green rooms.

I AM NIKON

The Nikon brand, keen to broaden its market from its heartland of high-quality digital SLRs, also introduced its own 'I am...' concept. The strategic background evolved from a technology/product focus to a more customer/user approach. People could embrace the idea, which, in turn, positioned Nikon as more modern, engaged and, of course, *authentic* in the process. It worked especially well with social media: an 'I am...' Facebook picture-sharing application allowed customers to share their own 'I am' moments with each other.

By using 'I' and 'we', the verbal branding becomes far more personal than the traditional, third-person style of most corporate-speak. The knock-on effect of this move to more personal, *possessive* branding, if you like, is that more and more organizations are trying to become increasingly 'human'.

One observer called this the 'tyranny of we', as we are bombarded with friendly messages from the moment we wake up. [29]

And it can cause problems linguistically, too. Waitrose have a 'my Waitrose' card – yet at the checkout you are asked 'Do you have *your my* Waitrose card with you'. [30]

My	My Waitrose
Your	My Waitrose
Her	My Waitrose
His	My Waitrose
Our	My Waitrose
Their	My Waitrose

Furthermore, you don't go to a cashpoint any more, you go to 'Cash out' (First Direct) or 'A Hole in the Wall' (Barclays). Machines are now replacing actual people in Barclays branches and are as likely to say 'Hello, I am Sally. Here's what I can do for you' as show you your bank balance.

What these corporations are trying to do, in a slightly clumsy way, is imbue their machinery with some sense of character, a hint of personality.

Whether anyone would actually, truly want to become 'friends' with their bank (and its cashpoint) is, of course, highly debatable.

The I/Me/We phenomenon:
McDonald's: I'm lovin' it
Reebok: I am what I am
IBM: I think, therefore IBM
Avis: We try harder
FedEx: We live to deliver
Innocent: Hello, we're Innocent
Obama: Yes we can
My Sainsbury's
Your M&S...

E. coli

Salmonella typhi

Schistosoma

Cholera vibrios

Hepatitis A

WATER.

charity: water

• Charity: Water / USA / from 2006 onwards

GETTING EVERYTHING RIGHT

A great example of brand thinking working perfectly on every level is Charity: Water. Its unique way of working developed when an early project to fund and repair a series of wells was followed up with an email to donors, containing visual proof of how their money was helping. The response was significant.

This gave the organization early and crucial insight: by setting itself up with state-of-the-art, start-up technology it made tracking and recording the funds donated its key reason to be – 'restoring faith to donors, inspiring giving and inspiring compassion. That is our why' (distilled into the phrase, 'water changes everything'). If we were filling out Charity: Water's brand 'map', it would read something like this:

Our ambition:	Re-invent charity (i.e., make sure the money gets to where it's supposed to) – 'a brand built around hope instead of guilt, instilling confidence in non-profits and building a community of generous world-changers'
Why we're here:	Water changes everything. Restore faith to donors, inspire giving, inspire compassion
What and how:	Supply clean water and make sure the projects are communicated with stories, images and feedback
What makes us different:	100% of the money donated goes to projects and donors can track their money, where it's going, what it's doing
Our values:	Helpful, optimistic, honest, adventurous, generous, grateful, creative, respectful
Our personality:	Inspirational, exciting, full of possibility, transparent, clear and simple

What's fascinating about this stance is that most water charities would have 'to provide clean water and change lives' as their *why*. But Charity: Water has flipped that around and realized that, actually, to keep its fundraising pipeline working, it must make the donors central to what it does. If you like, its purpose is to show where people's money is going – it's as simple as that.

This, allied to overwhelmingly positive imagery of the projects, simple infographics and a compellingly simple visual identity, completes a very well-thought-through and positioned brand, and one that has been hugely successful.

WHERE BRAND AND STRATEGY OVERLAP

In some boardrooms there is still a divide between traditional corporate strategy (mission and vision) and the new approach (led by agreed purpose, core values, and people talking about our 'brand' and 'personality'). For a traditional audience, accepting that 'brand' could actually have a profound, rather than a cosmetic, effect can take time. Done well, the branding process can help facilitate this change. By definition, a new or amended brand cannot be decided by middle management – it has to involve typically more conservative senior figures.

Usually, within Steps 1 and 2 of a project, these issues start to surface. If we return to the two 'ageing' brands discussed earlier, Gap and Billabong, re-aligning to their original audiences (in Billabong's case) or stopping being clothes for all (in Gap's case) would mean rewriting their entire strategies. If a brand such as Supreme decided to grow, it would have to abandon its cool status and scarcity model once its clothes were no longer seen as 'cult'.

The truth is, for *all* of the successful case studies littered throughout this book, strategy and brand are umbilically linked. If you're filling out the six questions with a team and you can't agree on your overall direction of travel, or key audiences, then how can you define your core 'why', or work out how to communicate? Conversely, there's no point in having the greatest and most carefully detailed 'emotional' brand definition if the 'what and how' isn't defined, or doesn't match.

DEC ☀

DISASTERS EMERGENCY COMMITTEE

☀ THIS IS WHO WE ARE: ACTIONAID, AGE UK, BRITISH RED CROSS, CAFOD, CARE INTERNATIONAL, CHRISTIAN AID, CONCERN WORLDWIDE, ISLAMIC RELIEF, MERLIN, OXFAM, PLAN, SAVE THE CHILDREN, TEARFUND, WORLD VISION. **TOGETHER WE'RE STRONGER**

The design stage can also play a crucial role in strategic decisions and leadership. For the Disasters Emergency Committee (the DEC), a 'pop-up' fundraising brand for 14 of the UK's largest aid agencies, it was only at the final stage of choosing the design that the strategic choice became clear.

Should the DEC choose the idea shown left, which expressed its constituent parts (the 'who', if you like) or the idea shown right, leading with 'why' it was jointly appealing for funds? The DEC correctly chose the 'why' and developed a system that allowed both the DEC and each appeal to be branded equally – but the combination of verbal and visual branding was critical to the process.[31]

BROADENING OUT OUR ORIGINAL DIAGRAM

The benefits of simplifying a brand down to six questions are that what can, at times, seem overwhelmingly complex becomes more manageable. Keep saying this to yourself: if you can at least define *something* in each of those areas, then you're doing a heck of a lot better than many other brands.

What we 'do' with this information is the next bit, and this is where we need to briefly expand our diagram a little more. For example, thinking harder about *who we're here for* often leads to 'segmentation' of markets, which, in turn, starts to suggest the different types of message that each segment needs. So a political party will agree its overall 'pitch' to a country, but will tailor the messages it uses when speaking at a Trade Union conference, or to a group of pensioners, for example.

Values are, of course, useful to define, but it's often just as useful to show and demonstrate how key values affect behaviour. If 'integrity' is a value, for instance, what does that really mean? Drill further into the what and how and you start to define actual products and services, and perhaps an organization's approach to innovation.

There are two overall approaches to this: either you can place all of the content of your agreed brand in the centre, and build out again across all 'touchpoints' – your 'voice', 'place', 'offer' or 'behaviour' (see below) – or you can keep extending our original box's key sections outwards (see opposite). We'll come back to some of this in Step 5.

BRAND COMMUNITY

As illustration: to include
Advertising
Identity and design
PR
Face to face
Digital
Sponsorship

As illustration: to include
Physical and digital space for:
Retail and trading
Workplace
Experience

VOICE   PLACE

BRAND STORY

OFFER   BEHAVIOUR

As illustration: to include
Products and services
Channels
Pricing
Fulfilment

As illustration: to include
Culture
HR policies and practices
Customer and employee service charters

This affects:
- How we define and segment our key external target markets
- How we define the key 'stakeholders' of our brand
- How we rank these

In turn, this affects:
- Precise messaging and product offering for each segment
- Tone of voice for each segment

This affects:
- The precise make-up of our products and services
- Which channels we use to market ourselves
- How we resource, price, or fund what we do
- How we approach research, development and innovation

This affects:
- How we match what we do (or what we do best) to our agreed target audiences
- How we can position ourselves away from our competition
- How we can create a unique and ownable 'space' in a market

Who are we here for?

What do we do and how do we do it?

What makes us different?

Why are we here?

What do we value the most?

What's our personality?

This affects:
- How we behave as an organization/brand/company
- How we behave as individuals
- What the 'outcome' of this behaviour will be
- How employees view us, and how future employees will view us

In turn, this affects:
- How we work with our employees
- Our human resources approach and practice
- Our charters

This affects:
- Everything we do – how we think, talk, create
- Our strategy
- How we're perceived by our key audiences and stakeholders

In turn, this affects:
- How we present ourselves
- Our brand identity
- Our approach to advertising, communications and PR
- How we approach our digital/physical/retail spaces and experiences
- How and where we work

This affects:
- Our character – how we come across to audiences internally and externally
- How we communicate

In turn, this affects:
- Our messaging and our tone of voice

Our ambition

This is driven by: historical definitions of mission and vision, a brand's context, long-term strategic goals and objectives

SUMMING IT ALL UP

I started this chapter saying that it wasn't about writing snappy straplines and now, 50 pages later, I hope you believe me.

Of course, it can be fantastically useful to summarize what a brand stands for, in just a few words, and some of the famous slogans on the page opposite do exactly that. But it's just as useful to have an internal 'mantra' that helps an organization remember why it is there (such as Virgin Atlantic's 'everyday pioneers' or Nike's 'authentic athletic performance') and then allow external straplines to evolve, case by case, for tactical reasons, not strategic ones. We'll see later in Step 5 that telecoms brand O$_2$ has indeed had multiple external straplines in its 15-year life, yet the core idea behind the brand has remained the same.

THE JOURNEY

We've had to go deep into brand theory in this chapter. I hope you stayed with me and I hope it's been helpful. With luck, you'll be starting to see that Step 2 is critical to the future health of any brand and any branding project.

Without a strong verbal basis, a clear brand strategy and across-the-board agreement, a project is in danger and the visual work could be critically undermined before it has even begun. What this step illustrates is that with powerful definitions, manifestos, values and brand strategy, the stage is set for the creative work. And, as we will see, it often inspires and drives what comes next.

Summing up what we've covered in Step 2:
- *How to put a statement of 'why we're here' at the core of a brand*
- *The six key questions that our brand model has to answer*
- *How to use scenario writing to help the process and the rise of the manifesto*
- *How some brands take what they do and their 'product' as their reason to be*
- *How clarity about what makes a brand different, and who it is aimed at, is key*
- *How to turn boring old 'brand values' into powerful and usable tools*
- *How 'possessive branding' can work well, or can even work too well*
- *How narrative and strategy are intertwined*
- *How we can begin to broaden out our brand model*

The future's bright
I'm lovin' it
Beanz Meanz Heinz
We try harder
Think small
Think different
Because I'm worth it
A diamond is forever
The world's local bank
The ultimate driving machine
Vorsprung durch Technik
Impossible is nothing
Have a break...
Got milk?
Where's the beef?
Yes we can

This step wouldn't really exist if branding was always a linear, logical process. But projects can take twists and turns, and the line between stages can blur. The strategy in Step 2 should have a direct effect on Step 3, but sometimes the design process prompts new ideas. So, how do you bridge this gap?

2.5

BRIDGING THE GAP

raditionally, the branding business is set up to be a linear one. So this book is all about the process laid bare, a 'how to do it' in a few simple steps. Follow Steps 1, 2, 3, 4 and 5 pretty closely and, if I've written this properly and you've read it carefully, it should work.

But this half-step celebrates the parts of the process that can't quite be 'locked down'. In the crossover between the verbal ideas in the last step and the visual creativity in the next, there are often decisions to be made that involve both sides, sometimes simultaneously.

For example, a visual idea might crop up in Step 3, which, technically, falls just outside of the brief, but is so unusual and exciting that you might return to Step 2 and slightly rewrite some of the verbal ideas. Or the creative work in Step 3 may find a new verbal 'angle' on what has already been agreed and so it makes sense to return to the agreed script, as it were, and amend it.

Sometimes it's almost impossible to agree on the name of an idea or an organization until everyone sees the favourite names turned into visual ideas – it almost does a name a disservice *not* to see it turned into a design idea.

Some projects that involve the linking of many parts of an organization (sometimes called 'brand architecture'), and the visual process of diagrammatically articulating those parts, raise so many questions about strategy and structure that the narrative and design 'loop' has to begin again.

Blurring the lines between strategy and design takes courage and the willingness to leave things unresolved, at least for a while. If Steps 1 and 2 are about definition, and Steps 3 and 4 are about the creative, then this half-step is concerned with the translation of one idea into another.[1]

Define   Translate   Create

1 2   **2.5**   **3** **4** **5**

SHOULD YOU EVEN RECOGNIZE THE GAP?

It's a good question. Those of you reading this book and following its linear process are possibly thinking 'this man's a lunatic, you can't allow things to drift between the narrative and design processes'. And, yes, the narrative is normally 'locked down' at the end of Step 2 before you go onto the design stages. That fits well with most organizational structures – it's likely that serious grown-ups have been involved in either the agreement or even the authoring of Step 2, so why invite change? Why open the project out again, given the chance that some things might need to be adjusted?

The verbal and visual 'blur' implied by this step might scare some people and could imply that the decisions made in Step 2 weren't final – that they were just stepping stones towards the final outcome. But, allowing the stages to overlap, even planning for it, can be the key to great, and unexpected, brand solutions.

It's hard to say to an internal team or a client, as everyone gazes admiringly at the finalized brand narrative, 'now everyone remember this could change after the next stage', but that's the truth of it. Your choices seem to be either: pretend that it isn't going to happen or admit that things could change and manage expectations accordingly. In this book I'm trying to avoid 'what I've learned in 30 years' moments, but here's one – don't completely lock down the narrative stage as you enter the design phase. Leave the final, final sign-off until a little later, just in case...

HOW BRAND NARRATIVE CAN SOMETIMES FOLLOW DESIGN

There are many examples of Steps 2 and 3 getting a little muddled or following the 'wrong' order. What can happen fairly often is that organizations that may not have the budget to do detailed research and narrative 'jump' straight into the design process. This has its pluses and minuses as a strategy. In these cases, it's only within the design stage, or sometimes years later, that a coherent verbal narrative emerges.

So, for example, the re-alignment and re-design of Parc de la Villette's communications style was initially intended to give the park a better sense of *gestalt*, and present a coherent whole, not just the sum of its many parts (located in Paris, it contains a series of landscaped spaces, parks, architectural interventions, an exhibition hall, a science museum and a music museum). It was only after the initial re-design that the key phrase 'jardin des cultures' was brought to the foreground as a core idea to 'glue' its myriad activities together. For a decade the phrase did its job beautifully.[2]

▸ Parc de la Villette, Paris, re-brand / johnson banks / UK / 1999–2007 ▸ Parc de la Villette, Paris, verbal re-branding / Watermark & Co. / UK / 1999–2000

PARC LA VILLETTE

EMBOUTEILLAGE

COMPAGNIES LES COLPORTEURS ET FATTORE K.

GIORGIO BARBERIO CORSETTI
MISE EN SCÈNE

LE METAMORFOSI

PARC LA VILLETTE

CIRQUE TRIX
CIRKUS CIRKÖR & ORIONTEATERN

PARC LA

LICORNE

'Jardin des cultures' was a perfect verbal 'mantra' for Parc de la Villette for almost a decade. But the verbal idea followed, rather than preceded, the design into the public domain.

ÇA

CINÉMA EN PLEIN AIR

MACBETH
THÉÂTRE ÉQUESTRE
THÉÂTRE DU CENTAURE
D'APRÈS SHAKESPEARE

PARC LA VILLETTE

PARC LA VILLETTE

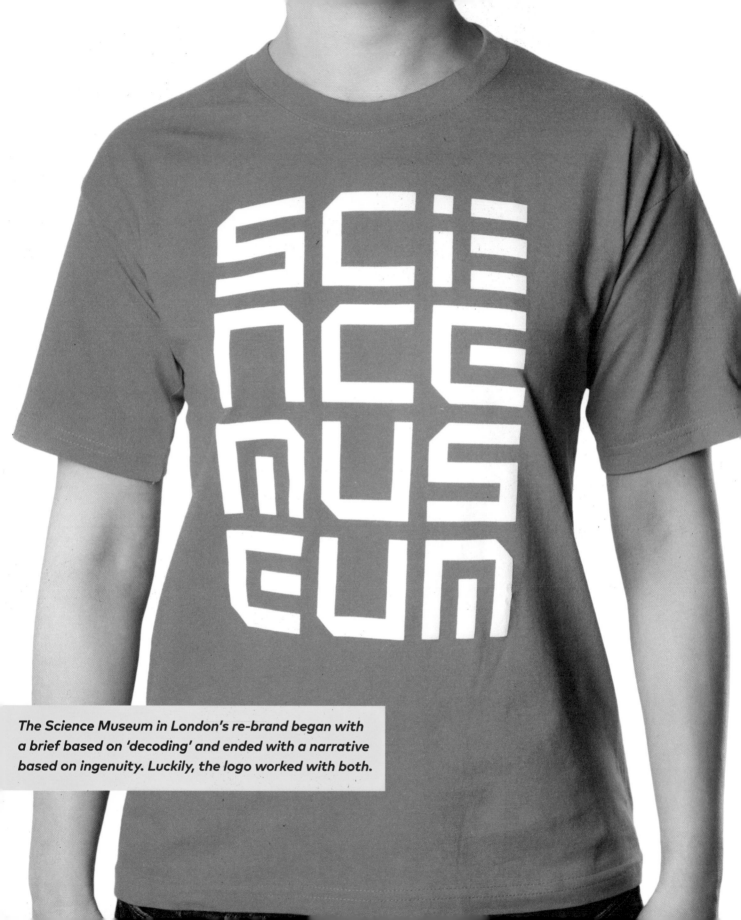

The Science Museum in London's re-brand began with a brief based on 'decoding' and ended with a narrative based on ingenuity. Luckily, the logo worked with both.

• Science Museum, London / johnson banks / UK / 2010 ▲ Verbal brand / Jane Wentworth and Associates / UK / 2011 ▲ Sendai Astronomical Observatory / johnson banks, Total Media / UK, Japan / 2008

London's Science Museum re-worked its brand identity after realizing that its 'stand-out' amidst the city's tourist attractions was pretty low. The first phase built on initial work on the museum's core offering that suggested its role was to 'decode science'.[3] Yet, not long after its launch, a more detailed piece of narrative work was commissioned that eventually culminated in a new core statement – 'the home of human ingenuity'. Luckily, the new narrative was able to complement the 'ingenious' nature of the institution's brand identity and did not unpick the now-complete design process.

HOW DESIGN DISCOVERIES CAN AFFECT NARRATIVE

In a similar fashion to the examples above, the design stage for a new observatory north of Tokyo began from a broad design brief rather than an established core narrative. It was only during the design process that an idea emerged that demystified the concepts of cosmology by using day-to-day examples.

The effect of a black hole was explained by drawing a visual analogy with a plug hole, the motion of Saturn's rings was explained by a hula hoop, the action of a double

star 'cluster' by two eggs in a frying pan, and so on. These observations led directly to the design route and, in turn, to the core idea of 'bringing the cosmos down to earth'. Ideally, of course, this idea would have come up and been agreed on as part of Step 2. As it happens, it was just mentioned as part of the 'preamble' to the design presentation, but soon became vital verbal 'glue' for the whole scheme.

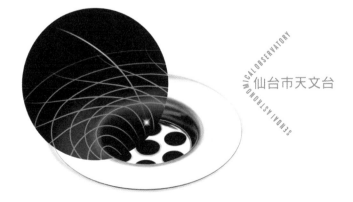

THE CREATIVITY OF BRAND ARCHITECTURE

Much has been written about the ways that organizations arrange and structure their 'brand architecture' and there are many models in existence to help us decide which is the right approach. The classic analysis and stratification is illustrated on the opposite page: when all aspects of a brand are led by the same visual identity, we see that as a *monolithic* solution. The example opposite shows that (in theory, at least) each of the London Science Museum's departments falls 'in line' beneath the dominant brand.[4]

The Olympic Games, in contrast, is a classic example of an *endorsed* model: each event, held every two years, is location-specific and yet is 'endorsed' by those famous rings – compelling each separate design approach to incorporate the design in some way.

Conversely, organizations such as Unilever have a *house of brands* model – most customers would have no idea that Marmite and Dove were essentially produced by the same company. Similarly, very few 'public' audiences have any idea that the LVMH empire (which stands for Louis Vuitton Moët Hennessy) technically reaches far and wide, across six different sectors, from wines to fashion and from perfume to jewelry. As you sip your Krug, there's no need to know that it's LVMH Krug, but there is a clear 'luxury' link across all of their activity, should you wish to search for it, which is summed up by their descriptor: *the world leader in luxury.*

These formulaic models help organizations decide how much linkage there should be between their brands. In practice, these models quickly become more hybrid, often because a group name only works for part of a customer base. For Marriott Hotels, there has clearly been a decision to use the group name at the mid- and low-end of the market, but not to bother Ritz-Carlton visitors with the news that they might be staying in an up-market Marriott – the Marriott name will only 'stretch' across 75% or so of their portfolio.[5]

For some of the more sprawling Asian conglomerates, brand architecture poses a serious challenge. Samsung's brand currently has to stretch from washing machines to mobile phones. Tata's organization has a very broad reach, from steel to telephony to tea. Establishing any sense of linking values across these vast empires becomes quite a task for the brand managers charged with establishing any connectivity.

◂ Marriott diagram / Martin Bishop / 2009

Monolithic – *each constituent follows the master brand's lead.*

Endorsed – *there's a clear link between master brand and constituent brand.*

'House of brands' – *the sub-brands take precedence and the master brand (in this case, Unilever) moves to the 'back of the pack' or the boardroom.*

Pew's brand structure allowed for three states of the 'core' mark, with each initiative then having its own variant. This broke all of the 'rules' of brand architecture in the process.

▾ Pew Center for Arts & Heritage, Philadelphia / johnson banks / UK / 2010

Some organizations have to find ways to link their work together in more unexpected ways. When the Pew Center for Arts & Heritage in Philadelphia decided to bring its many activities (shown immediately left) together under one name, there was significant 'pushback' from the various project teams and initiatives (spanning seven disciplines, including dance, theatre and exhibitions) to still recognize their role.

Now, was this a *strategic problem* (i.e., the way each department links together) or a *creative problem* (finding a design that all parties were happy to use)?

In the context of this chapter, it was probably both. By exploring the various ways that the organization could link together, yet still allow the initiatives to have some independence, the Pew Center merrily ripped up the conventions of brand architecture and adopted multiple models that best suited each circumstance. At the top, most 'corporate', level, there were multiple variants of the core mark that allowed the Center to talk about its enterprises at various levels of detail. Then each initiative, in turn, had a 'reshuffle' of the core elements, so that it could become dominant but the group could remain supportive.

On paper this created a hybrid of the monolithic and endorsed schemes – a perfect example of the 'blur' between strategy and design, with an end result that couldn't have come about without knowledge of all the arguments simultaneously, and a preparedness to collectively search for a more unusual solution.

▴ (PRODUCT)RED / Wolff Olins / USA / 2006

The (PRODUCT)RED scheme is another groundbreaking approach to brand architecture. It raises money for The Global Fund (which fights AIDS, tuberculosis and malaria) by creating an unprecedented series of affinity partnerships with the likes of Apple and American Express. Each brand is presented 'to the power of RED' and becomes part of the collective and yet remains resolutely itself.

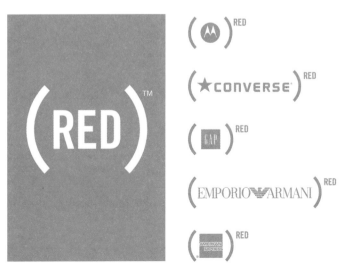

QAGOMA took two organizations with
8 characters between them and reduced them
to one name spelled with six characters.

CHRIS LAMONT
Senior Curator

CHRIS LAMONT
Senior Curator

ASK EVERY
QUESTION

QUESTION
EVERY
ANSWER

ASK EVERY
QUESTION

GALLERY OF MODERN ART

ART IS
ALL ABOUT
PERSPECTIVE

WHAT'S
YOURS?

GALLERY OF MODERN ART

Other examples of how strategy, design and brand architecture can drive a design solution are the Queensland Art Gallery (QAG) and the Gallery of Modern Art (GOMA), its sister organization. They are two related, yet distinct entities, but by sharing the 'G' of their two names, the linkage is visually established and their names are truncated from 38 characters to just six.

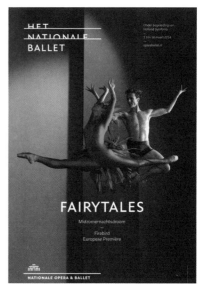

The Dutch National Opera & Ballet faced a recurring issue with multiple organizations sharing the same space for performances. They needed to create a brand identity for three separate and yet related entities (The Dutch National Ballet, The Dutch National Opera and the combined entity). This was achieved by carefully using typography and a clear photographic style.

The merger of contemporary dance school, Laban, with music conservatoire, Trinity, proved to be challenging for two educational organizations with very different mindsets and approaches. As with QAGOMA, their visual identity helped to make the interrelationship between the two organizations concrete. This time the logo turned to emphasize either dance or music and yet their educational 'partner' was ever-present.

For nearly a decade, designers have been experimenting with design solutions and brand architecture that illustrate organizational breadth and scale. One of the forerunners was Roppongi Hills, a vast scheme in Tokyo.

HOW NAMING BLURS THE BOUNDARIES

The generation and filtering of names is another part of the process that falls into the odd, blurred world of Step 2.5. Millions of names have already been registered by hundreds of thousands of companies across the globe, so creating and protecting a name takes a unique combination of different creative and administrative skills.

For every 'Google', named by accident because the person doing the name-checking misheard the suggestion of 'Googol' (a very large number: ten to the power of 100 or 10^{100}), there are countless other projects that take months, sometimes years, to generate, edit and choose a name for because of the difficulties of this work.[6]

So, to find or create names that might stand a chance of being registered, it helps to take a 'creative' look at the process and allow (and fight to keep) names that, on paper, seem odd, but when turned into 'brands' seem entirely plausible.

The name of Brazilian telecoms company Oi might seem particularly brutal on paper in English, but it works perfectly well in application and has the huge benefit of being extremely short, memorable and distinctive (surely three of the key criteria of any name-generation exercise). As a name it becomes a key piece of attention-grabbing communication in its own right.

SIMPLES ASSIM

Googol

What happens when you mishear a name in a brainstorming session? Google could have been Googol...

flicker

The advent of 'made-up' names has come about since so many names are already registered and there is a clamour for ever-shorter names (and hence shorter URLs). Most companies may still wish for a 'real' name such as Barnes & Noble, or even Amazon, but more often than not such names are simply unavailable. This has led to various new naming strategies. Twitter's co-founders discovered to their amazement that the name Twitter was actually available – it seemed to chime perfectly with the process of tweeting a short burst of song, just 140 characters long.[7]

When naming its online photography site, the team found that Flicker was unavailable, so truncated it to Flickr.[8] The name of the visual scrapbooking site Pinterest comes from a mashing together of the idea of a 'pin' and 'interest'.

Paradoxically, this trend towards mashed-up names (think You/tube, Face/book) or made-up names (Spotify) has been so strong in the last decade that naming conventions have been turned on their heads. Even if a real name is actually available, it may not be chosen. (Imagine the boardroom conversation: 'I love it, but, well, it's just too much of a real name for me. I really wanted one of those funny made-up ones.')

NAMING ON THE GLOBAL STAGE
Internationally, the naming challenge is significant for companies looking to establish a global reputation. Since the 1950s,

Japanese technology companies have had a permanent export focus, so names such as Wii will have been carefully chosen to have some form of resonance worldwide and, of course, it sounds like the English word 'we'.[9] Other names such as VAIO have more complicated provenance: the V and the A purportedly stand for a wave-form and the 1 and the 0 represent binary code.[10]

◂ Flickr / Ludicorp / Canada / 2004 ▾ Sony VAIO / Sony Creative Centre / 1996

In the last few decades Japanese brands have explored similar naming thoughts. The beautifully apt DoCoMo stems from an abbreviation of the phrase, **'do co**mmunications over the **mo**bile network'. The name also relates back to the compound word *dokomo*, which means 'everywhere' in Japanese.

The next challenge for emerging Asian and Arabic brands is to work out how to retain their national roots and yet have names that are pronounceable in the West. The name of the Qatari brand Ooredoo stems from the Arabic for 'I want' and is charmingly pronounceable.

عيد مبروك

inwi

INWI sounds similar to the French for 'incredible' and stands out a mile in Morocco.

▼ INWI / Naji El Mir, Publicis Royalties / France, Morocco / 2015

In an international context, re-naming presents both a challenge and an opportunity. When Wana, Morocco's third largest mobile operator, suffered commercial and technical setbacks, it needed to present a new and refreshed 'offer'. In an inspired move, it chose a new name, INWI, deliberately reminiscent of the French word 'inouï' (which means 'incredible'), but still suitably international. The four-letter name, simple design and limited palette mean it stands out well among the visual maelstrom of modern Morocco and successfully positions INWI away from its domestic competition.

WAH-WHAY?

As Chinese brands begin to establish themselves on a global stage, many face naming challenges going forward. For Huawei, the challenge is simply how to make its name pronounceable (it's actually pronounced 'Wah-Whay').[11] This is a major stumbling block that isn't going to go away. Conversely, Alibaba's name has no cultural link, and arguably this makes the brand appear more international as a result.

Brands such as Lenovo face fewer verbal challenges since their names are relatively phonetic and don't have any obvious cultural associations. Lenovo's challenge is that it could come across as large, 'Eastern' but of no clear, fixed abode.

◀ Lenovo / Saatchi & Saatchi / USA / 2015

Its recent re-brand updates its wordmark and uses a holding rectangle to offer a glimpse into its work and audiences.[12]

Xiaomi was only formed in 2010 and yet was selling 18 million handsets by 2013. The company allegedly paid $3.6 million for the mi.com domain address and has abbreviated its name accordingly, offering up the rationale that 'MI' stands for 'mobile internet' (rather than 'small rice', which is actually the translation of *xiaomi*). It's early days, but as it expands its international reach this may well be $3.6 million well spent.

REDUCE, REDUCE, REDUCE

In an environment where a shorter name is always better, many are under pressure to find an abbreviated form (unless you can cannily use both, such as with this example of The Metropolitan Opera in New York).

> # The Met ropolitan Opera

Truncating is usually a logical process, so when Federal Express adopted its nickname, FedEx, it made sense and helped modernize the brand. 'International Business Machines' was never going to succeed in the way that 'IBM' has. Yet the issue of acronyms is often a thorny one in the global boardroom. Because of the kudos sometimes attached to an acronym, organizations can create, or hold on to, acronyms when they aren't really helping them. So, while reducing 'Bangladesh Rural Advancement Committee' to BRAC made a lot of sense (the arrangement was quicker and easier to say), Médecins Sans Frontières (Doctors Without Borders) used their French acronym, MSF, for many years, but eventually realized that their name, in full, was more powerful. In addition,

when translated it 'fought' with the MSF acronym (which only made sense to French speakers). As increased globalization leads to the increased use of Doctors Without Borders, MSF slowly becomes just shorthand for those within the business and an anachronistic mystery for those not. Francophile NGOs such as Action Contre La Faim (ACF) face a similar paradox: as the organizaton becomes increasingly global its French acronym makes increasingly less sense.

Others in the international NGO sector are rejecting their acronyms altogether. The International Rescue Committee used its formal-sounding IRC acronym for decades, but in a bid to explain itself it has reverted to its full name, while heavily emphasizing the 'Rescue' part. The message is clearly: 'if you're going to remember one part of our name, remember this bit.'

MEDECINS SANS FRONTIERES
DOCTORS WITHOUT BORDERS

MEDECINS SANS FRONTIERES
ÄRZTE OHNE GRENZEN

MEDECINS SANS FRONTIERES
LEGER UTEN GRENSER

▾ The Metropolitan Opera, New York / Pentagram / USA / 2006 ▾ BRAC / CDT / UK / 2010 ▾ MSF / 1995

HOW THE NAMING PROCESS WORKS

As the last few pages have illustrated, finding, generating, choosing and even purchasing the 'right' name is becoming critical for modern brands. So here are some simple notes on how to go about naming projects.

The right name is now critical

This goes without saying, but prior to the internet (and subsequent importance of domain names) a less-than-perfect or overly long name was not a branding disaster. Now that a name is also a web address it becomes the first port of call for any audience.

Some ground rules

First establish some clear criteria and objectives from the beginning: so, ideally what 'kind' of name will suit, what broad territory it needs to inhabit and how you want people to feel when they read or hear the name for the first time.

It needs to align with the agreed brand strategy and narrative (assuming this has been written and signed off); if it hasn't been agreed, then it's risky to start. But, in the spirit of the 'blur' of this chapter, it might be worth looking for names that inhabit different territories, and attaching varying types of name to brand scenarios.

Many hands, hard work

It's a tough and arduous task. There's no option but to generate *lots and lots* of names, pause, and then generate lots more. You have to stay positive at all times and never lapse into a 'that'll never work'-type mentality. Get as many people involved as you can (for multiple perspectives), but especially writers, and hold lots of workshops.

Never fall in love

It seems to be impossible for people to do this without adopting 'their favourite'. In my experience *never fall in love with a name*. As soon as you do, someone will prove that 'your favourite' is already owned worldwide by a Mongolian multi-national, or means something unspeakable in Azerbaijani, or both. Also, stay objective. Try to keep assessing what you have from the perspective of the brief, *not* 'do you like it?'

Be aware of the hurdles, but not in awe

The issues of name registration, obtaining web domains, checking name availability and precise meanings in multiple languages are all significant hurdles. But if you let the constraints overwhelm you, then nothing good will come. It's better to generate unusual and interesting ideas and then test them rather than not to push at all.

THE TYPES OF NAME THAT ALREADY EXIST

Reduction of unwieldy name to shorter

Federal Express	FedEx
Pan American	Pan Am
The National Art Collections Fund	Art Fund
Acumen Fund	Acumen
Unique Clothing Company	Uniqlo
Thomson-Houston Electric Company	General Electric
Southern Pacific Railroad Internal Network Telecommunications	Sprint

Brand names that have become generic terms

Kleenex, Tupperware, Velcro, Zipper, Dry Ice, Ping-pong, Cellophane, Thermos, Trampoline, AstroTurf, Biro, Chapstick, Ziploc

Names that have become generic verbs

Hoover	Tarmac	Rollerblade
Google	Jet-ski	Tipp-Ex
Skype	Photoshop	Sellotape

New 'real' (or apparently real) names

Twitter
Oi
Amazon
Uber
Cahoot
More Th>n
Swatch
Orange
Egg
Yahoo
Pitchfork
Wonga
Monday
Alphabet
O_2
Apple
Blackberry
Innocent
Quora
Tinder

Radically short names

7	David Beckham Unicef Fund
Oi	
Mi.com	Xiaomi
The Y	YMCA
3M	Minnesota Mining and Manufacturing Company
3i	Investors in Industry

-ly names

Bitly.com
Friend.ly
Tattly
Bonusly
Neighborly
Flightly
Weebly

Naming systems

BMW 3,5,7 series

Audi 2,3,4,6 series

iPod, iPad, iMac

Cupcake, Donut, Eclair, Froyo, Gingerbread, Honeycomb (Android operating systems)

New 'made-up' names

VAIO
Wii
Trivago
Flickr
Google
Skype
Pinterest
Spotify
Accenture
Tumblr
INWI
Kodak
Etsy
Häagen-Dazs
Happn

Generic names

Hotels.com	Booking.com
diy.com	Made.com
Nuts.com	Photobox.com

Names of geographic origin

Nokia	The river and town
eBay	Echo Bay
Andrex	St Andrew's Mill
Cisco	from San Francisco
Adobe	Adobe Creek
Fuji	Mount Fuji
Amazon	The river

Names of historical, fictional or mythical origin

Starbucks	from *Moby Dick*
Phileas Fogg	from *Around the World in 80 Days*
Yahoo	from *Gulliver's Travels*
Olympics	Olympia
Nike	Greek goddess of victory
Venus	Roman goddess of love, sex, beauty and fertility

New mash-up names

YouTube

Facebook

PayPal

InnerWill

BuzzFeed

Intel – Integrated Electronics

Vodafone – Voice, Data, Telephone

Amex – American Express

Groupon – Group Coupon

Reduction of unwieldy names to acronyms

PricewaterhouseCoopers	PwC
International Business Machines	IBM
Oxford Committee for Famine Relief	Oxfam
Bangladesh Rural Advancement Committee	BRAC
America Online	AOL
British Broadcasting Corporation	BBC
Wire & Plastic Products	WPP
Victoria and Albert Museum	V&A
Museum of Modern Art, New York	MoMA
Fabbrica Italiana Automobili Torino	Fiat
The National Biscuit Company	Nabisco
Consumer Value Stores	CVS
Yoshida Kogyo Kabushikigaisha	YKK
Hongkong and Shanghai Banking Corporation	HSBC
Columbia Broadcasting System	CBS

Names of Latinate origin

Aviva

Altria

Converium

Centrica

Consignia

Zeneca

Engie

Diageo

Hovis

Nike

Sony

Sonos

Verizon

Nivea

Volvo

Audi

Reduction of unwieldy names into equally unwieldy acronyms

Anheuser-Busch, Interbrew, Ambev, South African Breweries, Miller Brewing: AB InBev/SABMiller

United Cannery, Agricultural, Packing, and Allied Workers of America: UCAPAWA

Rainey Kelly Campbell Roalfe / Young & Rubicam: RKCR/Y&R

From founders' names

Boots

Mars

Aldi

Hewlett-Packard

Marks and Spencer

B&Q

Adidas (Adolf 'Adi' Dassler)

Hermes

M&Ms

Taco Bell

Chrysler (Walter P. Chrysler)

Jack Daniel

Names created from other names

Haribo	Combination of founder's name and location: Hans Riegel, Bonn
IKEA	Similar: Ingvar Kamprad, Elmtaryd Agunnaryd
Garmin	Combined from its founders' names: Gary Burrell and Dr Min Kao

WHAT KIND OF NAME SHOULD YOU CHOOSE?

Here are just a few of the types of name you could be searching for:

Real names

The 'go-to' solution, especially for professional services. The downside is that companies such as Boase Massimi Pollitt (BMP) soon only included Boase.[13] The merger of Rainey Kelly Campbell Roalfe with Young & Rubicam led to the rather cumbersome RKCR/Y&R.

Names that describe a product or service

Pinterest doesn't need much explanation: it's about visually 'pinning' something that interests you. Even YouTube is fairly descriptive when you think about it. Booking something on Lastminute.com is also pretty self-explanatory (but arguably limits the company to a particularly short-term offer). Or you could search for a name that describes the 'end benefit', for example, Uncommon is an unusual name for a chain of schools but is understandable if the desire is to teach children who stand out.

Real names that allude to something or are metaphorical

O_2 doesn't immediately make sense as a name, but implies a hidden idea of oxygen. Oi is a great name for a telecoms provider. Twitter is, in retrospect, the perfect name for a short burst of chatter. Thames & Hudson is the perfect name for a publisher based near famous rivers in both London and New York. When and if Uber takes over the world, then perhaps a name that means 'best' will make sense after all.

Names plucked out of left field

Names such as Apple and Blackberry are now imbued with a lot of meaning, but initially meant only one thing. Taking a name from one place and re-appropriating it in a new context has the benefit of involving a known entity (i.e., I know what a 'pitchfork' is), but may need some work to explain *what a pitchfork has got to do with music*.

Names that are Latinate in origin

A rich seam for naming specialists for some time – search for the Latin roots of known European words and then slightly tweak or twist them. In the case of Diageo or Aviva, produce names that are strangely familiar and yet technically new (hence registrable). This is now seen as a very 'corporate' approach and is falling slowly out of fashion.

Names that are made up or misspelled

The most fun, but the hardest to assess. Who is to say whether Wii was a good name or not. The Flickr/Tumblr trend for amended or misspelled names (that technically includes Googol/Google) looks set to continue for some time yet.

The 8 steps of the naming funnel:

1 Establish some criteria, e.g.,
- it needs to convey an agreed 'feel'
- it needs to match with the narrative and strategy
- it needs to be understandable (or can be made to be understood)
- it could be a springboard into the design
- it needs to be legally viable (or there's a clear route to it becoming viable)

2 Filter your top 70–100 through your criteria; do initial low-cost legal checks and check domain name availability

3 Watch 40–60% fall at this hurdle

4 Shortlist 15–20 (and/or generate more). Carry out further and deeper legal checks

5 Shortlist 6–10. Test with brand narrative, generate messaging/tone of voice examples for each name

6 Do final legal checks

7 Take 2–4 into design

8 Choose

LOOKING AT THE PROCESS AS ONE

So far in this half-step we've looked at many of the ways that Steps 2 and 3 can merge into one another. This could be because (for some reason) the design has been done *before* the strategy, or the overwhelming need to solve a project's *brand architecture* issues means that design and strategy have become necessarily intertwined.

Alternatively, the process of generating and *picking a name* becomes both the verbal summary of a brand's reason to be and the platform for the design creativity of Step 3: the name itself bridges the gap, if you like.

Sometimes the blur between these stages can be exploited to produce a better project outcome. For example, in a bid to clarify exactly what it offered to its community, campaign harder and offer hope and positivity, Alzheimer's Australia developed an approach that was designed to 'cut through the clutter of the charity landscape' and allowed it to talk about all of its work in an insightful and unusual way.

The strategy, writing and design all take place simultaneously with an approach such as this. Just written plainly on a PowerPoint slide, the idea wouldn't have the power that it has as a final, mostly typographic, design. The continual prefacing of its formal name with active, 'doing' phrases would only have made sense when seen as a fully formed design scheme.

UNDERSTAND **ALZHEIMER'S** EDUCATE **AUSTRALIA**

BEAT **ALZHEIMER'S** TWEET **AUSTRALIA**

GOODNIGHT **ALZHEIMER'S** WAKE UP **AUSTRALIA**

FIGHT **ALZHEIMER'S** SAVE **AUSTRALIA**

CONQUER **ALZHEIMER'S** CONNECT **AUSTRALIA**

RESEARCHING **ALZHEIMER'S** FUNDED BY **AUSTRALIA**

AGAINST **ALZHEIMER'S** FOR **AUSTRALIA**

DISCUSSING **ALZHEIMER'S** ACROSS **AUSTRALIA**

STOP **ALZHEIMER'S** GO **AUSTRALIA**

Another example is Orange, which, nearly 20 years after its launch, sought to refresh its brand approach by tackling the problem from an entirely customer-centric point of view. Six themes were pulled out as critical to people: *family, fun, home, work, money* and *wellbeing*. Then the design and language established a 'frame' for the customer question, need or observation, which was duly filled by Orange's services and products. All entirely logical and driven by a 'what do our customers really need' approach, rather than the 'who are we, what do we do' approach that marked the company out when it launched 20 years earlier.

MERGE THREE, CREATE ONE DIFFERENCE

When three Istanbul arts organizations (Platform Garanti Contemporary Art Center, Garanti Gallery, and the Ottoman Bank Museum and Archive) looked to merge, the key sponsor wanted more of a 'return on investment' than just a nice bookshop and café. There was an ambition to become something far more engaging, which marked out a clear point of difference with its view of the world and its view of the future.

This desire to stand out soon found its voice in a radical strategic proposal – 'the institute of difference', which hardwired learning, debate and ambition into the core purpose. Then the task was both to name and design a brand identity to fit: an equally unusual route was chosen. First the name 'Salt' – 'like salt on food, they want to make a difference to how people experience life, making it more piquant, stimulating and complete';[14] secondly, a brand identity expressed through a deconstructed, ever-changing typeface that sidesteps any formal 'design' of the Salt name, in a traditional 'logo' sense.

Even though technically the product of two different agencies, there's no perceivable gap between narrative and design. The two functions have merged and blurred together seamlessly, and the 'difference' is seen throughout the entire process.

Why are we here?

The Institute of Difference

'Like salt on food...making it more piquant, stimulating and complete'

As we've seen, deciding whether narrative, name, brand architecture or design should 'lead' a project isn't always obvious. We've seen examples of all four and we've even seen projects that manage to juggle all the elements simultaneously.

But, to finish this step, perhaps we should share a few serendipitous examples. A team developing computer-based language products was searching for ideas for a name and chose 'Rosetta Stone' after the famous artefact (now in the British Museum in London) that enabled the decipherment of Egyptian hieroglyphics. What a great choice for a language product.

When two development and regeneration companies (Development Securities and Cathedral) were planning to merge, they looked into the history of one of their sites, a disused wharf. They discovered that a union, whose motto was 'Be United and Industrious', used to meet in a pub on the site . They soon realized they could truncate and adopt this as their new company's name, U+I, creating both a great back-story for launch and a highly differentiating brand stance.

When David Beckham and Unicef decided to join forces to create a global fund for children, there was a clear favourite as a name – the number seven, which marked the shirt Beckham had worn at Manchester United where he first made his name. But it was only by chance that it was possible to use one of the shortest ever domain names – by applying, in writing, to use 7.org.[15]

The blur that this step has described is controversial and some see it as distinctly non-linear. It means that teams have to work together, not apart, and sometimes re-examine ideas previously agreed, maybe even signed off. But this type of thinking can often produce uniquely differentiating and unusual ideas by forcing all parties out of their comfort zones into unknown and often exciting territory.

> *Summing up what we've covered in Step 2.5:*
> - *The key conundrums faced when merging narrative and design*
> - *How narrative sometimes follows the design stage*
> - *How studying brand architecture models informs both strategy and design*
> - *How to create names that work for 21st-century branding*
> - *How the blur between narrative and design can help – and not hinder – the process*

A one-character URL? 7.org

3

DESIGN

The branding business often gets boiled down to the contents of this step. The creation or change of someone or something's brand identity can cause huge debate and massive heartache, especially if people can't agree or it goes wrong. But conversely, done well, this is the step that can make people, companies, organizations and products famous the world over...

o this is where we are: we've researched the market; we've understood the gaps and decided what differentiates our product, service or organization; we've agreed why we're here, what we're going to do and who we're doing it for; we've decided what we value the most, what we believe in and how that affects our character and personality. A name, or amended name, has been agreed and someone has checked that it's available.

Now the talking has to stop and the designing has to start. If you've just jumped straight to this step thinking that *this* is where brand projects really start, then I'd encourage you to have a good look at the previous 169 pages. Take a moment to think: if you do not have the answers to all the questions in the paragraphs above, perhaps it's time for more work on the verbal brand. If you do have the answers, then pencils at the ready, team, and let's begin.

'Well, I don't love it, but maybe it will grow on me.'

Apparently, this is what Phil Knight said when first presented with the Nike swoosh.[1]

· A typical ad agency brief / Based on an old BBH example / BBH / UK / circa 2009

STARTING SOMEWHERE: THE ROLE OF THE 'BRIEF'

This step should start with a briefing of some sort. It can be entirely verbal but is more often written down (and, some would say, set in stone).

There are different schools of thought on the design brief itself, how long it should be and how much detail it should contain. One view is that all the relevant information – who it's for, what it does, what the core idea is, what we are really trying to do, etc. – should be written on *one piece of paper*.

This is an approach often used in the advertising industry,[2] where a team of account managers and planners will have toiled and haggled for months over the precise words on that page. The underlying thought is that the creative mind just needs a few prompts and key words to help with the spark and more detail can be added later. (There's another implicit thought here, too, which is that 'creatives', primarily visual not verbal people, might not read much more than a page.)

At the other end of the briefing scale is the 160-page PowerPoint file and a three-hour meeting, with no stone left unturned. The benefit of this approach, in theory, is that many bases have been covered and all eventualities discussed.

SO WHAT'S THE IDEAL?

The ideal is probably something in the middle: a short document that can be referred to when ideas veer wildly off-brief. It should have enough background briefing so the market, competition and context for the project can be understood.

Ideally, someone should be on hand at all times to answer questions and clarify (one of the best writers I ever worked with had his own personal mantra – 'always question the brief' – and he did, relentlessly[3]); and, while we're on ideals, being involved in some way in the project beforehand (e.g., attending key workshops and meetings) can help the creative team understand the context for their work.

It's worth pointing out that, oddly, *knowing less* at this stage can sometimes be a benefit. Those involved in the previous stages might be unconsciously carrying bits of 'baggage' with them – a key client doesn't like this approach, another doesn't like those colours... Knowing too much can almost hold people back at this point.

The benefit of fresh eyes at this step is that someone can come in, ask 'why not?' and challenge any preconceptions in the brief thus far. But for this to work, those carrying around the project 'baggage' need to be flexible enough to listen to those difficult questions, of course...

Title	The product is...	The brand is...

WHAT key business challenge does the brand face?

WHO are we trying to engage and what competes for their attention?

WHAT'S the role of communication?

WHERE and **WHEN** will communication have most power?

HOW does the category engage creatively and how could we challenge this?

Practical considerations

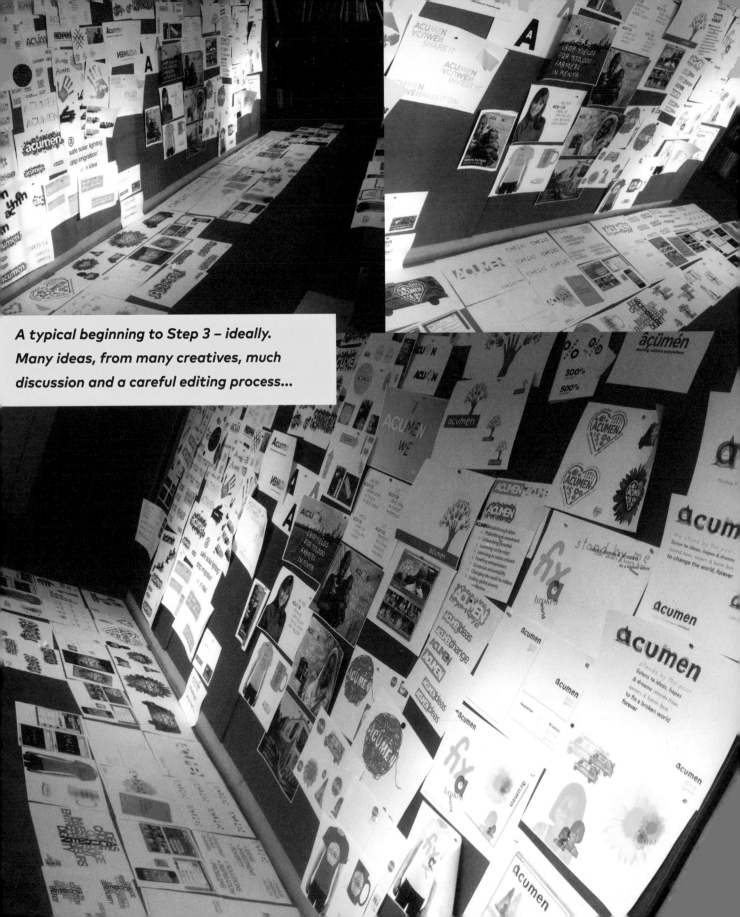

A typical beginning to Step 3 – ideally.
Many ideas, from many creatives, much
discussion and a careful editing process...

AN ENVIRONMENT OF POSSIBILITY

There are, of course, many different ways to approach the design or re-design of a brand's visual identity. Some companies have hierarchical structures whereby one creative is appointed to a project and off they go with x number of days allocated to 'crack it'. The account team retreat, hoping that creative sparks and multiple eureka moments are imminent. Meanwhile, the overworked creative director waits, no doubt hoping that the appointed creative is going to come through with that pioneering, and yet grounded, step into the future.

Indeed, this *vision of the future,* this *step into the unknown,* has been sold pretty hard, so now is the time to deliver.

No pressure.

What seems to occur to almost no one is that this places an inordinate amount of pressure on one, usually young, creative, especially if they are having a long-running row with their landlord or going through a torturous split from the love of their life.

Many companies (including mine) have therefore developed 'team' approaches to the critical early design steps of a project. And when I write 'critical', well, it's true. This is where all the hard graft of Steps 1 and 2 (and maybe 2.5) has to find some visual form. You could have the finest strategic thought and the most differentiating core idea on the planet, but if the creative work doesn't cut the mustard, then you're in trouble, and, worst of all, that fantastic name you laboured to get through or that great core idea isn't even going to be noticed.

Working in teams has its ups and downs. Some teams populate their walls with multiple designs and this means that editing, crits and discussion have to take place almost constantly, sometimes with the client, sometimes not.

And it's a Darwinian process – the great ideas rise to the top, get developed and presented, while the duff ones don't. One creative can take an overlooked idea off the board and make it work better than the original choice. If someone is off their game, then all of a sudden none of their ideas are getting selected – and this can affect the ideas they present next time. (In fact, research has shown that, in the face of constant rejection, it's human nature to present progressively *fewer* creative ideas.[4])

The onus on those who are 'managing' this process is to be as encouraging as possible, cast a suitably wide creative net, but then be crystal clear about which are the most appropriate and most differentiating designs to develop further.

The key ideas are the really disruptive ones that cut through, question convention and change all our perceptions of what brands can do. This book is full of brand ideas that seemed odd at first...before they were universally accepted. The genuinely new is, by definition, hard to judge.

For example, strategically desperate to re-position itself away from its early 'dial-up modem' roots and pedestrian original identity, AOL was in serious need of refreshing its brand. A young designer, who was only a few years out of college (albeit at a world-famous consultancy), came up with the idea that AOL is effectively 'invisible' until revealed by content. The designer was still young enough to show potentially 'crazy ideas' and deal with the knock-backs.[5]

LOOKING FOR THE SPARK

It's hard to pinpoint exactly which are the best words, images or phrases that will provide an impetus like this. Some designers respond to verbal prompts and use them as their starting point; for others, it's all about the imagery and they will almost immediately build 'mood boards' of images as a way of scrapbooking themselves into the process (indeed, some companies work this into their briefing procedure).

Of course, a brand identity project will eventually involve 'traditional' elements – there's a piece of type to be designed, there's a symbol to be redrawn – but it certainly seems to help to keep the visual 'net' as wide as possible at first and not throw anything out, even those things deemed to be wildly off-brief.

It could be that the spark is something tiny: the prompt for the Science Museum in London's entire scheme was the realization that the 'I' and 'E' of 'science' could be a ligature (i.e., a combined letterform), making the two words six characters each, which would lead directly to the stacking effect of the letters and eventually the form of the logotype and complementary typefaces. Or it could be something physical: the Brighton Dome famously has a scalloped roof, and these scallops were eventually echoed in the serifs of the venue's D-shaped monogram.

▾ AOL / Wolff Olins / UK / 2009

▾ Science Museum, London / johnson banks / UK / 2010   ▴ Brighton Dome / johnson banks / UK / 2013

Brighton Dome

Brighton
Dome

How a scalloped roof eventually became scalloped type.

WHEN THE JUMP IS INTO THE UNKNOWN

Merging letters or channelling the architecture of a building are fairly logical routes to a design solution, but sometimes something completely different is what is needed. A good example is this luxury five-star Hollywood hotel that mixed European grandeur with Los Angeles's after-hours spirit.

The solution, bizarrely, was a troop of capuchin monkeys. First they invade the hotel's crest and then re-appear throughout its décor, in a Planet-of-the-Apes-meets-London-club mash of influences. The monkeys are a form of metaphor, showing that the hotel is a 'playground for them to indulge in mischief' – both the monkeys that look on and the 'elite' visitors who will be drawn to this particular playground.[6]

SLS HOTELS

BEVERLY HILLS

THE STAGES IN THE PROCESS

Many consultancies have developed their own approaches to the design stage and have clear views regarding when work is shared with the client.

Some develop multiple routes and then select the best three to five to share. Others might, for instance, show all 15, good or bad. Then there's a hard core of companies that select their 'favourite' internally and work that one up – a no-holds – barred, all-or-nothing strategy; what we might call the 'we're the professionals here, trust us' approach.

So which works best?

Perhaps the answer lies on the other side of the fence – which approach best suits the client group? If they are 'partnering' with their consultants and truly collaborating in the process, then sharing the design 'journey' not only offers an insight into the process, but also enables democratic decisions, builds trust and (in theory, at least) avoids people taking positions 'for' and 'against' routes in key meetings.

However, if the relationship is a little more hands-off, then it could be that a shortlist of two to three routes with a clear recommendation might actually be the best way forward. And 'one route'? It can work brilliantly. Until it's rejected...

BUILDING TOOLKITS, NOT LOGOS

One of the key shifts in recent brand identity thinking has been the realization that as brands become more complex and multi-layered, all aspects of a brand's purpose, positioning and activity cannot be distilled down into a logo or symbol alone. As branding's remit has broadened away from 'just' logos and symbols to one that occupies a key visual and verbal role at the hub of a brand, the spokes that drive off the core are many and varied.

In a way this creates a paradox: branding is increasingly important, increasingly central and no longer just 'stuck on' by the marketing department, and yet how do we imbue all of these things into a core brand identity?

Well, the truth is we can't. All that logos and symbols can do is supply something to put on the flag at the top of a building, or the 'signature' on an email or website. It's the responsibility of the rest of the scheme to deliver on all the aspects of a brand. This is where the 'toolkit' has become crucial, allowing a brand to be recognized as much for its attitude to imagery, choice of photography, tone of voice, personality and writing style as for its logo. The best branding schemes have a clear approach to their entire communication, not just the logo that goes in the corner.

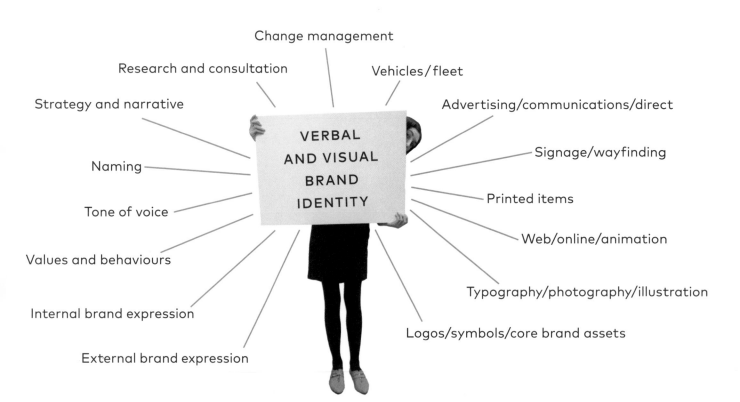

Change management

Research and consultation

Vehicles/fleet

Strategy and narrative

Advertising/communications/direct

Signage/wayfinding

Naming

VERBAL AND VISUAL BRAND IDENTITY

Printed items

Tone of voice

Web/online/animation

Values and behaviours

Typography/photography/illustration

Internal brand expression

Logos/symbols/core brand assets

External brand expression

▴ Tama Art University, Tokyo / Kenjiro Sano, MR_Design / Japan / 2013

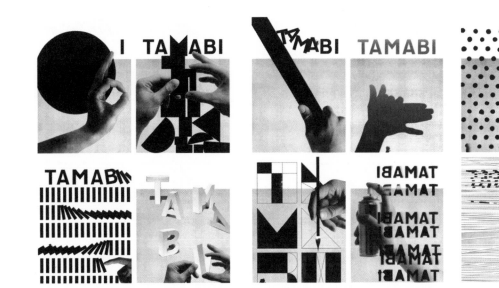

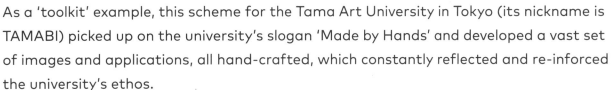

As a 'toolkit' example, this scheme for the Tama Art University in Tokyo (its nickname is TAMABI) picked up on the university's slogan 'Made by Hands' and developed a vast set of images and applications, all hand-crafted, which constantly reflected and re-inforced the university's ethos.

In order to keep the broader requirements in mind (however tempting it is to dive straight into the specifics of logotype or symbol), ideas need to be general enough to encompass a whole range of related thoughts and applications.

So, identifying some key applications (let's say, web page, bag, vehicle, sign and so on) early in the process will make everyone involved see that the breadth of an idea is just as significant as the button at the top of the website. Multiple applications help client teams 'see' how ideas that might be obvious to designers extend out and develop over multiple and varying channels.

Shelter

∵ Shelter / johnson banks / UK / 2004 ▴ Mobil / Chermayeff & Geismar / USA / 1964

DESIGN APPROACHES BASED ON TYPOGRAPHY

The design basis for a new scheme can be founded on various approaches. Over the next dozen or so pages we're going to examine some of the options. While the branding originally used on cattle was often symbolic or based on combinations of letters (monogrammatic), in the last few decades brand identity design has often concentrated on letterforms and names. This isn't because of a design obsession with the precise spacing of pieces of type, but the hard and fast realities of the 21st century. A company's 'front door' is now their website domain name, itself a verbal, written destination. In an airport, the way an airline writes its name on name boards helps quick and easy recognition – the same applies to products in a supermarket or on a price comparison website.

What this means is that, for many branding or re-branding projects, the journey often starts here. If, somewhere within those few words or letters, there is an opportunity to 'plant' an idea, a visual hook, a mnemonic device (i.e., something that aids memory), then that can be very powerful. This is what we call a logotype.

Mobil's wordmark is almost painfully simple, but the US oil company's choice of red, white and blue is intentionally patriotic and the single red 'o' provides a visually memorable element that, crucially, aids recognition.

For decades, Shelter, the British homelessness charity, had used a piece of 'typewriter' typography that fitted with its 'agit' roots, but it didn't encapsulate the

charity's work 30 years later. The idea of the 'h' being in the shape of a house with a pitched roof means that the word 'Shelter' is now visually linked to the idea of 'a roof over someone's head'. In a way, impossibly simple, but sometimes impossibly simple is what's needed.

DESIGN APPROACHES BASED ON MONOGRAMS AND ACRONYMS

There seems to be a human need to shorten names into more easily said initials, making the designing of various collections of letters sometimes unavoidable.

Most reductions of names also reduce meaning. So on the one hand, a name becomes drastically shorter, but on the other, it becomes less meaningful, placing more pressure on the design to find a way to communicate meaning.

The brand identity of the Mauritshuis, the famous home of Dutch Golden Age painting in The Hague, takes its cue from artists' initials and simplifies what translates as 'Maurice House' into an 'Mh' mark. This, coupled with colours that echo the collection and subtle, close-up details of its famous portraits (including those by Rembrandt and Vermeer), is both elegant and appropriate but also 21st century – all at the same time.

▾ Mauritshuis, The Hague / Studio Dumbar / The Netherlands / 2014

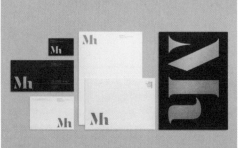

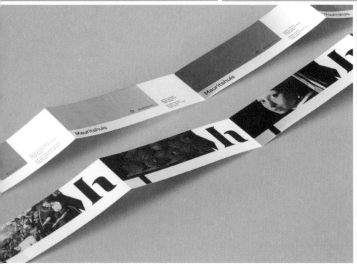

◂ ◂ English National Opera / CDT / UK / 1990 ▴ Opera Australia / Interbrand / Australia / 2013

The need to design memorable and yet meaningful acronyms is a recurring issue across the arts. They are popular because, carefully handled, they work. Think of MoMA (the Museum of Modern Art in New York), the V&A (Victoria and Albert Museum in London), or M'O (Musée d'Orsay in Paris). They are all world-famous, but few are quite as expressive as English National Opera's ENO, where the three letters *double as a singing face*. Some designers have even been able to design for the best of both worlds: Opera Australia's brand system opens up both opera *and* its own name. With a series of expanding and contracting typographic marks, it is flexible enough to cope with any design requirement.

DESIGN APPROACHES BASED ON SYMBOLISM

While the pressure of registering a brand name has always been at the forefront of people's minds, symbols and symbolism still have their part to play in 21st-century branding. It's not an accident that Starbucks has been carefully tweaking and adapting its mermaid symbol for nearly

Twin-tailed siren (15th century).

five decades – although the reason why a mermaid/siren symbol was chosen will have been lost long ago on the vast majority of Starbucks visitors.[7]

Some may link its name to the chief-mate of the whaling ship in *Moby Dick*, but most won't make the connection between a two-tailed mermaid and the company's origins in Seattle. Nearly all of the implied original meaning of the symbol has been lost and replaced by something much simpler: green mermaid = coffee. It's that easy. The ubiquitous white cup with the green circle can be spotted half a mile away on a busy city street. It is a simple visual identifier that we no longer question, just as we stopped questioning the 'shell' symbol at petrol stations decades ago.

Ideally, a symbol should have at least some meaning, some relevance to an organization, but that meaning can be hidden quite deeply. Few people know that NatWest bank's symbol represents a forgotten merger of the National Provincial Bank and Westminster Bank – the meaning is long gone.[8]

The symbol chosen by Open Knowledge, the pioneers of open data, is actually based on information from one of its key projects, the Open Data index, which measures how open (green) or closed (red) 72 of the world's governments are with their statistics. Most people won't know, understand or, perhaps, even care, but to the core team this is *their* data, which effectively drew *their* symbol and created a powerful sense of ownership.

▾ Starbucks / Lippincott / USA / 2011 ▸ NatWest / The Partners / UK / 2003

▴ Michelin / UK / 1979 ▸ Optus / RE; Marco Palmieri / Australia / 2013

Sort ○ alphabetically ◉ by score	Transport Timetables	Government Budget	Government Spending	Election Results	Company Register	National Map	National Statistics	Legislation	Postcodes / Zipcodes	Emissions of pollutants	Total Score
United Kingdom											940
United States											855
Denmark											835
Norway											755
Netherlands											740
Finland											700
Sweden											670
New Zealand											660

OPEN KNOWLEDGE

Physically creating a symbol that has genuine and yet unique and differentiated meaning is one of the toughest challenges a designer can face.

The benefits of having such a symbol are undeniable but simply creating one out of thin air and persuading a client group to adopt it takes inspiration, perspiration and guts.

Most symbolic devices that come to mind immediately have often been developed over decades, for instance, Bibendum, Michelin's tyre man. But recent pioneers in the digital space, such as Twitter (and its bird) and Evernote (with its cleverly chosen elephant, an apt symbol for 'never forgetting' note software), have shown that designing and adopting a visual device is still possible, giving their brands a character and warmth that a piece of type on its own will always struggle to deliver.

Just because symbols seem a little unfashionable, it doesn't mean creating them isn't possible. This suite of symbols (below) for the Optus telecoms brand has a charm and humanity that's almost impossible with traditional imagery and succeeds in supplying a 'human' touch to the service.

In their search for a universal symbol, Airbnb's designers consulted with semiotic experts to find a device that could be adopted, recognized and understood globally and not offend anyone.[9]

Conversely, it was *too much* adoption, use and misuse of its name that pushed the retail chain Habitat into developing a visual symbol to accompany its famous logotype. The charming house/heart symbol, drawn using one continuous line, instantly provided another key brand 'property' to be used on bags, flags and fascias (and a 'love your home' narrative whenever it was needed). But it also, crucially, gave Habitat something visually unique and legally protectable.

Habitat's new design was driven by the need for legal protection, but the brand also received a very fine new symbol in the process...

DESIGN APPROACHES COMBINING WORD, MONOGRAM AND PICTURE

The demands of an online environment have placed unique pressures on the branding business. Yes, brands need an agreed form for their name (be it, for instance, Google, Facebook, LinkedIn or Pinterest), but they also need 'short-form' versions. These have become critical online manifestations: think of Skype's 'S', Facebook's 'F', Pinterest's 'P' – the 21st-century equivalent of the branded monogram stamped onto pixelated, but not real, cattle. For any organization that is regularly searched for or compared online, how well it functions at tiny sizes has become crucial.

While brands mostly, and logically, use the first initial of their name, some can use symbolism to better effect. In a way, this was always part of a brand designer's remit – to design the 'small use' logo – and now the usage is just as small, if not smaller.

The readability and resolution of a brand icon at 48 pixels or less starts to become critical, and the trickiest test of an online presence is actually a brand's 'favicon', the miniature 16 x 16 pixel symbol that appears next to a web address in most browsers. It's here that a brand stands or falls as it is reduced to its tiniest and yet most recognizable elements. Here are just a few for you to try and recognize...

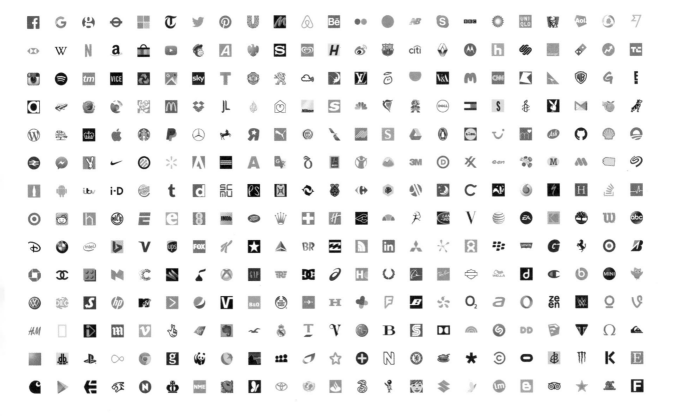

Know Canada.

DESIGN APPROACHES USING FRAMEWORKS AND 'CONTAINERS'

Imagery can often provide critical 'glue' for a scheme, but it needs to be in context. Faced with a challenge to dispel the preconceptions surrounding Canada, especially from a North American perspective, a Canadian design firm realized that the country's clichés were more intrinsic than they originally thought and promptly took all their local designers off the project. They then concentrated on dispelling the many long-held prejudices about the country, but they did it without attempting to 're-design' or 're-brand' Canada.

The visual answer is almost impossibly simple: the two red bars of the Canadian flag are the only constants. Between them, and in place of the classic maple leaf, is a view through to the beauty of the country's diverse and 'multi-everything' culture.

OCAD UNIVERSITY

IMAGINATION IS EVERYTHING

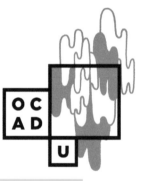

OCAD's frame is the perfect device to showcase the university's work.

FACULTY OF LIBERAL STUDIES

HUMN 4B03 EXISTENTIALISM

CONGRATULATIONS Ms. PAIGE STEEL!

DATA WITH SOUL

▾ OCAD-U / Bruce Mau Design / Canada / 2011 ▴ NYC / Wolff Olins / USA / 2006

The 'Know Canada' scheme is a relatively recent (and very well executed) example of a design approach that has been explored in detail over the last decade.

The principle is a simple one: for organizations that are multi-faceted and multi-functional, it seems inappropriate to distil this down into a single piece of type or a single symbol.

A different approach has gradually developed where the brand identity performs a 'framing' or 'container' function into which (or through which) the myriad activities can be seen. Some of the best examples are shown on this spread. In theory the NYC identity

allows all of New York to be shown and seen. The Frieze Art Fair is neatly summed up with the corners of a frame that then are used to crop information or overlay images.

For OCAD University in Toronto, a window-style framework becomes a showcase for students' work, recording their ideas and aesthetics and allowing the scheme to modulate over time. For London's Natural History Museum, we look into

a bold 'N' to see different aspects of the natural world, every time.

This visual approach, being very powerful and supremely flexible, has, in the way of many design trends, been appropriated worldwide. So you will see these ideas repeated and reflected in many other lesser campaigns, and for some years to come.[10]

FedEx ®

◂ FedEx / Landor / USA / 1996

DESIGN APPROACHES USING THE ART OF THE INVISIBLE

One way to add an extra 'dimension' to a brand's identity is to use some of the principles of optical illusion to 'hide' designs or shapes inside a typographic mark or symbol. Probably the most famous example of this designer 'sleight of hand' is the FedEx logo, which subtly incorporates a white arrow between the 'E' and the 'x'. If you hadn't seen it before now, don't feel bad – a huge number of people don't see it straightaway either. But once they do, then another 'layer' of the FedEx brand is revealed to them. Does it enhance the brand? Probably, because the symbolism is very apt for a global delivery organization. Look

around and you start to see dozens of examples. Take the Toblerone logo – have you always seen the 'Bern bear' dancing in front of the mountain? How many people spot the peacock's head in the NBC logo? And

Baskin-Robbins, famous for its 31 flavours – have you always seen the pink numerals in its logo?

Some of this is extremely subtle, but once you 'see' the mouse (below), or the colours of the Swedish flag (right), you will always see them – they are almost blindingly obvious. The approach can even be used to 'trick' the brain to see letters that aren't actually there: the logos shown opposite actually remove the 'i' in 'child', but our brains 'read' the negative space as a letter and so we think we see the whole word.

iiS

INNER WILL

CAN WILL

DESIGN APPROACHES BASED ON LANGUAGE

As branding as a discipline matures, and the narrative skills and insights we highlighted in Steps 1 and 2 develop, it's unsurprising that some of that language starts to seep into full design schemes.

When developing and choosing a name for its new leadership not-for-profit, InnerWill chose a name that reflected the tough and inquisitive personal journey on which its work takes people. A core language was developed that clearly explained what it offered to delegates and the wider societal context and a collection of related phrases: 'I can', 'I will' and so on. These verbal approaches carry over into a series of typographic assets that can be used throughout the work.

In contrast, the University of Cambridge needed to appeal to its alumni and philanthropic audience for funds, so that it could continue to have the same impact on the world that it had managed in the previous eight centuries. Most of the campaigns carried out in this sector make

fairly pedestrian and generic claims – to be *the most innovative*, or *the most future-facing*, or to be *the most creative*, etc., etc. There was a clear 'gap' in this market for something less corporate and more personal.

So the university developed a unique 'letter to the world' – 'Dear World... Yours, Cambridge' – which swiftly became the verbal and visual format into which it could talk about past and present achievements, and yet still talk about future aims. The simple palette, restricted graphic toolkit and clear copywriting style 'carry' the scheme forward, giving the university a far more approachable public image and, crucially, attracting key donors to be part of its future.

Dear Quentin,
Black, no sugar.

Yours, Paul

Quentin Stafford-Fraser (Gonville & Caius College 1986) and Paul Jardetzky (Darwin College 1993) about the first webcam in 1991, to keep an eye on the coffee pot. cam.ac.uk/YoursCambridge

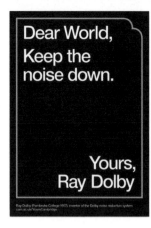

Dear World,
Keep the
noise down.

Yours,
Ray Dolby

Ray Dolby (Pembroke College 1957), inventor of the Dolby noise reduction system. cam.ac.uk/YoursCambridge

Dear World,
Thought this
might take off.

Yours, Frank

Frank Whittle (Peterhouse 1934), inventor of the jet engine. cam.ac.uk/YoursCambridge

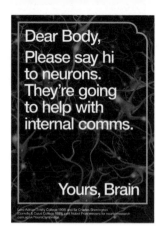

Dear Body,
Please say hi
to neurons.
They're going
to help with
internal comms.

Yours, Brain

Lord Adrian (Trinity College 1908) and Sir Charles Sherrington (Gonville & Caius College 1885), joint Nobel Prize-winners for neural research. cam.ac.uk/YoursCambridge

To: Ludwig
Re: attachment

There's nothing there.

Yours,
Bertrand

Bertrand Russell (Trinity College 1890) argued with Ludwig Wittgenstein (Trinity College 1911) about the presence of a hippo in the lecture room. cam.ac.uk/YoursCambridge

To: Bertrand
see attachment

📎 hippopotamus.jpg

Yours,
Ludwig

Ludwig Wittgenstein (Trinity College 1911) argued with Bertrand Russell (Trinity College 1890) about the presence of a hippo in the lecture room. cam.ac.uk/YoursCambridge

Hi Mr Attenborough,
Call me Trig.

Trigonophorus attenboroughi, one of 11 species named after David Attenborough (Clare College 1945). cam.ac.uk/YoursCambridge

'Ello
I wish to
register a
complaint.

John Cleese (Downing 1960), Graham Chapman (Emmanuel 1959), Eric Idle (Pembroke 1962), Norwegian Blue (Deceased). cam.ac.uk/YoursCambridge

Dear World,
I'm doing my
best here.

Yours,
The Sun

Richard Friend (Trinity College 1971), Cavendish Professor of Physics and researcher into artificial photosynthesis to capture solar energy. cam.ac.uk/YoursCambridge

Dear Samuel,
Saw some
nice daffodils
today.

Yours, William

William Wordsworth (St John's College 1787), poet and friend of Samuel Taylor Coleridge (Jesus College 1791). cam.ac.uk/YoursCambridge

Dear World,
You can blame us for
the offside rule. Sorry.

Henry de Winton (Trinity College 1842) and John Charles Thring (St John's College 1843), developers of the Cambridge Rules of Football at Trinity College in 1848. cam.ac.uk/YoursCambridge

Dear World,
What goes
up must
come

down.

Isaac Newton (Trinity College 1661), mathematician, physicist and originator of the theory of gravity. cam.ac.uk/YoursCambridge

To: Humans
cc: Apes

So I've been thinking
about these finches.

Yours, Darwin

Charles Darwin (Christ's College 1827), naturalist and author of On the Origin of Species. cam.ac.uk/YoursCambridge

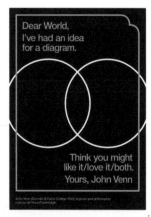

Dear World,
I've had an idea
for a diagram.

Think you might
like it/love it/both.
Yours, John Venn

John Venn (Gonville & Caius College 1853), logician and philosopher. cam.ac.uk/YoursCambridge

Dear
Sir/Madam,
Why do Sir
and Madam
always come
in that order?

Yours, Laura

Laura Bates (St John's College 2004), founder of everydaysexism.com. cam.ac.uk/YoursCambridge

Dear Robots,
Can we be friends?

Yours, Humanity

Huw Price, Martin Rees and Jaan Tallinn, co-founders of the Centre for the Study of Existential Risk, examining threats to humanity from technology and elsewhere. cam.ac.uk/YoursCambridge

Dear Shakespeare, Stick at it, you have talent.

Yours, Marlowe

Christopher Marlowe (Corpus Christi College 1580), playwright and seminal influence on Shakespeare
cam.ac.uk/YoursCambridge

These guerilla posters covered the city's railings with imaginary celebrations of past achievements.

Dear World, We designed that t-shirt you love.

Yours, Jocelyn and Antony

Jocelyn Bell Burnell (Murray Edwards College/New Hall 1965) Antony Hewish (Churchill College 1942) discover first radio pulsar (discovered later by Joy Division) cam.ac.uk/YoursCambridge

DESIGN APPROACHES BASED ON ANALOGY, METAPHOR OR DIAGRAM

Branding ideas that embed conceptual thoughts and hidden messages are all very well (and all very clever), but sometimes a brand identity needs to *demonstrate* why it is here and what it can do.

In clichéd terms, this can mean a preponderance of pointing arrows for delivery companies and train tracks for railway services, but in more imaginative hands the results can be dramatic. Alzheimer Nederland has adopted a unique approach to its visual identity that alludes to the fateful process of losing one's memory (or perhaps

providing a source of light and hope). The use of gently fading typography means the effect is just legible enough and profoundly moving – almost poetic.

Swanswell is a drug and rehabilitation service saddled with an unfortunate name. But its visual approach takes its cue from the 'well' at the end of the word and crumples all before it: whether by using words, phrases or people, it becomes a visual metaphor for the journey that its clients go on to become well again.[11]

Alternatively, it may be that a simple diagram is what is needed: Anthony Nolan, a bone-marrow donation register, kept its historical name, but confused many of its target audiences

by concentrating on the blood disease leukaemia (just one of the reasons to donate bone marrow). Put simply, bone-marrow donation is an exercise in 'matching' – simple DNA samples are taken and if the DNA of a donor on the register matches that of someone in need then an operation could save that someone's life. Anthony Nolan's revised branding illustrates the 'matching' principle in its letterforms and carries that idea through into applications.

The diagrammatic approach has also been used in other sectors. The Bahamas adapted a form of a stylized 'map' as an overall symbol for the islands, which could then be broken down piece by piece to represent each island in the chain – a neat and effective way to show both the whole and the constituent parts.

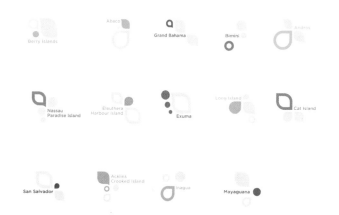

EVOLVING A BRAND FROM WHAT'S ALREADY THERE

Many designers entering the branding business assume that every day will be spent dreaming up and creating brand identities from scratch. Most clients, of course, realize that branding and re-branding usually affect products, services, companies or organizations that already exist and already have substantial brand 'equity'.

In some projects this creates an immediate tension – the desire for a 'clean slate' versus the logic of an evolutionary approach. In fact, the ability to look at an existing brand, take the good and quietly drop the bad is a skill in itself. Take Amazon's previous visual identity: lowercase type, two weights and an orange swoosh under the lettering. It looks perfectly fine, but it's pretty unmemorable.

In many respects, the revised version looks very similar in terms of typeface and palette, but two things have changed: the type is a little stronger, and the 'swoosh' has become an arrow linking the 'a' to the 'z' and forming a smile.[12] So with subtle changes, Amazon's desire to be a company about everything, not just books, is supplied by the 'A to Z' device, and the swoosh indicates that things arrive (happily) on time. Many established customers might not even have noticed the change, or seen the A to Z.

▾ Amazon / Turner Duckworth / USA / 2001 ● Coca-Cola / Turner Duckworth / USA / 2008 ● Levi's / Turner Duckworth / USA / 2014

Similar approaches have worked well to revolutionize other established brands. This work on the Coca-Cola brand came at a time when its packaging and promotional materials were cluttered and clichéd – the essential things that made Coke 'Coke' were getting lost. The solution? To radically simplify Coca-Cola's design by ensuring that only the most important elements were retained, in a classic 'return to simplicity' approach with a carefully re-drawn and re-crafted toolkit: the red, the white, the script logo, the 'swoosh' device, the bottle shape and clear supporting typefaces. Since the designs were no longer hampered by endless drop shadows and flying bubbles, the support collateral and designs soon began to have fun again and reflect the positivity and optimism at the heart of the brand.[13]

For Levi Strauss, faced with a proliferation of logos and design approaches worldwide, the recommendation was to identify and simplify the iconic brand devices that could truly be called 'property of Levi's' and use them consistently on a global basis.

HOW PLACES CAN BECOME 'BRANDS', TOO

As the principles of 'how to brand' something have spread from 'branded goods' to 'branded companies', it is logical that we should start to see 'branded cities' and even 'branded countries'.

Architects have long understood the innate power of memorable visual forms: iconic buildings such as Bilbao's Guggenheim Museum or Paris's Pompidou Centre attract on pure design alone. It's no surprise that the Pompidou's logo is simply a representation of the building's form – in a way it couldn't be anything else.

New York's High Line also has a 'logo', but it's the *idea* of the High Line that currently attracts five million visitors a year, who take an elevated stroll above 20-odd blocks of Lower West Side New York. In just a few years it's become a key tourist attraction by dint of the unique perspective it offers on the hubbub all around and below it, while itself driving renewed gentrification along its route. One day it may be a 'canyon' through an entirely changed district.

▲ Pompidou Centre, Paris / Piano & Rogers / Italy, UK / 1977

▲ Guggenheim Museum, Bilbao / Frank Gehry / USA / 1997   ▲ The High Line, New York / Diller Scofidio & Renfro / USA / 2009–14

Branding cities is notoriously difficult since there are so many variables that affect citizens' and visitors' perceptions. You may have the finest ever poster campaign at an airport welcoming visitors, but if the train into town is dirty and smelly or your taxi driver is rude, then little can be done graphically to counter that.

Sometimes city brands are almost created by accident – the famous 'I love NY' symbol started out as a doodle on a scrap of paper, done during a cab ride to a campaign meeting. Without any strong copyright protection in place it has been adopted and adapted by many cities worldwide, slightly reducing the power of the original thought.

A better controlled example is that of 'I Amsterdam', a powerful and simple idea coined to help the city keep itself competitive compared to other European cultural destinations such as Barcelona and Berlin. It is the three-dimensional form of the logo that is most memorable, inspiring a host of copycat versions around the world and supplying an almost instant picture opportunity.

Sometimes entire regions can tackle preconceptions, both good and bad, head on. West Bengal may be known to some for its intellectual tradition and great vegetarian food, but it was also seen to be 'investor-unfriendly' by others. So a brand campaign based on the principle of 'Everyone's Bengal' was developed to help drive enthusiasm and interest from both tourists and investors.

PERSON AS BRAND

It's equally possible to see, watch and learn from historical and modern examples of how people brand themselves, whether knowingly or unknowingly.

Roman emperors were at great pains to see their profile on coins after Julius Caesar rejected the previous approaches (portraits of ancestors, the bust of Roma or

symbolism from his family history). He became the first living emperor to circulate his profile across the empire, in what was arguably one of the first pieces of 'personal branding'.

But it was the presentation and cultivation of image by the English monarchs in the 16th century that demonstrated mastery of both the words and pictures associated with a public figure.

Elizabeth I's father, Henry VIII, carefully controlled images and portraits of himself, but Elizabeth was the one who really understood how to 'codify'. Whereas early portraits depicted her in styles of the time, it was Nicholas Hilliard's first miniature that started to

establish the 'rules' of the 'face pattern' that were then picked up by multiple artists and propagated through coins and prints, even through a portrait of her that appeared on the title page of the Bishops' Bible.

Hilliard is thought to have produced 16 miniatures, which were given away to key supporters. In tandem with canny control of her personal image (a council was empowered to destroy anything felt to be unseemly, i.e., off-brief), Elizabeth began to master the 'messages' that came with this powerful and almost ageless visual symbol – the famous notion of the Protestant 'Virgin Queen', selflessly dedicated to her country, in direct opposition to the 'Virgin Mary', and the new religious enemy of Catholicism.

In times of national stress, this imagery became either critical, proliferating at the time of the Spanish Armada, or a symbol of hate for enemies – Elizabeth's portrait was burnt, pierced and seeped in poison. Much as

▼ Henry VIII / after Hans Holbein / UK / late 1500s / early 1600s ▼ Queen Elizabeth 1 / Nicolas Hilliard / UK / 1595– c. 1600

▸ Obama mural, from Shepard Fairey design / USA / 2008 ▾ Obama poster / Felix Sockwell / USA / 2008

USA-haters would now demonstrate their anger by burning the Stars and Stripes on local television, Elizabeth started a far more personal trend, four centuries earlier.

The notion of head of state or politician as potent symbol endures to this day. Rather than presenting the standard, monolithic face of everyday American politics, Barack Obama's presidential campaign of 2008 allowed his messages to be tailored from state to state or from key audience to key audience ('Environmentalists for

Obama', 'Kids for Obama', etc.). The control of his typefaces, use of a 'sunrise O' symbol and a clear verbal message, 'Yes We Can', meant that his campaign was just as powerful as that of many consumer electronics brands, if not more so.[14]

But one element hadn't been planned. A Los Angeles street artist channelled a news photograph and some of the revolutionary spirit of Che Guevara into a print run of posters, originally titled 'progress'. The poster was soon picked up, the title changed to 'Hope', 50,000 copies printed and $350,000 swiftly raised for the campaign. The image became the unofficial symbol of people's support and was ever-present on social media, even inspiring hundreds of other designers and artists to produce their own poster designs.[15]

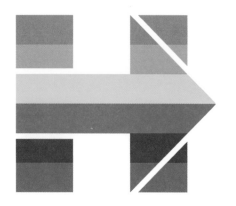

I'M WITH HER

Women for H
hillaryclinton.com

Hillary Clinton's brand is designed to flex and mutate from just two elements, an 'H' and an arrow pointing forwards.

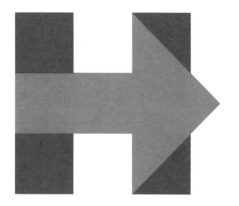

Eight years later, Hillary Clinton's 'brand' also questioned the status quo, and this time used the principle of forward motion: 'H' for Hillary and some of the flexible ideas we looked at on page 193 created an equally adaptable campaign brand, allowing her team to keep adjusting the messages and imagery as her campaign progressed.

This notion of 'person as brand' has now become ingrained into our everyday lives. From the original 'Air Jordans' to David Beckham's children's fund (see page 166), it's now almost assumed that a famous figure from one walk of life will then look to project and generally control their personal brand going forward. People such as Virgin's

Richard Branson and Facebook's Mark Zuckerberg become umbilically attached to the companies they lead – their 'values' and 'beliefs' are often intertwined with the organizations they started.

But even major personal brands need the occasional tweak. After five months in prison, five months of house arrest and two years of probation for alleged insider trading, even the mighty Martha Stewart needed a brand 'tweak'.

The bold sans-serif logo that previously emblazoned her products was replaced by a softer and friendlier circle of type and her narrative re-written as 'not just about lifestyle, but about essential tools for modern living'. In the short-term, Stewart's perceived and actual stock has fallen, so whether these subtle changes to her products and their communications will be strongly linked to her incarceration, long-term, is hard to judge.[16]

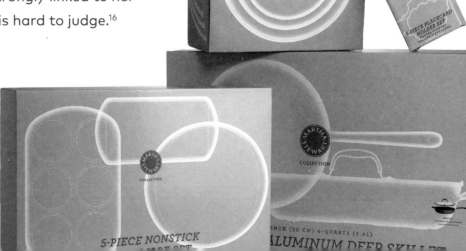

THE NUTS AND BOLTS OF GETTING IDEAS AGREED

For most of Step 3, so far, we've looked at how to *start* the design stage; how to look at and disseminate the myriad ways that any design brief can be solved. For the remaining few pages of this step, we're going to look at the hurdles that can stand in the way of agreement and some ways to get over these.

ALIGNING DESIGN WITH CLEAR STRATEGIC CHOICES

For most designers and clients, the editing of multiple design routes becomes an exercise in not only finding what matches the brief best, but also what maps most appropriately onto an organization's ambitions and future strategy. The reduced and simplified palette that we saw chosen by Coca-Cola on page 203 clearly matched an internal desire to clarify. The strategic choice faced by the DEC on page 128 was paralleled by design routes that both illustrated and informed its choice.

This is key to the future role that design, and design 'thinking', can play in a boardroom. Design and branding supply tangible, visual pointers to what the future looks like, either right or wrong, and can help massively with choice and with gaining the kind of agreement that is almost impossible with a 148-page PowerPoint deck.

It's not unusual to reach the denouement of Step 3 with two to three design routes still on the table. Having examined their relative pros and cons, the task is then to decide which one aligns brand, design and strategy, all in one.

HOW DO YOU DECIDE?

On being presented with the first Nike swoosh, Phil Knight allegedly said, 'Well, I don't love it, but maybe it will grow on me.'[16] This gives just a small insight into the issue of 'the decision' – this is almost always subjective territory and everyone has a view about change.

First, let's look at the dreaded 'committee decision'. Playing mix and match with the design routes very rarely works – any consultant worth their fee will have worked hard to make routes A, B and C quite separate from one another, so melding them all into one amorphous nothingness will remove their innate differences and just create a mess. But this is exactly what committees will try to do – mix, meld and muddle.

It almost never works.

SAFE	⟵————————⟶	RADICAL

Secondly, and sometimes related to point one, is the 'safe route'. Too many designers will present a continuum of designs, from the 'safe' (i.e., easily done, ruffles few feathers, is barely noticed but signals a degree of change) through to the 'radical' route (often the one everyone loves but it will receive a vast amount of flak). This approach is destined to failure since the polar extremes on offer will almost always force a group into the middle ground (unless the decision is being made by one person alone).

There's an implied responsibility here, for both designer and senior client, to try and see this coming and avoid these impasses or creative backwaters. And perhaps sometimes there is a need for ideas to percolate and permeate; for them to pass the 'day after' test and to grow on people.

THE ROLE OF CONSULTATION AND RESEARCH

For some organizations, especially those talking directly to consumers, testing may be the only way to truly ascertain which idea from the final three left on the table is the one most likely to succeed, and also deal with the implied risk of re-branding from a fiscal point of view.

▲ Unicef UK / johnson banks / UK / 2014

When tested, the Unicef campaign we saw on page 53 was preferred by seven out of eight focus groups, which provided vital evidence to help embolden a board decision. It can often be critical to have proof from a sample of key audiences that something 'could work'.

Of course, some view research as a block to creativity, and it's true that some truly 'out there' ideas are almost impossible to test if there is no valid frame of reference. The other block to creativity is the rise of 'risk analysis'. Once someone is brought into a meeting to analyze the 'risk' of the creative ideas on the table, you can pretty much pack your bags and assume that the project is dead and buried at that moment (since anything 'new' or 'unusual' will, of course, be deemed 'risky').[17]

ROUTES TO SUCCESS: BEING HONEST ABOUT CONSTRAINTS

In theory, every branding project starts with a blank sheet of paper, but in practice there are almost always some key applications that must be dealt with, unless the project fails. It's best to identify these early and design accordingly. An airline's brand identity could easily fail – not because of its livery, but because of how a proposed scheme works half an inch across on a price comparison website. So if you can 'crack' the tailfin design *and* the small-use electronic logo then that's a good start. (By the way, here's a great example of the perfect tailfin – Qantas's flying kangaroo, in use since the 1940s and developed and refined in this form since the 1980s.[18])

What if you're designing for a cultural or governmental identity? Putting its name across the headquarters in vast steel letters is a great ambition (and may happen one day), but it could be that final decisions are made on how it appears in a 'line-up' with its peers. Christian Aid wasn't happy with its previous symbol for many reasons, but was especially concerned about how it appeared adjacent to others. This had a direct bearing on the design. The charity chose to emphasize 'aid' over 'Christian' and ensured as much of the available 'real estate' of the logo worked as hard as possible.

Generic
and
meaningless
symbol
next to

Generic Piece of Type

By identifying the key applications early you stand a better chance of resolving the issues. You may, of course, unearth assumptions you didn't want to hear. I once spent a lot of time designing solutions for a new FTSE 100 company, purposefully avoiding all the clichés of the sector and the competition, all of whom seemed to have brands consisting of a quasi-abstract symbol next to some featureless sans-serif type.

But the initial designs were rejected out of hand.

'What's the problem?' we asked.

'Well, you haven't done what I want. I want a symbol next to a piece of type.'

'That's what everyone else has,' we fought back.

'Exactly!' came the triumphant reply.[19]

So what's the moral of this story? Check client or internal assumptions before starting expensive design stages.

SOME HARD-WON ADVICE

My personal view on this is to show multiple routes to the client working group (usually not involving the key board decision maker/s). The design 'journey' is then shared, but with a clear end-game in sight: the two to three stand-out routes that deserve the most attention can promptly be analyzed.

Details and nuances from other routes can be brought over and incorporated, but only if they fit. The aim? To have two to three clear favourites to take into serious meetings – ideally, clearly differentiated routes that help inform a strategic decision.

Importantly, these aren't routes differentiated just by colour or typeface – so the final decision is not made subjectively ('I prefer this colour', 'I like that typeface') but objectively ('This fits with our future aims' or 'This best suits our new brand narrative').

There's an inherent paradox here, of course, because the creative stage begins with a rational, well-worded brief that then collapses into creative chaos without any end in sight, before funnelling back towards a well-argued, rational conclusion. But, given that most boardrooms prefer rationality over chaos, this is the way it has to be.

STARTING OVER

For every ten projects that tick over perfectly, there may be one that goes awry, either at narrative stage or, more likely, design. The truth is that sometimes more time is needed, or those first ideas just helped to clarify the brief before a more developed stage of work could really nail it.

These things happen. Just because branding books are full of perfect, shiny, final product, don't believe for a minute that they all arrive perfectly formed from the designer's mouse or sketched that morning on the train. Sometimes the journey to the finalized design just takes a little longer than expected. Shown on this spread are just a few of the journeys that some brands went on before they reached their final form. There might come a point when there's no option but to start again. Even though, at the time, this seems like a catastrophe, it's remarkable how re-grouping and re-thinking can lead to something new, and quite often, something better.

As a famous graphic designer once said, 'No matter how many times your amazing, absolutely brilliant work is rejected by the client, for whatever dopey, arbitrary reason, there is often another amazing, absolutely brilliant solution possible. Sometimes it's even better.'[20]

For this project for an arts centre, it took time to find the best way to express the relationship between the overall centre and its eight constituent parts. The final version only arrived bit by bit (see the complete solution on page 144).

Acumen: the humility to see the world, but the audacity to envision the world that could be. Forged by optimism, tempered with grit, resilience & hard-edged hope. Learning at the edge, always standing by the poor. Breaking through bureaucracy, complacency, corruption and cynicism. Using capital to work for us, not control us. Doing and saying what others won't, or wouldn't dare. Bound neither by tribe nor ideology, seeking a new kind of courageous leader ready to unleash potential. Our aim is simple — change the way the world tackles poverty & uphold the dignity of every human being. A huge task but we're unafraid. Because together, we can change the world.

Acumen: determined, well-informed and persistent. Always questioning, always probing, never blindly accepting. We roll up our sleeves, get out there and get on with it., pushing each other to greater heights, and greater goals. We're happy to be smart, but unhappy to be smart-ass. We imagine and dream, but ground it with business skills. We're driven by what we do, see a better way and believe we can create a better world. Actually, we know we will and won't be thwarted. We're fearless and a little bit obsessive. But in a good way.

The idea of a 'manifesto' style approach was preferred, but it took a lot of experimenting to find a final design (see page 98).

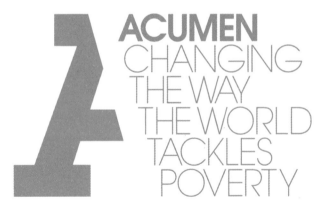

The core idea was agreed upon early on and then multiple typographic approaches informed the final decision (see page 78).

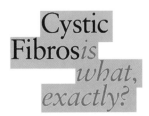

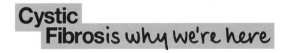

WHEN BRANDING GOES WRONG

What should be clear after 215 pages of branding theory and practice is that, as a general rule, it works.

But there are, of course, some examples of branding change associated with corporate failure. Enron's famous logo couldn't save them, and Royal Mail suffered general ridicule in suggesting they might re-name as 'Consignia'.[21] British Airways' 'tailfins of the world' could have done without the then Prime Minister Margaret Thatcher draping her handkerchief over the design as shown on a model.

Sometimes a re-brand just suffers from bad timing. There was nothing 'wrong' with this re-design of the Monotype (international type foundry) brand – it just suffered from being introduced six months before a change of ownership that swiftly resulted in another change of logo. A stylish re-design of the marque for London football club Queens Park Rangers's was intended to be a better match for a more stylish manager. Unfortunately it was kicked into touch when said manager lost his job.[22]

With the advent of the web and the ability to create 'mass' protests overnight, more schemes are falling foul of online pressure. It seemed that Gap was on the verge of modernizing its logo, yet, when leaked, the proposed design unleashed a torrent of negative press.[23] The proposed new icon for the University of California was also scorned, and equally swiftly dropped, leaving just the typography.[24] These online issues set a difficult precedent: should boards, companies and organizations 'bow' quite so fast to peer pressure? Gap's brand was surely in need of a refresh, and the University of California now finds itself without a compelling visual identity. The key to this is making clear decisions and then standing by them.

▲ British Airways / Newell and Sorrell / UK / 1997 ▼ Monotype, QPR / Johnson banks / UK / early 1990s

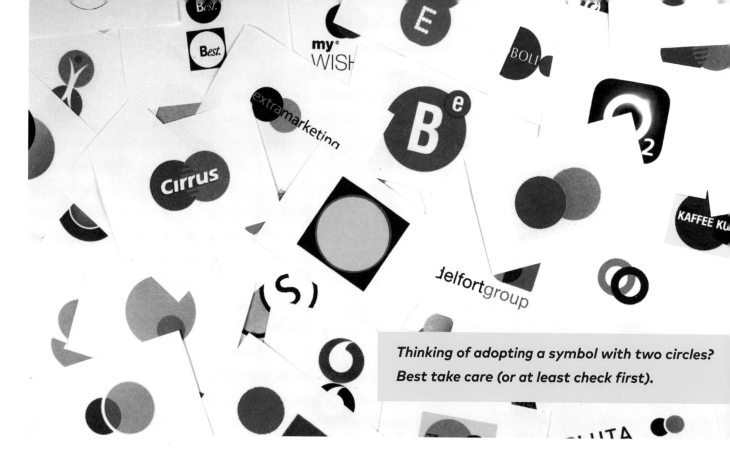

Thinking of adopting a symbol with two circles?
Best take care (or at least check first).

THE LEGAL BEAGLES

Eventually, when final decisions are close and the end of this step is looming, it's wise to carry out trademark checks. Search for similar names in existence and for similar (or crucially, *too similar*) marks that are in existence.

The slight paradox of this is that some shapes are deemed to be 'generic' and hence can't be protected. So, if you want to design something in a square, you won't have any trademark issues because a) there are millions of square trademarks out there and b) none of them can really sue one another. It's the type placed in the square that creates the trademark and that initial™ and the eventual®.[25]

Likewise, if you search for designs using a circle and a square, you'll find hundreds. And if you design something similar to MasterCard's overlapping circles be very careful – this symbol is registered in 23 different categories. Across the world.

Because few can afford to register themselves in this way, similar trademarks can occur in different categories. Orange guitar amplifiers have nothing to do with Orange phones, for example. Apple computers and The Beatles' company Apple had an agreement that both could use the name, as long as Apple kept out of music.[26] So the advent of iTunes led to multiple lawsuits and a very long gap until all was settled and 'Love Me Do' finally appeared in the iTunes store.

How do you deal with this? How will a junior designer know that the logo they've spent three days lovingly crafting is *way too close* to something else? Someone, somewhere on the design team, needs some sense of the 'canon' of graphic design to avoid any embarrassing incidents. And, if something's been done before, that someone has to be prepared to step up and say 'that's too close'. The simplest solution, of course, as the designer of this truly extraordinary scheme for the Jewish Museum in New York has said, is to aim to 'create something unique each time...'[27]

THE REALITY OF STEP 3

So this part of the process is where a brand stands, or it falls. It's where ideas can be conceived that help create thousands of jobs, millions of dollars of profit, or billions in funds and donations.

Yet, as we've seen, the design 'process' can't be completely controlled. Creativity doesn't really match up with time-keeping and Gantt charts.

It's an unpredictable business, usually done by unpredictable people.

I've tried to explain, as best I can, how it works – but some of the leaps into the unknown recorded in this chapter don't always start from a logical, rational place.

That's, in part, the frustrating side of this. But also, the fun.

Summing up what we've covered in Step 3:
- *How to brief a team and set up a healthy environment for good ideas*
- *How to help designers jump off into the unknown*
- *How to produce design solutions based on typography, initials and monograms*
- *How to use symbolism, systems and language as the basis of schemes*
- *How to evolve brands out of what already exists*
- *The potential and the pitfalls of getting ideas through, and getting them legally checked*

*Following Steps 1 to 3 well
can take a huge amount
of time and energy, but
Step 4 is arguably the most
important. All that verbal
planning and verbal thinking
has created something good,
but to become great it
must be easily understood,
and easily used...*

IMPLEMENT

There is no doubt that it's a genuinely great achievement for a branding project to have got to this point. If the steps have gone at all closely to what I've suggested, then you are now months into a project. And for larger projects, it's not unusual to be entering year two. So congratulations just for getting here.

But this next step is critical to the success of properly finishing and properly using a verbal and visual approach.

Without a good implementation plan and without a clear sense of what needs to be done, and in what order, ideas can be introduced too fast. They can then get quickly 'lost' within a company if no one is driving the project, or the driver isn't using a decent map. And there's sometimes a temptation for a team to take their foot off the gas, to continue the analogy. 'Well done, everyone, it's agreed, let's have a drink.' All fine for project camaraderie,

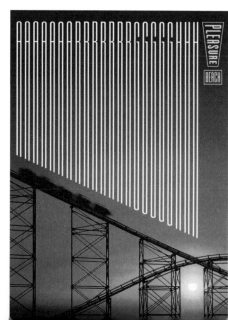

but there's an important reason why there is at least one more stage in the process: now the idea has to be crafted and turned into a working scheme (even if, in the words of the poster shown right, everyone's reaction is AAAAAAAARGH).

Great ideas wither and die without support, or if the design team keep using their 'visuals' to explain the scheme to others rather than actual, made-it-into-the-real-world applications. The aim is to create genuine applications that make the original visuals appear pedestrian in comparison.[1]

HAVE A GREAT SUMMER

AMAZING!

OUCH

HELLO!

FABULOUS

Look at these one by one. They don't look like they've changed much until you compare the first to the last...

WHAT ORDER SHOULD YOU DO THINGS IN?

First of all, you need to finish what you started. The pressures of achieving sign-off, attending tricky board meetings and/or getting positive research results can distract all parties from answering some basic questions and resolving some fundamental issues. Before we can go any further all this needs to be done.

So, in basic brand and identity terms, this means that 'core' visual assets such as logotypes and/or symbols have to be finalized for all eventualities, not hastily bashed out. This is where craft is still king and, unless the idea is impossibly simple, some time and thought is often needed. The 'lips' symbol (shown opposite and below) for an artisan ice-cream manufacturer went through countless design iterations, from the initial idea to finished rough, before being handed over to a hand-drawn lettering expert who developed it even further.[2] The original idea was a good one – to embed the words 'ice cream' between the lips – but it was the details of the execution that raised it up to another level.

A full list of applications needs to be drawn up (this may already have been started in Step 3, since key applications should have been used for visuals) and, ideally, short-, medium- and long-term labels should be applied to each item. The benefits of this are many, since a very long list with everything marked 'urgent' hinders rather than helps.

If the work is to be divided across multiple agencies, or split between in-house and out-of-house, roles can quickly be identified. The list needs to be balanced with speed and project context: for example, if a manual will eventually be needed, but certain applications take precedence, then do a quick, short-form manual, move on to applications and do the proper manual later. For Step 4 to succeed, all members of the project team need to be nimble and flexible, and willing to amend standard procedure in order to achieve a good result.

THE HIDDEN DETAILS

Many of the final tweaks and changes done at this stage are almost imperceptible, but can make a huge difference. For example, the British Rail symbol appears to have been constructed with parallel lines (above right), but it actually uses optically widening lines to counteract the thinning effect of a 'true' drawing (right).[3]

What the eye sees as uniform letters are frequently a balance of thick and slightly thinner strokes. The cross-bars in typefaces are often fractionally thinner than the down-strokes – otherwise they look wrong, optically. Another example is type arranged in circles: if it's not tweaked, then it can look a little crazy. Normally type is

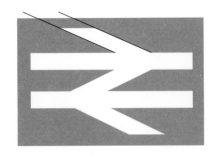

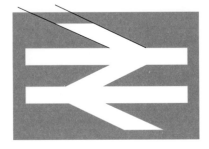

intended to sit on a horizontal 'baseline', but if that baseline is curved, then standard, 'correct' type looks anything but. So, for instance, the typography of the Martha Stewart symbol shown here is technically 'wrong' (e.g., the down-strokes of the 'H' are not parallel), but it looks far more harmonious because of its careful construction.

In some cases, key elements have to be adjusted in order to work better in a digital environment. While the UK government has embraced and pioneered its digital platform, its royal crest hadn't been revised

since the 1950s. Online it resembled something closer to a squashed pixellated beetle rather than a complex arrangement of historical symbolism and heraldry. It may still be complex now, but now it stands a chance of being reduced down in size and remaining legible.[4]

▾ British Rail / DRU / UK / 1964 ▾ Martha Stewart / Doyle Partners / USA / 2007 ▾ HM Government crest / johnson banks / UK / 2003

Sometimes the arrangement and design of certain typographic characters need some close attention. Here's an example: the typography of the first 'Virgin Atlantic' logo below looks pretty resolved, doesn't it?

Shown immediately above is the typography as it *originally looked*, when typeset. The arrangement of the letters is difficult, so almost every letterform, every typographic 'tail' and stroke, had to be tweaked subtly to allow the letters to work coherently as unified elements, rather than to appear as an ungainly arrangement. This is a particularly extreme example – most names aren't quite as problematic – but it shows the extent to which some changes have to be made. It's worth it, though: Virgin now have a main logo and a 'stackable' version in two lines which looked particularly awkward before.

THE QUIET CRAFT OF CRAFT

Sometimes the final iterations of an idea can really take time. Look at this design for a London-based inward investment organization. The overall scheme that was approved was a reversed skyline: the iconic buildings of London are 'reflected' in the graphic 'water' of the River Thames. The new skyline shows representations of all the reasons to invest and set up your HQ in London, whether it be music, parks, football or ballet.

What wasn't clear at first was that the design would need careful tweaking and experimentation to achieve both the appropriate symbolism above and below, and the right balance of elements. In the end it took 18 goes (14 of which are shown here) and eventually contained 44 separate symbols. Each step may seem incremental, but the change from the first one to the final one is immense.[5]

Think London / Johnson banks, Circus / UK / 2006

THE ROLE OF THE MANUAL

For designers of a certain age, and probably clients too, the words 'design manual' send a collective shudder down the spine. This is probably due to a residual memory of endless shelves of ring-bound folders, full of prescriptive 'rules', 'do's and don'ts' and liberal use of scolding language – something akin to a cross nanny with a penchant for kerning.

One well-known designer even said once that 'when the design manual is finished, it's time to start again' – which sums up the somewhat relentless role of design documentation.[6]

So what's 'wrong' with a document that contains rules, pointers and tips? Well, nothing really, but what seems to be critical is the tone in which such documents are written. A good manual should inspire its user to create great things, not lower their head in boredom and/or despair.

For example, the Barbican Centre in London's meticulously constructed design manual was created as a perfect piece of typographic 'porn'. It was precisely targeted to external designers taking on the Barbican brand, gently suggesting to them that 'the bar is set high, don't mess with this', and was even collected by designers who didn't work on the project as an example of best practice.

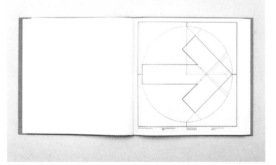

This type of manual has its roots in a particular style of document developed in the 1960s and 1970s as 'corporate design' emerged as a profession. On the left is a particularly famous example for the New York subway system – revived, re-printed and paradoxically popular again after decades in the ring-bound wilderness.[7]

▸ NYCTA design manual / Massimo Vignelli, Bob Noorda / USA / 1967 / Revival by Jesse Reed, Hamish Smyth / USA / 2014 ▴ Barbican identity guidelines / North / UK / 2007

Protecting the logo To protect the clarity and visual integrity of the logo, it has an exclusion zone. It must always appear legibly on a clear background.

Special case exceptions can be considered by contacting → printdesign@barbican.org.uk

12/13

Logo colour The logo colour is flexible, but clarity is always maintained by the use of contrasting colours. The following fundamental rules will help you achieve optimum definition.

To achieve good definition the logo full-circle must contrast with any background colour.

Likewise the word Barbican must contrast with the colour of the logo semi-circle. To maintain visual integrity, depict the name in either black or white or use a colour from your design see → pp.113–127

14/15

Lock-up typeface The lock-up information is set in Futura Book, which is a weight within our distinctive typeface.

In certain circumstances Futura Book can [...] Futura Bold (for example, when the im[...] and legibility is an issue).

The typographic values (tracking, leadi[...] the lock-up templates should not be adj[...]

20/21

Lock-up positioning The positioning of the lock-up on the Barbican grid has been defined for different formats including A5, A4, A3.

32/33

Much maligned, even hated for decades, design manuals are becoming respected, even desirable, objects in their own right.

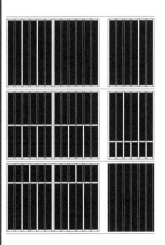

Using the column grid The column grid provides the flexibility for combining text with images in a number of ways, according to the needs of each marketing communication.

All elements should be aligned, balanced and proportional, creating strong professional communications.

36/37

Futura 108pt
Futura 96pt
Futura 84pt
Futura 72pt
Futura 60pt
Futura 48pt
Futura 36pt
Futura 30pt
Futura 24pt
Futura 18pt
Futura 14pt
Futura 12pt
Futura 10pt

Typeface introduction The Barbican typeface is Futura. It is at the heart of the Barbican identity and is the foundation for all Barbican branding. Clean, distinctive and legible, it is available in a variety of weights to express both contemporary and classical qualities.

The Barbican always uses a version of Futura that belongs to the Scangraphic font library. It is widely available and can be purchased directly from www.scangraphic-fonts.com Scangraphic Futura fonts (light, medium, bold etc.) are shown in detail on the following pages.

40/41

SM GRID

ABCDEFG

E E M U

abdefg

01234

A typical design toolkit, supplying fonts, logos, approaches to images, colour and layout examples.

abcdefghijklmnopqrstuvwxyz
ABCDEFGHIJKLMNOPQRSTUVWXYZ

BUILDING A USABLE TOOLKIT

The days of brands being summed up by a logo and one colour are long gone. Now brands need clear and flexible toolkits that can differentiate them from others, and allow multiple streams of work to take place yet still ensure they are coherently branded.

So it helps if the constituent parts can be clearly broken down: Coca-Cola has its script, its colours, the 'swoosh' device, the glass bottle shape (even when the drink isn't actually in a glass bottle) and the support typography.

The Science Museum in London's core identity is based on geometric, 'code'-like typography, and that approach is extended out into different weights of type. This gives the museum its own 'voice' for signage and publications, and is a clear identifier for the organization, alongside a colour palette, layout approaches and an identifiable tone of voice.

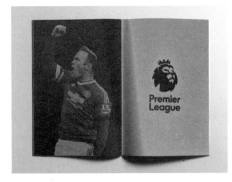

The Premier League's new identity is based on a bold new take on the league's lion icon. The symbol is part of the competition's heritage but has been re-engineered to meet the requirements of a 21st century digital brand. This is accompanied by a vibrant, almost fluorescent colour palette and iconic pattern, based on the lion's mane but determinedly flexible in its application.

For some brands, it seems to be more appropriate to keep the format of the documentation as approachable as possible. This brand guide for More Th>n takes the form of a small, pocket-sized booklet, deliberately written in a conversational way. The aim of the booklet is to explain, quite quickly, some important points about the brand (values, tone of voice, etc.), but to do it in a way that is engaging and entertaining.

We thought it would be useful to have our **own typeface.** It is.

It comes in two weights.
Regular. **Bold.** That's it.

Less is more, you see.

Having our typeface means we can be pretty consistent, and never get confused with other insurers. **Look at this page. Looks like MORE TH>N doesn't it?** It's amazing what a couple of colours and a typeface can do.

◄ Mathaf/Qatar Museums, Qatar / Wolff Olins / UK / 2011 and 2014

BRANDING IN A BILINGUAL WORLD

An increasing challenge when implementing brands globally is the need to be able to adapt famous marks into several languages. From soft drinks to tyres, designs have to work in languages as diverse as, for instance, Mandarin, Hebrew and Urdu. Very few are as lucky as Pirelli: as you can see, its world-famous mark adapts very well into Arabic, for example. Others adopt the classic side-by-side bilingual approach: the Mathaf Museum in Qatar and its overarching body, Qatar Museums, both use variants of this, coupled with symbolism that can work in English and Arabic.

It *can* be possible to combine languages together, although this is extremely difficult. The logo shown immediately left celebrated joint projects between the UK and Japan, and actually reads in two languages: by turning and twisting the letters for 'UK' and the characters for 'Nihon' (Japan), the letterforms can be read in both languages.[8]

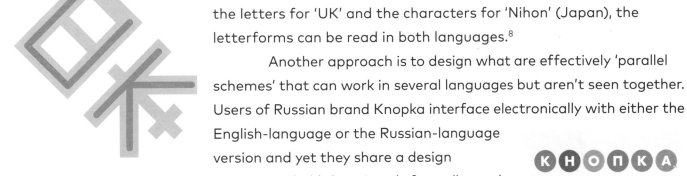

Another approach is to design what are effectively 'parallel schemes' that can work in several languages but aren't seen together. Users of Russian brand Knopka interface electronically with either the English-language or the Russian-language version and yet they share a design language. Zhuk's logo is only formally used in Russian, but applications exist in English and each language shares the same design style, typography and characterizations.

◄ UK Japan / johnson banks / UK / 2006

83% of companies close in the first year.

What makes you think you're any different?

ЖУК

ЖУК

Почему всё так?

КНОПКА

Включает всё. Для предпринимателей.

Why do you work so hard?

КНОПКА

The total business service, designed for entrepreneurs.

◄ Pirelli / Unimark International / Italy / 1970s ▲ Zhuk, Knopka / NB Studio / UK / 2013

There have been various experiments with bilingual typographic communication. Shown opposite is an experimental typeface combining Hindi and English (known as the Hinglish font) and shown left is a project embedding Japanese phonetic sounds into the Katakana-style font, allowing non-Japanese speakers to say the characters. As more and more Gulf and Asian brands look to the West to open up markets, the ability and need to find successful bilingual design approaches will become more and more pertinent.

Attempts to combine Latin letterforms and Arabic letterforms have generally been less successful – the approaches of both scripts are so dissimilar (one reads left to right, the other right to left, with fundamentally different typeface constructions) – but a few examples of typeforms are emerging that can work in greater harmony.

For example, this scheme for the Museum of Islamic Art in Doha uses the six writing styles of Arabic to populate one side of a three-dimensional cube, emulating both the richness of the culture and the unique design of the museum in the process.

▸ Phonetikana / johnson banks / UK / 2009 ▴ The Hinglish Project / Shirin Johari / India / 2012

▸ Museum of Islamic Art, Doha / Landor / Dubai / 2014

GO AHEAD, TYPE SOMETHING!

The Hinglish project

5.7 million tourists will visit India this year. The Indian Ministry of Tourism wanted to make India more approachable. Most of the street signs that tourists see are in Hindi. So we created a typeface that would make Hindi less intimidating and more friendly. Through this unique fusion-font design, you can tell the phonetic sound of a Hindi character by looking at the corresponding English alphabet superimposed on it. While this font cannot teach you how to read words as they are spelt in Hindi, it demystifies individual letters. Despite the superficial distinctiveness of English and Hindi, the two borrow from the same phonetic pool - the Indo-European group of languages. This type design playfully highlights these commonalities. To quote a now-popular phrase, "We're same same, but different!" With the Hinglish Project, the Indian Ministry of Tourism became the only tourism board in the world to help create a typeface for foreigners to familiarise themselves with native language.

english + hindi

a + अ = a

SHOWING THE BILINGUAL WAY

One of the great success stories of bilingual global branding is Uniqlo. Even the genesis of its name (the 'Unique Clothing Warehouse', which opened in Hiroshima in 1984) reveals its long-term aim to be both Japanese and yet Western-facing at the same time. The

organization is unusual due to its relatively flat structure and insists on carrying out its work in English.

Due to an administrative mistake in 1988, which now seems like a typographic masterstroke, implementation staff mis-read the 'uni-clo' abbreviation as 'Uni-Qlo' and the shorter name as we now know it was

born, with that all-important 'Q'.[9] For over a decade, Uniqlo presented a fairly neutral face to the world, but then in 2006 it decided to adopt a bilingual approach and its own customized font. Uniqlo continued to expand across the world, supplying 'everyday clothes for a better life' – simple, functional, quality products that are 'made for all' and beautifully presented – with meticulously trained staff in its stores.

It has become an international icon. The company still works primarily in English, but it remains determinedly bilingual and clearly Japanese – perhaps showing how Asian brands can succeed globally without losing their roots and slipping into a sea of ubiquity. As their founder says, 'We go to the world and global market as a representative of Japan-ness and Japanese culture. We realize contemporary Japanese culture in our clothing.'[10]

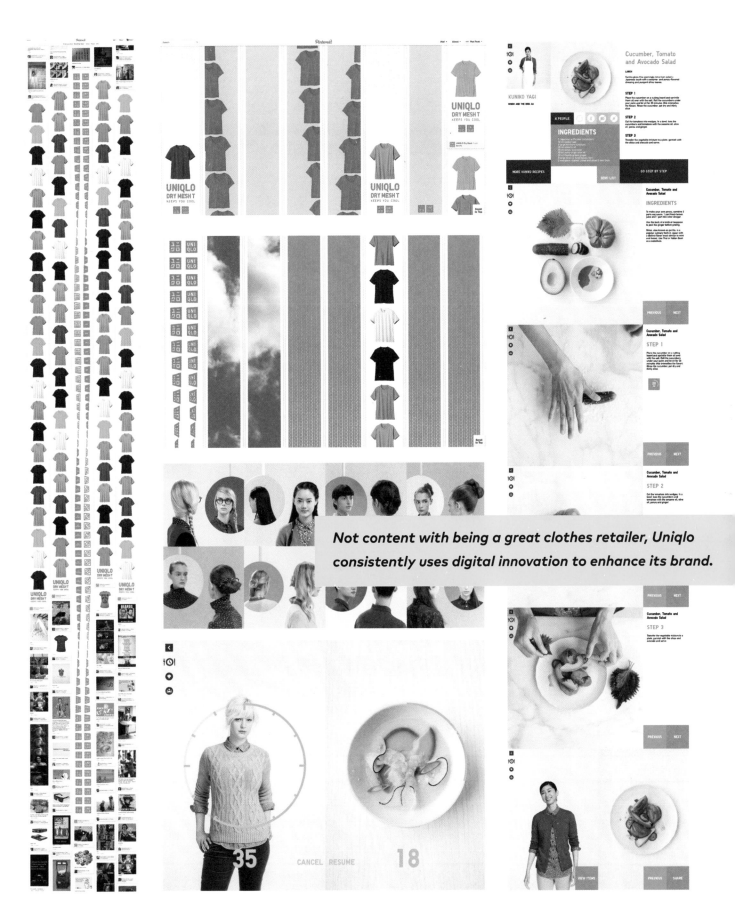

Not content with being a great clothes retailer, Uniqlo consistently uses digital innovation to enhance its brand.

IMPLEMENTATION IN A DIGITAL WORLD

While many of the core principles of branding that we looked at in Step 2 (defining a core why, what and how) remain sacrosanct, the biggest sea-change of the 21st century so far has been the need to strengthen, establish or launch brands in an ever-changing digital environment. Where once printed items were key, now early applications for every new project must prove that they can move and 'flex' on screen, and that an idea can work as well on a web page as it does infinitesimally tiny in a tweet, and so on.

Some of these challenges (such as the tiny icon challenge we examined on page 190) have always been there: instead of creating a logo for 'small use', a version of that logo is now needed for 'tiny use' at just 16 pixels across. Some of the issues are new: designers trained within a rigorous 'design for print' mindset find the problems of creating digital layouts that will be infinitely pushed and pulled by a user's browser, or squashed

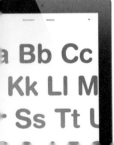

again on a smartphone, almost insurmountable. (The rise of more 'modular' design approaches online is a direct reaction to this design challenge.)

For brands born entirely into a digital age, a new mindset is developing whereby a brand is implemented *digitally first* and then physically. The best ideas are taking the opportunities that this offers and running with them. The approach for the telecoms company Ollo (left) has an entirely interactive form that allows the user/visitor to the site to 'play' with the logo to an almost infinite degree.[11]

Newsbeat, a BBC news service aimed at 16–24-year-olds, needed to re-align both its product and its brand to recognize more effectively the shifting preferences of its core audience. It developed a wordmark that spins as visitors scroll through the content, either cycling through its letters like a musical slot machine or else reacting to the speed of the music being played, cannily matching news per minute to beats per minute.

make food
affordable for
everyone /
إجعل طعام
بأسعار معقولة
لكل أشخاص
在公园和公交
上的长椅上放
置毛绒座 / put
plush seats
on park and
bus benches
/ idøm folk,
der smider
affald fra sig, en bøde /
לבנות שירותים ציבוריים נקיים
มีโครงการศิลปินพานัักในสวน
สาธารณะทุกแห่ง / werk en

l'étranger à
côté de vous /
woon   छतबगीचों द्वारा
in de-   बारिश के पानी
zelfde   को जमा करना /
gemeen-   Avere più
schap /   eventi artistici
create more gratuiti per
comfortable tutti / 歩行者用
shelters for の通りと自転
the homeless 車専用道路
population / を、全部道路
tocar música clásica より高く建設
en el metro / فواره های する / plant
／ بیشتری نصب کنید fruit-bearing
hupen durch Gesetze un- trees at street
terbinden / level / altyapı
parlez avec sistemlerini

tamamen ye-   criar arte pú-
niden tasar- blica em áreas
layarak /   negligenciadas /
şẹdá bósì tí 给无家可归的人提
àwọn èrò okọ̀ 供更多的庇护
şatókùn rẹ̀ / 所 / расши-
रस्त्याच्या काठ рить пеше-
ला फळझाडे ходные зоны /
लावणे / create dùng kỹ thuật
buses that   để tạo ra các
are powered dạng thức mới về
by the pas- sự cam kết
senger /   của công dân
ustawmy   / build under-
wokół miasta ground instead of
więcej kosz- above ground /
ów na re-   뜻밖의 장소에 작은
cyklizację   쉼터를 만들자

These two identities for the Solomon R. Guggenheim Museum in New York were entirely 'digital first'. 'LAB' is a touring project sponsored by BMW that allows visitors to 'tweet' their name into the logo. 'MAP' is a global art initiative sponsored by UBS, whose visual background is an ever-moving collage of the land masses of the countries and continents whose art is being curated.

Some revitalized brands are using the 'instant' aspect of digital platforms to their benefit. While the re-launch of the Airbnb brand allowed users and visitors to customize its new identity (a nice touch), a furore arose over the precise design of the new symbol and what it actually meant. Airbnb chose to deal with this head on and released an online 'Bélo' (the nickname for the new symbol) report, which, with good humour, tracked the launch, allowed Airbnb to poke fun at itself...and enhanced the brand at the same time.

A digital environment can even make us question what physical form a logo can or should take. An Indian charity raising funds to provide free cleft treatment uses simple keystrokes and emoticons to write its name :{ to :), in other words, from 'cleft to smile'. This communicates the entire idea by tweet, text or any form of typed or written language, neatly bypassing the need for a formal 'logo' entirely.

:{to:)

THE WORLD'S MOST TWEETED LOGO

How a small charity's type-able logo spread cleft awareness to millions across the world.

These digitally formed ideas can become a powerful rallying point by dint of their low cost and infinitely shareable nature. Protesting against the abduction of nearly 300 girls in Nigeria by the Boko Haram group, three Nigerians set up a campaign using the #BringBackOurGirls hashtag, which swiftly became a global meme and was endorsed by Michelle Obama and countless celebrities.

The Arabic symbol for the 'N' of 'Nazarene' (opposite), a pejorative Arabic word for Christians, was painted onto houses in conflict regions by ISIS soldiers in northern Iraq, which led to a mass exodus out of the city of Mosul. There are, of course, echoes here of the Nazis' use of the Star of David to badge Jews, and just as the star became a chillingly negative image then, so the odd, smiley-face Cyclops of this symbol has become potent now. Facebook and Twitter users have changed their profile pictures to feature the 'N', and widespread adoption of the #WeAreN and #IAmNasrani hashtags has been seen.

Although some of these campaigns have received criticism for propagating 'clicktivism', rather than genuine activism – providing a mechanism to be seen to support a cause via social media, but little else – they demonstrate how all preconceptions of naming and branding have to be re-examined in a digital context.

A B C D Q R S T
E F G H U V W X
I J K L Y Z 1 2
M N O P 3 4 5 6

Funciones

Sábado 17/9   15:00 hs. Autobiografía de Nicolae Ceaușescu
               18:30 hs. Presentación de Alan Pauls
               19:00 hs. Videogramas de una revolución

Sábado 24/9   15:00 hs. Videogramas de una revolución
               17:00 hs. Presentación de Alan Pauls
               17:30 hs. Autobiografía de Nicolae Ceaușescu

Sábado 1/10   15:00 hs. Autobiografía de Nicolae Ceaușescu
               18:30 hs. Presentación de Alan Pauls
               19:00 hs. Videogramas de una revolución

Sábado 8/10   15:00 hs. Videogramas de una revolución
               17:00 hs. Presentación de Alan Pauls
               17:30 hs. Autobiografía de Nicolae Ceaușescu

Más información en www.proa.org/esp/events

Informes y reservas: Agradecimientos:
auditorio@proa.org   Goethe-Institut Buenos Aires
4104-1000/1001   Buenos Aires Festival
                            Internacional de Cine
Fundación Proa: Independiente (BAFICI)
Av. Pedro de Mendoza 1929,
y Caminito Buenos Aires   Tenaris – Organización Techint

Fundación Proa   Educación
Av. Pedro de Mendoza 1929   educacion@proa.org
[C1169AAD], Buenos Aires   –
Argentina   Cafetería
[54-11] 4104-1000   cafeteria@proa.org
info@proa.org
                            Librería
                            libreria@proa.org
Horarios
Martes a domingo
de 11 a 19 hs   www.proa.org
Lunes cerrado

PROA

PROA
AUDITORIUM
FILMS

PROA

NOTICIAS
EXHIBICIONES
AUDITORIO
INFORMACION
EDUCACION
PRENSA
LIBROS/CAFE

TYPEFACE AS BRAND

While a logo and a symbol act as a clear 'signature' for an organization, there is an increasing realization that a uniquely drawn and constructed typeface can act as another key 'layer' and aid recognition.

    The Fundación Proa in Buenos Aires was inspired by a nearby riveted bridge and developed a bespoke typeface that embeds the 'rivets', graphically, into the logotype and font. This created an eyecatching visual style for all the museum's communications – and one that was entirely its own.

    Proa is a great example from the arts, while the typeface created for Oxfam, an international charity that fights poverty,

sums up its spirit and also helps it stand out. By using an intentionally hand-drawn and slightly imperfect typeface – which implies both that Oxfam is humanitarian and that its work is never finished – its 'voice' is now consistent and cuts through in an increasingly crowded market.

The Kröller-Müller Museum, near Amsterdam, wanted to drastically change public perceptions of it as a venue. It chose to do this with a dramatic approach featuring a specially created typeface that appears to open and is supplied in multiple degrees of 'openness'. This creates a beautiful and striking effect, while reflecting the museum's aim to draw in more visitors to enjoy its world-class product and subtly hint at the work on display both inside and outside the museum.

▲ ◄ Kröller-Müller Museum, near Amsterdam / edenspiekermann / Germany / 2013 ▼ El Banco Deuno / Saffron / UK / 2009 ▼ IBM 'Smarter Outdoor' / Ogilvy & Mather / France / 2014

Unique typographic approaches aren't limited to culture and charity. El Banco Deuno in Mexico deliberately positioned itself away from the more usual stuffy deference of the finance sector and drew on a brand idea of 'a new bank for a new Mexico', mining traditional Mexican art and design to create something entirely new.

Even though the relative cost of drawing unique, bespoke typefaces is much less than it used to be, it is still possible for organizations effectively to 'ring-fence' a widely available font as their own. IBM's consistent use of the Lubalin Graph typeface links to the 'slab' serifs of its logo and makes sense as the company font. Because IBM use it carefully, and consistently, worldwide, no other technology company can realistically use it.

It has become IBM's typeface by virtue of regular usage and repetition – even though it is widely available and there is no legal barrier to another tech company using it.

A B C D E F
G H I J K L M
N O P Q R S
T U V W X Y Z

Apple / USA / 2015 ▲ Miss Kō / GBH / UK / 2013

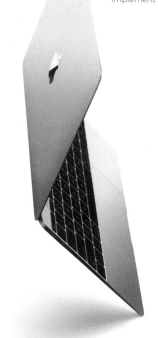

IMPLEMENTING CONSISTENT IMAGERY

For technology brands, the issue of presenting updates to products over many years (sometimes many times a year) is a marketing conundrum: do they keep constantly re-inventing their approach (and run the risk of seeming haphazard) or do they pick a clear and evident visual style to use and develop over time?

Consistent use of a particular approach to imagery can become key. While Apple's products are clearly Apple's by dint of their design, the way they have been consistently presented has become recognizable worldwide. Using photography of the highest quality shows off the products' physical beauty and attention to detail, and establishes a clear photographic 'look'. This then becomes very hard for competitors to appropriate without their ads (and products) looking like mere copies.[12]

It is apparent at a glance (see opposite) that these are Apple products – the perfect lighting, the sumptuous details. On these two pages, at least, only three Apple logos are visible, but the brand is summed up by its design and photography; the 'branding', from a traditional perspective, is almost nowhere to be seen.

A contrasting example of how imagery can make a brand is Parisian underground Asian fusion restaurant Miss Kō. The restaurant chose to emulate 'Yakuza' full-body tattoos and developed a set of unique images to use in all of its communications, meticulously photo-comping the tattoos on bodies, tongues and everything in between.

Disembodied tattooed body parts appear across all items from menus to business cards and, to redress any perceived sexism, there is also a male body tattooed. In an added, semi-surreal twist, a 26-metre-long table runs through the restaurant, projecting news from channels across the region right onto your sushi and miso soup.

MISS KŌ

ミス・コー

The visual effect of Miss Kō's tattoos is sexy and shocking, but it creates an undeniably strong brand identity.

▾ Library Foundation of Los Angeles / AdamsMorioka / USA / 2011

NEW-FOUND FLEXIBILITY

One of the accusations that has been levelled at branding schemes for years is that they are overly rigorous and lack flexibility. In the hands of world-famous designers, the post-war schemes for IBM and Olivetti, which established the ground rules for what was then 'corporate identity', seemed to have plasticity and interest built in, but this was almost entirely due to the skills of the designers driving the schemes.[13]

Come 'down' a level to everyday 'identity design' and the process quickly became a fairly restrictive list of do's, don'ts and never ever evers. Hence the invention of the phrase 'logo cop'. But as 'identity' slowly morphed into 'brand', so the seeds of a new

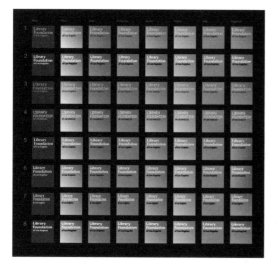

approach began to be seen: brand identities started to appear with ideas that could adapt to their surroundings. As TV pioneers such as MTV and the UK's Channel 4 showed, and continue to show with their on-screen idents, a certain amount of movement and flux not only added a bit of fun, but also added personality. Once Google had demonstrated that its masthead could change quite regularly to reflect anniversaries and world events, other brands began to experiment, too.

The Library Foundation of Los Angeles adopted a logo system that encompassed eight colours and eight typefaces (creating a mind-boggling choice from 64 variants when picking a logo).

The museum and gallery sector has also begun to realize that the image it presents to the world can be far more interesting and engaging. The Whitney Museum of American Art in New York developed a new identity that took one of its chief curator's views (note the value of good research) as its starting point: 'it would be much easier to present the history of art as a simplistic line – but that's not the Whitney'.[14] This proved to be a pivotal stepping stone for the visual idea of a 'zigzag', which finally became a 'W' that bends and squeezes itself into every available space.

▸ **Whitney Museum** / Experimental Jetset / The Netherlands / 2013

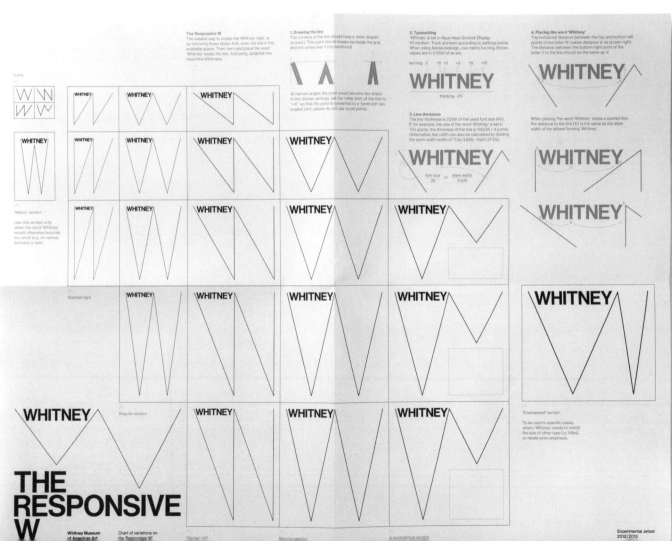

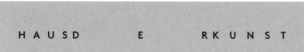

HAUSD   E   RKUNST

As if not wanting to be outdone, the Haus der Kunst Museum in Munich allows its logotype to stretch and be squashed into different horizontal spaces, breaking all the rules of consistent letter-spacing and principles of 'one logo' in the process. This sends a clear message about a museum in constant motion and flux.

The principle of continual change fits perfectly with technologically minded clients. MIT Media Lab, the sector pioneer, flirted with this when it unveiled its entirely 'flexible' 25th anniversary identity, which endlessly changed its form (in theory, always producing a unique symbol, from something like 40,000 permutations). But the Lab, perhaps envious of its sister organization, the MIT Press, with a logo that hasn't changed for decades, wanted something a little more permanent. It developed a mark based on the same grid as the anniversary logo, which had supplied much of that scheme's flexibility, but now providing a compelling design system *and* an immovable monogram.[15]

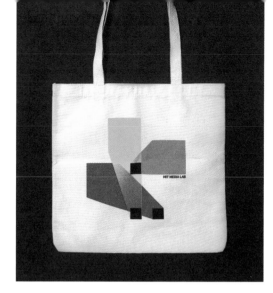

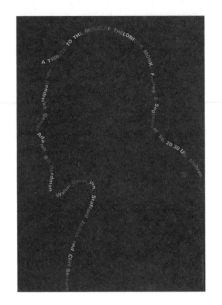

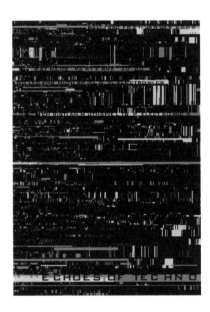

Still one of the greatest examples of the ultimate flexible cultural branding schemes is that of the annual Jazz Festival in Willisau, Switzerland. The festival's roots date back to a concert held in the town in 1966 by an amateur band from Zurich, which was organized by Niklaus Troxler, a jazz-loving designer.

As musicians such as Champion Jack Dupree and Evan Parker were then lured to play in the town, Troxler celebrated with vibrant posters. Even after the festival became a formal, annual event from 1975, and attracted increasingly significant names (such as Keith Jarrett, Chick Corea and Sun Ra), the posters continued and always eschewed any sense of formula or even a sniff of a regular, standardized logo. Each one was different from the last; each was exceptional. By combining his love of jazz and of poster design, Troxler carved out a piece of design history. He was presented with the keys to his town and has shown us all what unfettered flexibility can really look like.[16]

▴ ▸ Willisau Jazz Festival / Niklaus Troxler / Switzerland / from 1980s onwards

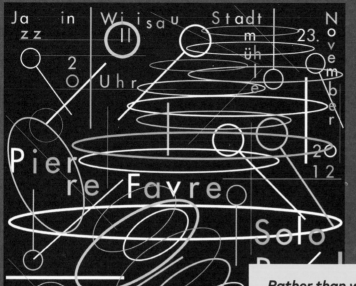

Rather than wait for the perfect client to arrive and grant him total flexibility, Niklaus Troxler just designed these posters himself.

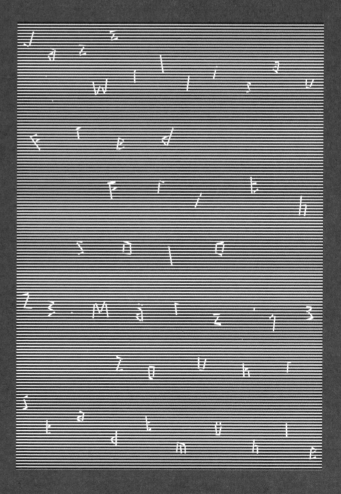

AVOIDING THE CURSE OF HOMOGENEITY

While the concept and principles of these dynamic identities seem naturally 'at home' with brands that value a shape-shifting, chameleon-like approach, the tactic is still very unusual in the retail and hospitality sectors.

For high-street, retail and hospitality brands, the time-honoured strategy has been to establish the 'core' of the brand – its consumer 'offer' – and then the key visual and environmental clues that go with it. So most Kentucky Fried Chicken shops will look similar, as will Starbucks outlets. It's the classic franchise model: establish what works and then replicate it. But what happens when you don't want to replicate; when individuality and originality are what you are looking for, albeit with some economies of scale?

Two very different, and yet related, examples of rejecting cookie-cutter branding in the search for more authentic 'experiences' for customers are Byron restaurants and Ace hotels. Byron, a British brand that has been going for less than a decade, sells up-market hamburgers in each of its 51 restaurants (and counting).

▸ ▸ Byron / Ben Stott / UK / from 2007 onwards

The critical difference is that, while each of these restaurants shares the same menu, they are presented as one-offs – different signs, different interiors, different music. Each is presented as an individual restaurant and, indeed, if a regular customer never strays from their particular patch, then they may never know that there are 50 other Byrons out there. The Soho Byron is suitably neon, the King's Road one very 'Chelsea', the Clapham one painted bright green, and so on.

The 'no-logo' approach has become a kind of 'badge of honour'. Even when three small shops on one street were turned into one restaurant, they still each received a different fascia. Of course, there's a question about how long Byron can keep this visual conceit going (and if their designers can keep creating a 'new' restaurant every time), but there's no doubt that it taps into the mood of anti-chain, 'pop-up' food stalls and the desire for what seems (at least at face value) to be 'the genuine article'.[17]

Ace Hotel: the closest thing to 'hipster in a bottle' that you can experience. And different every time.

Ace Hotel / USA, World / from 1999 onwards

A parallel example is the Ace hotel chain, which has somehow managed to bottle the concept of a hipster hotel and imbue each of its premises, all in carefully considered locations, with a huge amount of warmth and a feeling of authenticity. The name itself, chosen because the ace card is 'the high and low card in the deck', reflects the fact that even in the heart of New York they have cheap bunk beds on offer (as well as vast corner-room loft apartments at $800 a night).

Ace's style is led by a careful choice of building: Seattle's location is a former Salvation Army halfway house, Los Angeles's is on the historic United Artists site built in 1927, Panama's is a restored building in Casco Viejo. In New York a turn-of-the-century office building in the Flatiron District was turned into a mecca with shabby chic sofas and free Wi-Fi for those with hipster beards and the seemingly obligatory Mac portable.

RETAIL FLEXIBILITY

While much branding attention is placed on organizations, companies and products, the branding of places and spaces benefits just as much from this thinking. The results aren't as easy to pin down into logos, symbols and colours, but the principles are exactly the same.

For example, when London department store Selfridges was acquired in the 1990s, it was a pale shadow of what its founder, H. Gordon Selfridge, wanted in a store: innovation, fun and adventure. In re-inventing itself for the 21st century, Selfridges looked to liberate itself, continually refresh itself and re-capture some of its escapist and imaginative past. This was done by agreeing a new core purpose, 'exposure to the new', which became the verbal backbone of the store for a decade.

In terms of 're-branding', this didn't result in a change of logo, per se, but a wholesale change in attitude – the move to a 'house of brands'; the transformation of previously dusty departments. A comprehensive restoration project was celebrated with the world's largest photograph, by artist Sam Taylor-Wood, wrapped around the scaffolding.[18] Themed seasons such as 'Tokyo Life' became commonplace, while events such as Jerry Hall appearing in the window as Botticelli's Venus and 500 nude Londoners being photographed on the shop floor were just average days for the store.

Selfridges is about…

EXPOSURE TO THE NEW

New brands, new experiences, new behaviours – internal and external

We provide access, opportunity, knowledge. We act as both predictor and translator – maven and connector

▾ Selfridges brand strategy / Circus / UK / 2003 ▾ Selfridges hoarding / Sam Taylor-Wood / UK / 2008 ▾ Selfridges photoshoot / Spencer Tunick

The sheer fact that this photoshoot could even happen is proof of just how far the Selfridges brand has developed.

TO END: A HEALTH WARNING

We've ended Step 4 with some great examples of how 21st-century brands are implementing their core ideas in ever more unusual and innovative ways. Yet some of this flexibility comes with a warning: even the most well-intentioned design scheme and enlightened client *cannot rein in* a brand once it starts to get out of control. We briefly touched on design manuals and 'logo cops', but it's worth reiterating that some form of control is necessary to keep a brand identity from collapsing.

Often this isn't the fault of the end-users, especially if they are not trained designers. Instead of grumbling about 'how someone has ruined the scheme in PowerPoint', create some decent templates to help. Don't mutter about 'how Word makes everything look awful' – spend a bit of time learning how to make it great.

Conversely, another enemy can simply be boredom. By the time an internal team has nurtured an idea for launch (over the best part of a year) and then painstakingly implemented it (over several years), people have begun to move on, get itchy feet and want to tinker.[19] But, as a rule of thumb, it takes most brand identity projects about two to three years to even begin to become recognized by key audiences – in other words, just as an idea gets some traction externally, *internally* people will try to meddle. Ultimately, this can become the biggest enemy of brand building.

The brands that have always succeeded have been clear and consistent. The next generation of great brands will be the same and will embrace technology, seeing obstacles as things to be overcome or skirted around, and thriving on their ability to be nimble and flexible. This is what Step 4 is all about: building, codifying and subtly controlling an idea that is fit for purpose...and fit for whatever the future holds.

Summing up what we've covered in Step 4:
- *The importance of the last details*
- *The value of control documents and manuals, and the development of a design toolkit*
- *How to cope with the demands of a bilingual world*
- *The implications of digital and how to be 'digital first'*
- *How key elements such as typography and imagery can play a vital role*
- *How all manner of brands are building flexibility into how they look and what they do*
- *How to avoid the pitfalls of implementation*

ENGAGE OR REVIVE

Most of us involved in the business are only just starting to see how key this last step is. Either a new idea needs to be carefully embedded into an organization, or the time has come to take what's already there and give it a new lease of life...

n a way, this last step is several steps in one and it all depends where a brand is in its cycle. For example, for a new brand, created from scratch, which has progressed through Steps 1 to 4, the point has been reached where the strategic direction has been decided, a design has been chosen, and the 'roll-out' and implementation have begun.

Sometimes the temptation is to think 'job done', but this is where the long-term job *begins*, especially with larger organizations with layers of management and hundreds or even thousands of employees. If a new direction isn't understood internally, or people haven't been consulted, the task ahead may be an uphill struggle. This is where successful 'engagement' with an idea comes in.

Some brands may have been established for years and are slightly lifeless and in need of some resuscitation. If the issues a brand faces are terminal, then the brand may have to go back many steps. If you're reading this and in control of a brand that you sense is jaded, you need to decide whether or not to go all the way back to Step 2 to re-think your strategy, re-define your 'narrative' and work forwards.

Conversely, the contents of this step may make you decide that you *can* revitalize what you have, without comprehensive and far-reaching changes.

There is, of course, another scenario – which is that you don't have a good enough idea to embed, or you don't think you can revive what you have. This is a situation faced by products, companies, organizations and services that reach the 'end' of their useful life. This is sometimes called the end of the product's 'life cycle'.[1] It is either a huge problem, or a huge opportunity, depending on which way you look at it.

Now
what?

Apple Mac launch ad / Ridley Scott Associates / UK / 1984

EMBEDDING AN AGREED IDEA

This book suggests that there are five and a half clear steps, which is hopefully useful, but there is a strong argument that engaging with a new idea must start to take place as soon as it is agreed at the end of Step 3 – i.e., the process may be a little less linear. This is because internal take-up and adoption become increasingly critical for the long-term health and adaptability of a new brand, so establishing a clear link between the research stage and the engagement stage is vital.

If many levels of staff in an organization were consulted during the investigation stage of Step 1 (let's say, through staff workshops and staff surveys) then it's both polite and politically savvy to 'report back' regularly. And once strategy and narrative have been agreed, then this needs to be communicated with others; and once a visual approach has been agreed, share it.[2] And even if Step 4 is only just under way, staff can re-engage as soon as possible and, in some cases, in parallel with the implementation stage. It's possible that Steps 4 and 5 can almost take place side by side, if you wish.

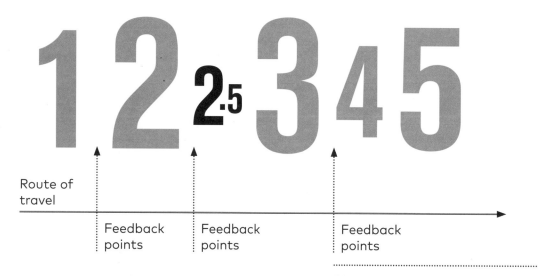

But for the purposes of the rest of this step, we're going to return to our more linear approach. So, you've got a great brand idea to share – what's the best way to do that?

One of the most time-honoured techniques is some form of roadshow/internal launch, with as much or as little razzmatazz as required. Apple famously chose to 'launch' its groundbreaking Apple Macintosh with one ad, aired only once, during the Superbowl. It took a direct pop, '1984'-style, at IBM, the then 'big brother' that dominated personal computing. It was the classic 'challenger' approach – ultra high risk (but ultra memorable).[3]

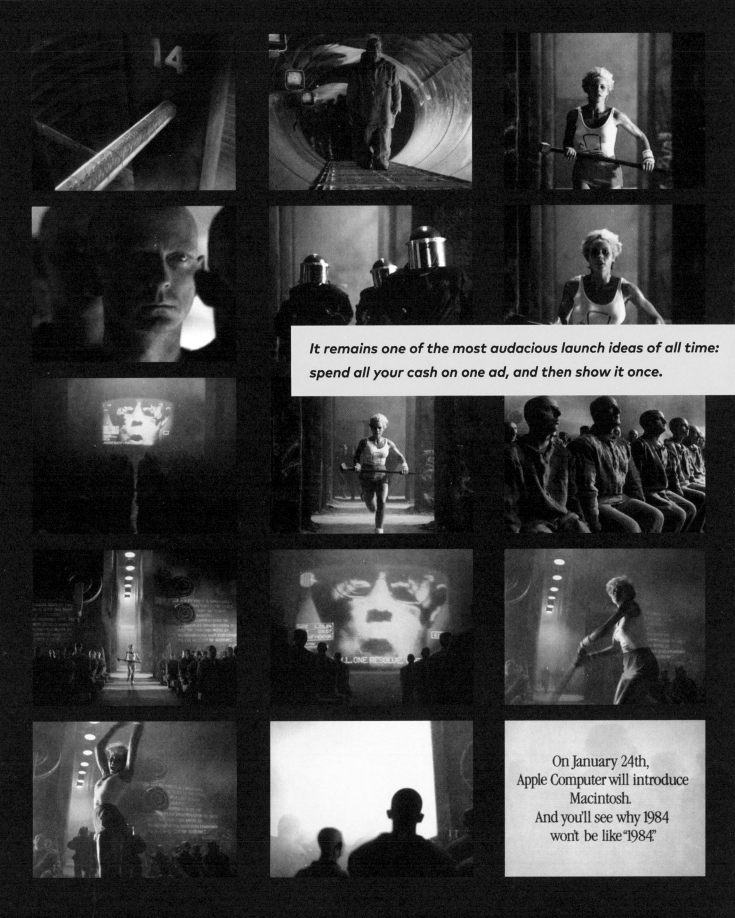

It remains one of the most audacious launch ideas of all time: spend all your cash on one ad, and then show it once.

On January 24th,
Apple Computer will introduce
Macintosh.
And you'll see why 1984
won't be like "1984."

• Dear World... Yours, Cambridge projections / Miguel Chevalier / France / Conceived and produced by Artichoke Productions / Scriptwriting and additional art direction by johnson banks / 2015

Some brand teams simply decide to hit the road. Way back in the early 1960s when Avis launched their radical new approach (page 42), they did a 300-city roadshow around the USA to explain the idea behind 'We try harder' to counter workers and attendants, and to encourage them to flaunt their hard-working buttons with pride.

When the University of Cambridge launched a global fundraising campaign (page 197) to hundreds of key donors, a central part of the launch was a carefully scripted series of short speeches, interspersed with narrated introductions from the likes of David Attenborough and Stephen Hawking. These were accompanied by immersive 270-degree projections played across the 16th-century ceiling of King's College Chapel.[4]

One-off adverts, immersive projections or roadshows criss-crossing a country are just three examples: it could be that a new idea is better 'soft launched' in order to let new thinking permeate more slowly.

ENGAGING BY DOING, NOT TELLING

One of the key tasks of this step is to take the words and ideas agreed in Step 2, and the designs agreed in Steps 3 and 4, then test and extend them in real, 'live' situations. For the visual aspects, workshops can be held where examples are brought, issues discussed and solutions sought. For the verbal elements (which crucially affect how a brand or organization communicates and behaves) and the decisions taken in Step 2 regarding future 'values', this is the perfect time to establish what those values will *really* mean, in everyday usage.

This is where engaging with the new brand can really make a difference: for instance, simple staff workshops that take each agreed value and then discuss how that affects their day-to-day lives. This can not only be incredibly helpful with brand definition, but also, crucially, it *involves staff in the process*. In simple terms: it helps massively with buy-in.

If there's a collective shrug of the shoulders internally, then the process won't be adopted with enthusiasm. The key is making the participants part of and shapers of the process and the final product, not just receivers of decisions made on high.

As an example, if a museum has committed itself to being 'enthusiastic', 'inspirational' and 'practical', but reception staff are bored, uninspired and offer no useful advice on what a family of four should do, then the message isn't getting through. If an airline has, say, committed to an internal mantra of 'living to fly' and yet its employees have no sense of joie de vivre, then something's not working.

Ideally, the new brand 'idea' will begin to cascade down within a company and, either formally or informally, staff will become 'ambassadors' for the new way of working. They can then begin to run groups with other members of staff and become informal 'explainers' of what 'that lot at head office have been up to'.

The work that can be done at this step, either internally or externally, can play a key role in expanding the brand model we explored throughout Step 2 (page 88). If we return to the bottom half of our model, then the implications are clear.

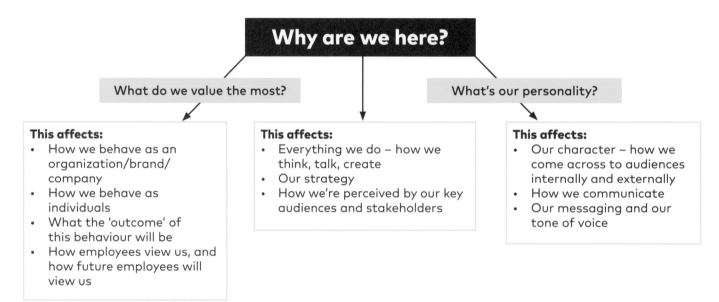

On the left-hand side, under 'what do we value the most', we can begin to flesh out how those values translate into how the brand and its employees behave.

Now, some of this might sound a little controlling, as in 'don't you tell me how to behave', but there is a reason why Starbucks employees go through a rigorous training programme – to ensure that *what they value* is then translated into how they *behave*. So the way a barista engages with you in Birmingham or Beijing should, in theory, be pretty similar. A Uniqlo employee should hand back your credit card with two hands, Japanese business card-style – a core *value* of Japanese-ness translated into a key mode of *behaviour*.

In the central 'box' above there is an interesting phrase: 'how we're perceived by our key audiences and stakeholders'. Now, again, this might seem odd written down, but if you start to note down what this could really mean – how you want people to see you – then it can be very useful and instructive, and spark lively debate.

Here is an example drafted for an art organization raising funds to keep art from being sold off to internationally (while offering discounts for museum members).

What we want the public to think I love art. I can see that this is a great charity for art, and a way for my small contribution to really help save art that's endangered. The benefits I get back are pretty good, too: they save art, I save money.	**What we want museums and galleries to think** Without them we'd be in trouble. We can turn to them and ask for their help, and they respond in a fast and fair manner. We understand why they want to be better known, so we'll help them, not stand in their way.
What we want the media to think I'm much clearer now – they are an independent art charity saving art for the nation, and campaigning on behalf of the arts sector. More people should know what they do. I think theirs is a story that we should tell more often.	**What we want volunteers to think** I love art. I know this is a great charity for art. I want to help them with my time. My small contribution really helps save art that's endangered. The benefits I get back are pretty good, too: they save art, I save money.

◂ Art Fund perception map / johnson banks / UK / 2006

THE IMPLICATIONS FOR MESSAGING AND TONE OF VOICE

If you've gone to the trouble of defining the core purpose of a brand and discovering an appropriate tone of voice, then how that translates into written words and applications becomes critical. This is where testing with internal teams is essential. There's no point in insisting that all communications should be 'agit' if there isn't enough internal anger to drive 'agitated' ideas through. Conversely, using a witty tone of voice only works, if, from day one, applications are engaging and carry that humour through.

Equally important is how the brand's core idea affects the 'messages' a brand uses and how they are tailored to each audience. By mapping a brand's purpose, personality and tone of voice onto different customers and audiences, it should be possible to build a messaging 'matrix'. Here's one example diagram of how to approach this, building on some of the questions we asked way back in Step 1, page 51.[5]

PROPOSITIONS	PROOF POINTS	PERSONAL STORIES...
What's the issue? A simple articulation of the problem or issue	Statistics and memorable facts to support the proposition	... that illustrate the human truths behind the issue
Why does it matter? To create salience, urgency or reason to engage	Facts to emphasize the urgency and seriousness of the issue	... that illustrate how it's affecting people
What are we doing about it? To position the organization and establish its right to talk about the issue	Information about the organization's programme, campaigning and fundraising work	... that demonstrate how the organization is helping people and bringing about change in their lives
What do we want to do? Calls-to-action	Information about why action is needed and evidence that it works	... that show how supporter actions can help individuals

TONE OF VOICE

One of the running themes throughout this book is that the *verbal* definition of a brand is as important to a brand as its *visual* representation. Capturing how a brand 'speaks' is vital, and supplying guidelines on how to do this is equally so.

Some brands have an inbuilt sense of how to communicate – it comes naturally. Pixar's warmth, wit and insight is second nature to them and instructs how they construct their films,[6] while Virgin's sense of fun is innate. But many corporations find it hard to 'overly personalize' and, while it may sound odd, guidelines on 'how to speak' become very useful.

Sometimes finding the right tone of voice happens by accident. The pages shown opposite from a brand book gently suggested to Shelter that its employees and collaborators take the words that they use just as seriously as the visuals. The line 'Keep reminding yourself that words like "stakeholder" or "constituency" remind normal people of either Dracula movies or politicians. Or both' was originally written as a joke, but it stayed in the book. It makes the point, with a bit of humour, that words are just as important as pictures.[7]

Increasingly, some form of structure for a brand's language is becoming important.

For several years, Save the Children based its communications around a three-stage 'messaging' mantra, *they/we/you*. So for each communication, Save the Children could identify the 'they' (*what the problem is*), the 'we' (*what we're doing about it*) and the 'you' (*what you, the reader, can do to get involved*). But beware of this desire to overly personalize – it can come across as a little, well, grating. Do you really want a bank to be your friend and talk about its cash machine as a 'hole in the wall' or use everyday vernacular such as 'cash out'? Perhaps not. The key to this seems to be to find an 'authentic' voice, one that customers believe, and, most importantly, one that can be maintained.

constituencies ~~constituencies~~
~~hypothetically~~
~~theoretically~~
~~objectified~~
~~ergo~~
~~alma maters~~
~~intrinsically~~
~~stakeholders~~
~~fundamentally~~
~~mutuality~~
~~dichotomous~~
~~paradoxically~~

~~interdependence~~
~~notionally~~
~~perceptionality~~
~~holistically~~
~~360 degrees~~
~~imagineering~~
~~bilateral~~
~~reciprocity~~
~~evolutionary~~
~~conjoined~~
~~applicability~~
~~opportunistically~~

simple   readable

It's not just how we look

It's how we talk as well.

Everything we write should be as positive, authoritative and intrusive as possible.

That's difficult if we use jargon, use impossibly long sentences (or use badly thought through ideas in brackets, like this, for example).

If you're writing for Shelter, keep it short. And make sure it keeps to the new copy-checking guidelines, coming soon.

Keep reminding yourself that words like 'stakeholder' or 'constituency' remind normal people of either Dracula movies or politicians. Or both.

Read it through. If it's difficult to read aloud, redo it.

Finding that voice may take some time, but the sparse, careful verbal tone used by German car manufacturers intentionally matches the 'precision engineering' of the product. Likewise, the long-running adverts for *The Economist* summed up the 'smart' target market the magazine wanted to appeal to (or to flatter).

Ideally, the words and pictures work in harmony. The communications for Optus (a fast telecoms service) use intentionally fast, fun and furious language that matches perfectly with its irreverent brand identity.

TM = Tasty Mixture

You should probably try opening this carton at the other end. Not that we're telling you how to run your life or anything, but it seems to work much easier when the drink comes out of the spout on the top.

people

burglars

welcome
to
fruit towers

home of innocent drinks

Innocent's secret? They really are like this, every day.

This hasn't been dreamt up by a marketing team.

a handy innocent guide to
AWKWARD BACK AT WORK CHAT

QUESTIONS YOU WILL GET ASKED	POLITE AND PROFESSIONAL RESPONSE	INTERESTING AND DANGEROUS RESPONSE
Did you have a nice Christmas?	Yes thanks. And you?	I shaved a puffin. It's a family tradition.
Did you get anything nice?	An electronic book reader. So useful.	The Fifty Shades of Grey pop up book. And a harpoon.
Annoying being back though, isn't it?	Yes but we had a good long break this time, didn't we?	I don't even work here. I'm Mi5.
Do anything for New Years?	Nothing much, just stayed in with Jools Holland.	How do my eyes look? I've not slept in 56 hours.
Cup of tea?	Yes please. Do you have green tea?	Pint of coffee. Twenty sugars.

innocent
fresh yoghurt drinks

▲ ▾ Innocent / In-house team / UK / from 1999 onwards

For brands such as Innocent, the challenge will be to keep their irreverent and copy-led approach vital as the company expands. Started by a group of Cambridge University graduates, Innocent initially sold its smoothies on a stall at a music festival. A sign next to the stall asked people if they thought the stakeholders should give up their day jobs. Customers could vote by putting their empties in the relevant bin – one was marked 'yes' and the other 'no'. 'At the end of the weekend, the "yes" bin was full, so we resigned from our jobs the next day.'[8]

From a purely 'brand' point of view, Innocent has become quite organized, with a core purpose ('to make natural, delicious food and drink that helps people live well and die old') and a vision ('the earth's favourite little healthy food and drinks company'), but in truth many of its branding 'strategies' have been spur-of-the-moment decisions.

Take the hidden messages on the bottom of bottles and cartons – they were discovered by chance (but soon exploited). And what about the idea of witty copywriting on the labels? It wasn't part of a grand marketing scheme – it just filled an empty space on the label.

Soon this chance idea of embedding stories, facts and jokes onto the 'real estate' of the packaging became Innocent's tone of voice. Even when the company finally hired a marketing director, his first suggestion was not a traditional marketing scheme, but to knit thousands of woolly hats and place them on the bottles to mark a donation to charity (this has since led to five million knitted hats and raised close to £2 million). Innocent has also successfully transferred its wit and speed of thought onto digital platforms: when lobbied by a follower to establish a Penguin Awareness Day, that's exactly what they did.

Even now, when it's useful to have established the kind of 'core values' we talked about in Step 2, Innocent has managed to boil its approach down to just three things: *being natural, being honest and being engaging*. And there's always a phone number on the labels and those calls go through randomly to different people, so every single person in the office must be ready, willing and able to 'be' the Innocent brand, on the phone. That's what you really call embedding a brand into the way its employees behave.

EMBEDDING WHILE CONSTANTLY CHANGING

For some organizations, embedding a brand's 'idea' has to take place 'in public' – you can't go off for a corporate retreat to 're-visit and re-boot' if you're open 364 days a year. This is a huge challenge in the cultural sector where museums and galleries are, in effect, 'containers' into which the content is periodically dropped. It's little wonder that the internal mantra of the groundbreaking re-brand of the Tate Gallery in the UK was 'look again, think again'. The logotype that was chosen even moved in and out of focus. Keeping a brand reacting and adapting to ever-changing content is a huge challenge, but by using flexible toolkits it has finally become possible to keep revitalizing and reinventing. Paradoxically, this comes about by being less dogmatic.

The famous poster above for the launch of the Musée d'Orsay in Paris introduced a beautiful new symbol and a new design style...but the imposition of a vast, cropped logo onto every poster eventually proved inappropriate.[9] However, the Victoria and Albert Museum in London, which had long wanted to treat its identity as a more flexible though still dominant item, only managed to free up its design style by insisting that its famous logo be ever-present, and often vast, on every document and poster. Then, rather than letting the brand retreat back into the corner, the museum made sure that the experience of visiting lived up to the chosen core idea of *inspiration that inspires creativity*.

▲ Musée d'Orsay, Paris / Bruno Monguzzi / Switzerland / 1987 ▼ Tate Gallery / Wolff Olins / UK / 2000

▼ David Bowie posters / V&A / UK / 2013

Publishing bespoke maps of famous people's selections from across the museum isn't surprising – part of the V&A's 'reason to be' is to inspire with their collection.

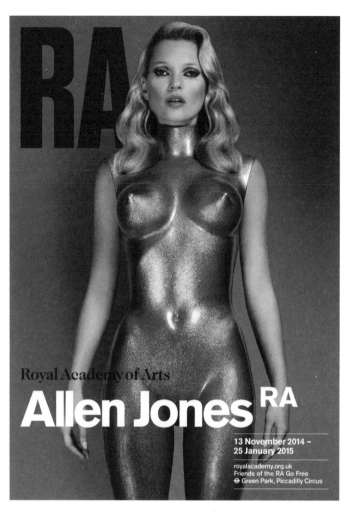

RA

Royal Academy of Arts

Allen Jones RA

**13 November 2014 –
25 January 2015**

royalacademy.org.uk
Friends of the RA Go Free
⊖ Green Park, Piccadilly Circus

Ai Weiwei

Positioning the Single Line Logotype with significantly larger text

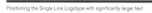

1.

Royal Academy of Arts

Anish Ka

2.

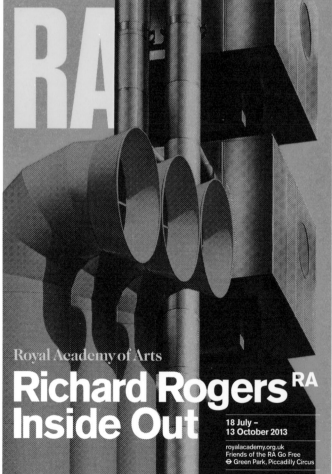

RA

Royal Academy of Arts

Richard Rogers RA
Inside Out

**18 July –
13 October 2013**

royalacademy.org.uk
Friends of the RA Go Free
⊖ Green Park, Piccadilly Circus

▲ Royal Academy of Arts, London, brand strategy / Jane Wentworth Associates / UK / 2012 ▼ ▶ ▶ Visual branding / Pentagram / UK / 2012

Within the context of Step 5, the Royal Academy of Arts in London has managed to introduce a new brand purpose, engage with its staff (and members), and revitalize its brand identity, all within the space of a few years. By engaging fully with both its employees and its Royal Academicians, a careful process broke down internal silos and let internal teams appreciate the values of cross-cutting ideas and approaches.

By building on their unique structure – an institution led by renowned artists – the academy is now reasserting a strong voice for both the understanding and appreciation of art, its practice and its practitioners.

Having agreed on its core verbal definition (*living artists, leading art*), the next task was to translate this into a viable visual toolkit.[10] Initially this might look limited – the 'RA' monogram, the full name, one sans-serif typeface – but because of the simple 'bookending' approach of the design, the documents and applications have a framework in which to breathe, and there is freedom to convey the uniqueness of each individual application. The constituent parts can be expressed while always clearly being part of a whole. This allows the academy's myriad events, exhibitions and activities to knit together in a coherent yet curated way.

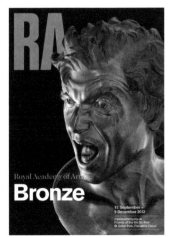

SHOULD WE STAY OR SHOULD WE GO?

So far, the case studies we have seen in this step have concentrated on how a new approach to brand identity can permeate and infuse itself across an organization, either through the words used (through tone of voice and messaging) or the brand toolkit that has been adopted.

For some brands, an uncomfortable point is reached where they know that their fortunes need to change, but it's difficult for an internal team to reach a clear consensus about what form that change should take, and who should implement it.

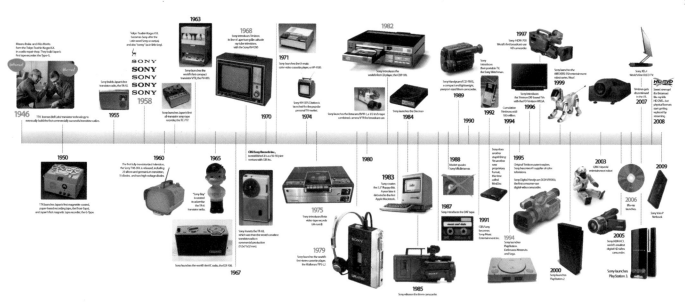

For example, this slightly infamous timeline of Sony's key products by the website Gizmodo[11] concluded that, while the world has loved many of their goods and gadgets for decades, 'their technology…is just me-too. No spark, no true revolutionary innovation. Just a giant, surviving in a world where other brands now carry the torch they had for decades.'

Harsh, perhaps, but possibly true, and backed up only a few years later with the demise of the VAIO sub-brand.[12] For a company defined by its innovation, the reputation of the Sony brand is in some danger.

Usually some form of review will reveal how a brand is performing in its market, and this is where 'tracking' research can offer fascinating insights into how a brand is 'perceived' by its different audiences. This can provide invaluable evidence if it's suspected that a brand isn't firing on all cylinders, and, coupled with more nuts and bolts data such as sales figures or funds raised, can propel a change.

BRANDING CAN'T SAVE EVERYONE

In the technology sector, the fortunes of brands can change ferociously fast, especially if mishandled. Myspace was one of the earliest online brand successes, but the attempts to rescue it seemed to come too late. It had become a bloated and blurred online offer with no clear sense of purpose, and its newly commercial mission

following its purchase by News Corp in 2005 didn't help. It was swiftly outdone by other forms of social media offering more 'social' usability (such as Facebook) or better music-sharing functionality (such as SoundCloud) or better music opinions (such as Pitchfork).

Even when it was re-launched in 2013, with an extensive ad blitz and launch party, there still seemed to be no reason for Myspace to exist. Even though, visually, the revised brand seemingly delivered something engaging and different, the pure 'product'

offer continued to confuse. As one observer said, 'It suffers from an existential question – what is it?' It was bought for $580 million and sold six years later for $35 million.[13] Even the

grooviest and most alluring brand identity can't paper over the cracks of a product that has no clear sense of why it should be here.

Meanwhile, Myspace's nemesis, Facebook, has been carefully tweaking its public face ever since its first days as 'the facebook' and its initial target market of Harvard students. Slowly and surely it adapted and evolved its core assets, often in a way that few of its users would actually perceive. Similar to the way that Amazon and Google have gently 'evolved' their brands, the giants of online have actually pursued quite conservative brand strategies – gentle brand evolution coupled with assiduous and forensic testing of even the tiniest of changes to interface and navigation.

STARTING AGAIN WITHOUT STARTING AGAIN

For brands such as Adidas, keeping their brand front of mind, appreciated and desired by millions worldwide needs constant brand 'tinkering'.

Adidas got an early break only two years after it was founded (by German brothers Adi and Rudolf Dassler), when Jesse Owens wore Adidas shoes while competing in the 1936 Olympics in Berlin.[14]

Another break came half a century later when Run DMC's anthem, 'My Adidas', propelled the name into rap fashion,[15] and then into high-street sports and fashion. The creative collaborations continue – with Stella McCartney, Missy Elliott and Yohji Yamamoto, and with controversial footballer Luis Suarez for a campaign titled #therewillbehaters.

From a brand identity perspective, Adidas's 'assets' are a series of wordmarks and symbols, linked by similar typography and the iconic use of three stripes. In fact, in 2008 Adidas won a lawsuit, forbidding other clothing manufacturers to use even two stripes on pieces of clothing. In other words, Adidas has managed to 'own' the use of stripes by arguing that, in consumers' eyes at least, stripes = Adidas.[16]

For other organizations it takes time for them to realize what their core brand assets and core 'offer' really are. When the National Art Collections Fund realized that it actually had at least three names (its full name; an unwieldy acronym, NACF; and a commonly used abbreviation, The Art Fund), it took the initial decision to shorten it to 'The Art Fund' and rally its members around its cause, protecting art (we glimpsed some of its messaging on page 277). But within a few years, a change of director led to another name change and now it is just Art Fund.

Normally, it isn't ideal for a name to be changed so quickly, but with the second change came brand clarity: its key differentiator was the card that enabled its members to access dozens of museums at a discount, and from there a much clearer and understandable message evolved.

Problem   **Solution**

The National Art Pass. Free entry to over 200 galleries and museums across the UK and half-price entry to the major exhibitions.
Buy yours today at artfund.org

ArtFund

National Art Pass

▲ Adidas logo / Germany / 1996 ▼ Art Fund logo / johnson banks / UK / 2006 ▼ Art Fund advertising / 101 / UK / 2012

Jack **Queen** **King** **Ace**

The National Art Pass. Half-price entry to the major exhibitions and free entry to over 200 galleries and museums across the UK. **Buy yours today at** artfund.org

ArtFund

Mission **Accomplished**

The National Art Pass. Half-price entry to the major exhibitions and free entry to over 200 galleries and museums across the UK.

Buy yours today at artfund.org

ArtFund

Strings **No strings**

The National Art Pass. Half-price entry to the major exhibitions and free entry to over 200 galleries and museums across the UK.

Buy yours today at artfund.org

ArtFund

Target is another perfect example of how brand 'thinking' can completely turn an organization around. After a 30-year run, and a decade of the 'Expect More. Pay less' promise,[17] Target had a chain of stores in the US but little to differentiate itself from other discount retailers. Essentially, its offering was indistinguishable from the likes of Walmart and Kmart.

The answer wasn't to undertake a wholesale re-invention of its visual identity, but of the whole brand, as Target began to carve out a more differentiated direction. An iconic dog (called, of course, Bullseye) was introduced, with a suitably retouched and targeted eye, who has proved to be a long-standing and durable icon. There followed an exclusive private label of products developed through pop-up stores on a boat in New York, followed by a carefully

aimed pop-up called the Bullseye Inn in the Hamptons. A value food line was introduced (Eat Well. Pay Less) and then a premium meat brand.[18] Soon they were developing fashion lines with Isaac Mizrahi and Fiorucci and by the end of the 2000s, Target was doing tie-ups with Liberty of London and planning a range of Missoni clothes, swiftly followed by link-ups with Isaac Mizrahi and Fiorucci, and photoshoots with *Vogue*. Marketing knitting kits for 'together sweaters' just seemed like a normal day at the office by 2014.

All in all, an amazing 15-year brand revival and a lesson in how to take a previously humdrum brand steadily up-market. Its new, up-scale nickname is 'Tar-zhay' (imagine a stylish Frenchman saying 'Target': 'Tar-gé').

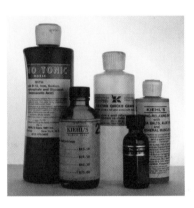

Kiehl's

SINCE 1851

Kiehl's has carefully 'not' changed the way it goes about its business: a brand built on quirky authenticity, generosity, honesty and service.

GIVING AN IDEA TIME

Some brands can take decades to find and exploit their core offer. Kiehl's is an example of the 'long game'. The premium cosmetics retailer has slowly and steadily ploughed its own furrow for over 150 years. It presents a quasi-medical image to the world that reflects its apothecary origins – a 'real brand that started as a real apothecary in New York City, at a specific address...not just from an idea, from an actual place and an actual purpose'.[19]

Even after it was acquired by L'Oréal in 2000, the company continued its trademark approach – no advertising, and a culture of modesty and honesty reflected in its un-designed, almost surgical, packaging with predominantly two-colour labels. Kiehl's welcomes male customers (who are traditionally thought to be pharmacy-phobic) and offers samples in a 'try before you buy' tactic that encourages the cheapest and most effective form of promotion – word of mouth. Even the shops feel authentic and quirky; some have a vintage Ducati in the window just because the company founder liked them.

We can examine the Kiehl's brand through the lens of another branding 'diagram' (I'm trying to avoid too many different models but this is an interesting one). This 'prism'[20] helps us look at the brand through its relationship with its customers, as reproduced below, and represents a useful additional model for retail brands – especially those looking hard at who they are and how they want to be perceived.

Physique
Apothecary-inspired skincare and hair care. Efficacious products from nature and science.

Personality
Expert innovator. Honest and authentic. Adventurous. Eclectic.

Relationship
Respect. Service. Generosity.

KIEHL'S IDENTITY PRISM

Culture
All-American with New York roots. Community. Pharmaceutical expertise. Spirit of adventure.

Reflection
Person who seeks healthy skin. Cares about the environment and product safety.

Self-image
I look and feel healthy.

Physique: the basis of the brand; *Personality:* the kind of person it would be if it was human; *Relationship:* the handshake between the consumer and the brand; *Culture:* symbolizes the organization, its country of origin and the values it stands for; *Reflection:* the ways others see the brand's users; *Self-image:* the way consumers see themselves

The re-invention of the sports brand Puma didn't happen overnight; it is another example of the long-term strategy that some brands need to take of their development, and the benefits of a mutually beneficial relationship with one key design supplier.

At the turn of the 1990s, Puma was just an also-ran in the sports retail pantheon – a slightly forgotten shoe brand that hadn't managed to carve out a clear identity for itself, with a flawed distribution model and a lack of its own stores to showcase its products. And in light of massive competition from the likes of Nike and Adidas, this was a serious problem.

The work started at a basic level – asking fundamental questions about the brand. Was it a sports brand, or a lifestyle brand?

The earliest initiative involved the installation of a moving, projected, actual puma into retail environments. This became a two-decade-long project that, bit by bit, has seen Puma's market share grow by articulating a new direction of 'sports lifestyle'. This wasn't done by taking the expected, big ad budget route, but by investing time, thought and creative ingenuity into every single aspect and application of the brand, from phones to underwear, from yacht livery to football kits, from packaging to container-style retail outlets (while steadily expanding from seven to 250 of their own stores, worldwide).

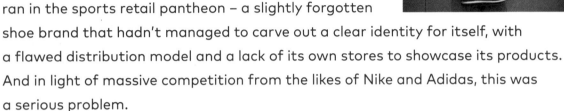

▸ ▸ ▸ Puma applications / GBH / UK / from 1995 onwards

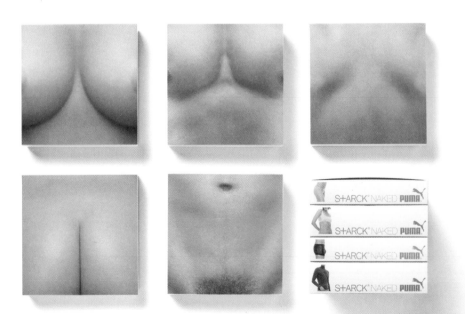

TURNING TRADITION INTO ADVANTAGE

For brands that have been in existence for decades, the key issue they face is to keep revitalizing and re-interpreting the elements they have at their disposal. For two completely different icons of American publishing, the response has been remarkably similar – to use the coloured borders that have become their visual 'catchphrases'. *Time* magazine ran a series of campaigns that showed how it could,

almost literally, re-frame an issue by using the magazine's iconic red frame and placing oversized versions into images, hence suggesting that 'everything inside that red border is worth knowing, and whatever is outside of it, less so'. Another brand with a famous border, *National Geographic*, has been utilizing its distinctive colour with its own 'Frame What Matters' campaign, encouraging everyday explorers to use the yellow border

around the things that matter to them, whether they are moments, memories, people or places.

When looking at its brand identity, British rail operator First Great Western delved into its 182-year heritage and rebadged as 'GWR' (Great Western Railway), purposely adopting an approach that suggested a 'renaissance of rail' and rejected the garish colour scheme and graphics that preceded it.

For Saks Fifth Avenue in New York, the re-development of its visual approach first took a step backwards to a previous logo, but then converted this into a vibrant and tessellated scheme by cutting, dicing and splicing the revised logotype into an ever-changing patchwork of black-and-white images. Instantly recognizable as Saks, and yet constantly altering, it was a perfect analogy for the store's ambitions and approach.

SAKS
FIFTH
AVENUE

Saks Fifth Avenue
1946

Saks·Fifth Avenue
1955

Saks Fifth Avenue
1955

Saks Fifth Avenue
1973

By reproducing and presenting Old Masters outdoors, one gallery took 'public art' to a whole new level.

The new current of mobile communication.

O2

Music through your mobile. Whenever. Wherever. Digital Music Player.

O2

Be more dog

bemoredog.com O2

◄ O2 advertising campaigns / VCCP / UK / from 2001 onwards

THE TACTICAL ADVANTAGE OF ADVERTISING

Another way to encourage re-appraisal is by using traditional advertising techniques to regularly embolden and enhance a brand. The telecoms brand O_2 (see page 54) has subtly amended its positioning every few years, while retaining its core brand idea and overall identity.[21]

Other more tactical routes eschew the traditional channels of print and TV, and can gain far greater (and cheaper) media attention in the process. With the support of Hewlett-Packard, a long-time sponsor, the National Gallery in London printed a host of its treasures and then displayed them throughout London in a 21st-century recreation of a 'grand tour'. But the tour was limited to the city's backstreets and sought out its public rather than vice versa (see opposite). This tactical idea worked nicely for the

gallery and its sponsor, imbuing both with a wit and charm hard to pull off in a traditional gallery environment.

The paintings were accompanied by captions with phone numbers to call to hear curators' comments. The idea of utilizing phones within a campaign was taken a step further several years later when an agency tasked with marketing an exhibition at the New Museum in New York on the artistic breakthroughs of the early 1990s, turned 150 phone booths throughout the city into geo-located information booths. Passers-by could listen to oral histories pertinent to that corner, or that neighbourhood, once again taking a gallery's content and making it publicly available.

D WNING STREET SW1
CITY F WESTMINSTER

Another excellent example of hijacking the everyday was a campaign to encourage blood donation, specifically types A, O and B. Those letters were simply removed from signs, mastheads and packaging. The *Daily Mirror* newspaper became the D ily Mirr r, Waterstones bookshop became W terst nes, and even Downing Street joined in and became D wning Street.[22]

◄ National Gallery, London / The Partners / UK / 2007 ▲ National Blood Week / Engine / UK / 2015 ▲ New Museum, New York / Droga 5 / USA / 2013

▸ Caterpillar brand and applications / USA / from 1989 onwards

BRAND EXTENSION

One time-honoured route to extending a brand's life and broadening its appeal has been the concept of the 'brand extension' or sub-brand. Classically, Coca-Cola extends into Diet Coke and Coke Zero, while popular chocolate bars broaden out to ice cream and hot drinks. But in the 'corporate' world brand extensions are fairly rare.

In fact, a branding project usually helps bring diffused organizations back together rather than spread them back out again. Even giants such as Virgin have a mixed record – for every venture that succeeds (airlines, mobiles, money) there will be a hastily forgotten example that doesn't. Virgin Brides anyone? British retailer Next tried 'extending' its brand into furniture, hairdressing and cafés. The problem was that

consumers associated them with one clear offer – clothes – and couldn't really extend that brand 'trust' over into sofas, haircuts and cappuccinos.[23]

Conversely, an example of a brand extension that has really hit home is Caterpillar. Founded in 1925, it is known the world over for its distinctive yellow and black livery and its CAT logo. In the mid-1990s Caterpillar made a pretty bold move to take the ethos behind its core brand – durability, reliability, machinery that is 'built for it' – and extend it first into footwear and then into clothing. Everything features the CAT logo, and retail interiors are carefully designed to look rough and ready – even a CAT watch features bulldozer tread lines on its metal band.

From one point of view, this is quite a leap: the company that spent decades making earth movers now sells the product of earth moving – baby wear. From another this is a classic illustration of the difference between 'brand' and 'product' – the tractor and the boots are completely

different things, but the 'ready for anything' idea projected by the Caterpillar brand is elastic enough to imbue countless products with its ethos.

For cultural brands, creating co- or sub-brands has to be done carefully, to avoid confusion and cannibalization of the master brand.

While Brighton's Dome is open 11 months a year (page 177), its festival spans only three weeks, and yet it needs to maintain a subtle link to its parent brand. The solution echoes the Dome's 'D', but this time there is a bold and brutal 'F' that takes over the town every year through banners and posters, and adds to Brighton's cultural mosaic without muddying it. Another approach is effectively to have no master brand and design each event independently, as with this scheme for the 17th Biennale of Sydney which is completely different from the ones that preceded or followed (and is completely unfettered and free as a result).

Other brands discussed in this book have also carefully experimented with slightly 'loosening' their brand rules to create brand extensions or affiliations. So there's a Paul Smith Leica, for example – both brands benefit from some mutual reflected glory. And the Rapha cycling brand we examined on pages 120–21, which principally brands everything 'Rapha', has found its product adopted by the Team Sky road racing team, while developing a 'Wiggins' endorsement with Sky's most famous rider, Bradley Wiggins. These are all logical 'affinity' approaches where both parties share similar values and each brand benefits the other.

MORE TH>N

MORE ;-) TH>N :-(

LESS
STRESS
MORE
TH>N

↖ More Th>n / Brand Guardians, johnson banks / UK / from 2001 onwards

THE BRAND IS DEAD – MOVE ON

For other brands, the prospect of a 15-year gradual turnaround in fortunes simply isn't quick enough. The insurer and pension provider Royal & SunAlliance (RSA) was eyeing the burgeoning 'direct' market in the late 1990s (then dominated by phone sales), but was unable to make its 'Dad's pension' brand viable in a very different (and very competitive) arena. It simply wasn't 'elastic' enough in its customers' eyes to stretch to this new and burgeoning market.

After one attempt to use the core brand, which failed and left them the 13th most popular provider,[24] the decision was taken to 'create' a new brand that offered something different in this market.

After a long and painstaking naming exercise, the new brand was created and it was called More Th>n.

MORE TH>N
MORE TH>N THEM
MORE TH>N YOU'D EXPECT
MORE ICING TH>N ISA'S
LESS STRESS, MORE TH>N

This was both an unusual piece of naming in the market and an interesting 'comparative' positioning (always offering, doing and saying 'more than' its competitors). By virtue of its name and core purpose, it could immediately begin to offer 'more than' other providers, while establishing a memorable name and visual identity to boot.

So what was the result? Within three years the new brand was safely established in the top three, and it remains there 15 years later.

HOW DO YOU DECIDE WHAT'S NEXT?

Many examples in this chapter have illustrated how extending, revitalizing and re-launching can succeed. Some brands such as Kiehl's have aimed for slow and steady, word-of-mouth growth, while RSA and More Th>n concluded that entire product reinvention was necessary.

What is clear is that strategic and brand decisions can only be made in parallel, not completely separately. Time and again throughout this book, great branding has been proven to go hand in hand with great 'product'. The newest Apple or Tesla will probably sell itself, but Myspace's offer was outflanked by its rivals – the greatest re-brand in the world couldn't have saved it from its slow and painful demise.

WHAT ORDER SHOULD YOU DO THINGS IN, AND WHEN?

This book has, in a way, followed a relatively conventional structure by explaining the key stages that most brand and brand identity projects need to go through.

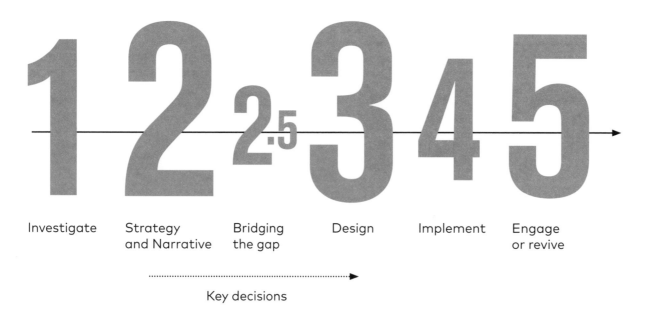

| Investigate | Strategy and Narrative | Bridging the gap | Design | Implement | Engage or revive |

Key decisions

Yet, as we reach the end of this journey, it's fair to say that *this is not the only way.*

For example, Step 2.5 (between Steps 2 and 3) hinted at the fact that the hard lines between strategy and design can sometimes blur. Or, on occasion, nearly all of Step 1 (and perhaps even Step 2) might have been done 'client-side' and the onus is then to *begin* the project with the design stage; in other words, the problem is understood, the strategy is agreed, so *let's get on with it.*

Another key factor can be speed. The typical process described above might need at least two months per stage, so 10 months in total. It's not unheard of for major brand identities, especially those at the larger scale, to need *years*. There is often a good reason for this – either the sheer scale of the consultation needed at the first step is vast, or the strategic work gets held up.

But what if you need to get to market fast?

What if you need your new brand in weeks – not months?

This is when you have to adapt the model to work more quickly and become a little leaner, a little more agile. The answer seems to be to concentrate on the key decision-making stages of Steps 2 and 3.

There are various strategies for this. One is to split the steps and commit to them in parallel. For example, if it's clear at the end of Step 1 that a new name and a new visual identity will be needed, it might be possible to start that work while in parallel agreeing the strategic route. This can be a bit of a gamble – if the naming and design go in one direction and the strategy in another, then that's not ideal.

A less risky approach is to work through Step 1 at speed and then approach the whole of Steps 2 and 3 together. So, rather than working through multiple verbal scenarios, narrowing them down and then gaining agreement for one, before proceeding to design, work on brand narrative, naming (if appropriate) and design *simultaneously*. So, entire visual and verbal scenarios happen in tandem, not apart.

The benefit of this approach is that a verbal thought can be carried through to its logical visual conclusion and virtually complete schemes can be judged against one another – so, in a sense, still scenario planning, but with fully worked-up brand strategies *and* designs on the table. These might also be researched in this form to help inform the decisions that must follow.

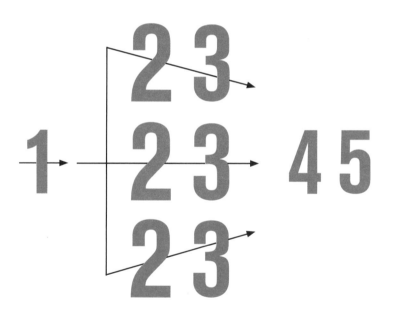

What are the implications of working like this? It's nimble and more work is happening, simultaneously, and quickly. In sheer woman and man hours it will be more expensive, but it can lead to some very interesting decision-making – not just pitting one logo against another but *an entire ethos* against another. And at the decision point the emphasis clearly falls onto leadership: a core individual or team must step up and decide which way to go. If the work has been done correctly, then an entire strategic direction, narrative, name and visual toolkit is there to compare and contrast with another, equally formed route. Branding and design become the cornerstone of a company, a start-up or an organization's future and it's at this point that, in my experience, the penny can really drop about how fundamental this work, and its implications, can be.

DOES BRANDING WORK?

Shown opposite are some examples of the impact of branding on just a few of this book's projects. They make an impressive case for branding's effectiveness.

If an organization gathers enough data about itself pre re-brand and then gathers again post-change, a brand project *should* see more awareness, more funds raised, more products sold (whichever indicators have been deemed to be key).[25] But it's also true that branding, or re-branding, carried out in isolation cannot provide an 'instant answer' to the question 'why are we here?', or drive customers towards an undesirable product. That's why the early steps of this process are so critical – to identify or help define what's truly unique and truly differentiating about a company, product, person, or organization, long before any design begins.

BRANDING GOES FROM STRENGTH TO STRENGTH

Paradoxically, branding's power is now so great that decisions on its definition have moved 'up' from mere departmental level into the boardroom. Once, in the days of 'corporate identity', logos were designed to last for decades – merely 'there' as visual identifiers, not the tips of huge branding icebergs that they have now become. A lesson to be drawn from this entire book is that by looking at the complete 'iceberg', as it were, branding has become one of the most powerful strategic, competitive and tactical tools that a company can draw on.

How you commission this, as a client, or how you do this, as a consultant, is of course up to you. What about my five and a half steps, and the last 300-odd pages? Well, they should have served to explain and demystify at least some of the best (and worst) practice. If I've done my job correctly, you should now be at worst intrigued, at least better informed, and at best inspired. I hope it's the latter.

Summing up what we've covered in Step 5:
- *The value of a great launch*
- *How our brand model extends out into tone of voice and messaging*
- *How organizations can plan for constant change and build toolkits accordingly*
- *The pressures of staying ahead when building digital brands*
- *How brands can revitalize and develop their brands over months or decades*
- *The tactical value of advertising and the case for sub- and co-brands*
- *The case for starting over and branding's impact*

Paul Smith
From one shop in 1970 to 300 worldwide, and an annual turnover of £200 million.

Shelter
Pre re-brand, it reached 80,000 service users. Ten years later it was reaching 5 million.

DEC
Pre re-brand, its Gaza appeal raised £8 million.
Post re-brand, a new Gaza appeal raised £25 million.

Innocent
Its founders have sold the majority of its shares to Coca-Cola –for £95 million.

TED
By 2011, TED videos had been viewed 500 million times. By 2012, it was one billion.

Macmillan
Within a year, spontaneous awareness was up by 9% and within three years the funds raised had increased by 22%.

Avis
Positioning and strapline retained for half a century.

We try harder.

Apple
In 2014 it became the first US company to be valued at over $700 billion.

Royal Enfield
Now exporting to over 30 countries and opening exclusive stores worldwide.

Miller Lite
Raised market share and increased profit by over £30 million following re-design.

Amazon
The logo has been printed over 100 billion times on packaging since its re-design.

V&A
Has tripled its visitor numbers within a decade.

Charity: Water
Grew from $0.7 million turnover to $36 million, in just six years.

SUMMING IT ALL UP

As a kind of memory-jogging guide over two pages, here's a quick run-down of what we've learned in our five and a half steps towards better branding.

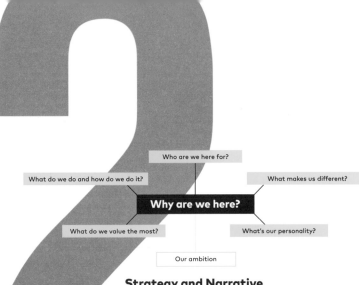

Who are we here for?

What do we do and how do we do it?

What makes us different?

Why are we here?

What do we value the most?

What's our personality?

Our ambition

Introduction

We learned that brands and branding, in different forms and guises, have been around for longer than one might think. Then we looked at why people re-brand and at the definitions of the discipline before highlighting just how powerful it can be... in the right hands (and in the wrong).

Investigate

Before you can decide where to go, you need to know where you are. So we looked at how to audit and review, and thought about the best ways to ask the right kinds of questions. We looked at how to 'map' a market and then look for gaps (as long as there was a market in the gap, of course). We dug further into brands to see if their history could provide a direction, or whether their product could provide the answer. Done well, the investigation step can often provide the answer (or at least the beginnings of the answer).

Strategy and Narrative

A good investigation suggests some directions, but it's Step 2 where, verbally at least, decisions are needed. We looked at a simplified brand model that asked six key questions and then immediately examined strategy, narrative and manifestos. We looked at the brands that say they aren't branded (even though we have a clear idea of what they stand for in our heads – work that one out if you can). We asked if values are still valuable and then looked at the good, the bad and the ugly of 'authenticity' before broadening our model out a little further.

Bridging the Gap

The step that shouldn't exist – or the most important bit of the lot, depending on how you look at it. If Step 2 defines and Step 3 creates, then this half-step helps translate, for both sides. And there are definitely a few key issues such as naming and 'brand architecture' that fall into the blurred area of Step 2.5. It's all about the interface between the verbal and the visual work, and, increasingly, they're happening together...

Design

This is where the visual fireworks start (well, in theory at least). We looked at how to brief, without briefing too much, and what makes a good creative environment. We talked about toolkits, not logos, and then examined the myriad different ways and routes to a design solution (whether typographic, symbol-based or something else entirely). We asked if people and places could also be brands and looked briefly at the politics, pitfalls and possibilities of this step.

Engage or Revive

It's not enough to have a great design idea and implement it well; increasingly, making sure an idea is fully embedded into a company or organization is critical to the long-term health of a brand. This is where launches can engage employees, and those same employees get the chance to explore and extend the brand idea. Linked to this is reviewing and renewing a brand – keeping it both vital and revitalized, whether through sub-brands, or advertising, or long-term collaborations. It might even be time for a brand to cut and run – to shed its clothes and begin again.

Implementation

It's all very well having a fantastic core idea for a brand and a killer bit of creative, but, if it isn't implemented consistently and carefully controlled it can swiftly fall apart. We looked at the dull stuff like manuals and how to make them a little more interesting with flexible approaches and broader toolkits. We examined the challenges of branding in multilingual environments and how consistency can come as much from images and type as from logos.

Unless I've forgotten something, that's basically it (except if you're one of those people who loves references and bibliographies, in which case you'll be in heaven if you turn the page).

REFERENCES

Step 0

1 There is a dedicated list showing the variety of books on both sides of this topic on page 314.

2 That's the Manet, on page 12, in case you hadn't realized. Look hard at the bottom right. Is this an early example of product placement?

3 This Bass example is the one most cited, but, to be really pernickety, the world's first trademark system was actually French (1857), and there was an American attempt to begin a similar system in 1870, which met legal hurdles until a new trademark act was introduced in 1881.

4 'Spencerian' script was the commonly used (and taught) style of cursive writing for business correspondence until the advent of the typewriter. Both the Ford and Coca-Cola logos are clear descendants of this writing style.

5 Wolff Olins (based in London in the 1970s) pioneered this deeper style of thinking into the personality that corporations expressed to the outside world.

6 This chart has been compiled from many sources, but one key driver was Interbrand's four ages of brand defined as: the Age of Identity (post Second World War), the Age of Value (from the late 1980s, i.e., Interbrand's first brand valuation), the Age of Experience (which coincides with the birth of the Internet) and the forthcoming Age of You (coincides with Social Media). *Brand Management Research Theory and Practice* is also worth cross-checking for its 'eras of brand' approach.

7 This is a whole other question. There are some useful video definitions here for graphic design www.designcouncil.org.uk/news-opinion/video-what-graphic-design.

8 You might think that 'branding' has been around forever, and in many respects it has, but the use of the terms 'branding' and 'brand identity' has only really been prevalent since the 1990s.

Further references for the definitions on this page:
Philip Kotler/Gary Armstrong, *Principles of Marketing*; Leslie de Chernatony, *From Brand Vision to Brand Evaluation*; Rita Clifton and Esther Maughan (eds), *The Future of Brands*; Marty Neumeier, *The Brand Gap*; Giep Franzen and Sandra E. Moriarty, *The Science and Art of Branding*; Debbie Millman, *Brand Thinking and Other Noble Pursuits*; and www.janewentworth.com/who/profile/jane-wentworth, sethgodin.typepad.com/seths_blog/2009/12/define-brand.html

9 This was, in effect, a long and tortuous battle over the use of the 'Andersen' name. It's too complex to summarize here, but suffice to say that it led to the renaming of the consulting arm. The process was led by Landor Associates with the final name being created by Kim Petersen in their Oslo office. Legend has it that payment came in the form of a golfing trip to Melbourne. Here's some commentary from the time of the re-brand: www.theguardian.com/theguardian/2001/jan/08/features11.g2

10 We were going to feature the Google/Alphabet story further here, but they, er, wouldn't grant us permission to use their pictures. So you can read about it here instead: googleblog.blogspot.co.uk/2015/08/google-alphabet.html

11 My thanks to a certain Mr Michael Bierut for fact-checking this piece.

12 It's fair to say that most of this merging of various European and North American myths had solidified by the beginning of the 20th century: it was just his precise colour scheme that still changed.

13 While the red coat had appeared before, it was Sundblom's 1931 painting that fixed it and, as this link confirms, Coca-Cola played a key role in Santa's re-branding: www.coca-cola.co.uk/stories/history/advertising/coca-cola-and-father-christmas-the-sundblom-santa-story/

14 Abercrombie & Fitch was technically bankrupt in 1976. It was bought for $1.5 million in 1978 and by 2006 revenue was up to $3.3 billion.

15 I'll come clean: I recently saved up enough cash to buy a Leica. Fantastic camera, but I'll admit that I didn't want people to know that I was carrying something worth thousands of pounds around my neck. Once I had taped over the logos the camera somehow became less visible. And you could also see people taking pity on me: 'poor chap, stuck with that old-fashioned-style camera...'

16 At one point the Leica M-P cost about $1,000 more.

17 There's a great article by Michael Bierut on this here: designobserver.com/feature/the-smartest-logo-in-the-room/6237/

18 Oddly, the logo was designed quite late in Enron's story and yet it became the key icon of the company's fall. It demonstrates, perhaps for the first time in this book, that corporate strategy and corporate branding go hand-in-hand (for good and for bad).

19 Here's Armin Vit's view: 'The reactions to Yahoo's 30 Days of Change stunt were mostly negative at worst and skeptical at best. No one came out and said "This is going to be great! Yahoo has my undivided attention for 30 days!"'

20 Until its appropriation by Hitler, the swastika was enjoying itself as a symbol of good luck: www.bbc.co.uk/news/magazine-29644591

21 Occupy in the UK adopted an official logo designed by Jonathan Barnbrook in 2011.

22 There's more on this here: www.theguardian.com/world/2014/sep/30/-sp-hong-kong-umbrella-revolution-pro-democracy-protests

23 Gerald Holtom himself said this of his design, 'I was in despair. Deep despair. I drew myself: the representative of an individual in despair, with hands palm outstretched outwards and downwards in the manner of Goya's peasant before the firing squad. I formalised the drawing into a line and put a circle round it.'

24 There's more about Jean Jullien here: www.wired.com/2015/11/jean-jullien-peace-for-paris/

25 Read more here: en.wikipedia.org/wiki/Lewes_Bonfire

26 Unfortunately, although writing about Burning Man is fine, we can't use any images of it. Go figure.

27 Famously used by Led Zeppelin's Jimmy Page.

28 More here: www.bbc.co.uk/history/people/william_iii_of_orange

29 There's more here on the neatly named: stuffdutchpeoplelike.com/2010/11/30/no-7-orange/

30 This also links to the same William of Orange mentioned above in reference 28.

31 This diagram shows 18 different saloons and 18 different 4x4's, which are then stepped and repeated just to confuse you further.

Step 1

1 You could argue this works the other way around, of course: that mass transit rarely has competitive underground systems so it's to the customer's benefit that they all look the same.

The terrible straplines are:
Ask Why: Enron; *Be Your Way*: Burger King; *Distilled in Hell*: Bacardi Spice; *High performance. Delivered*: Accenture; *High performance. Amplified*: Deloitte; *Cutting through complexity*: KPMG; *Live your life*: American Eagle; *Intelligence everywhere*: Motorola; *Delivering on the promise*: Skoda Minotti; *By knowledge, design and understanding*: Buckinghamshire, Milton Keynes; *Tomorrow's answers today*: AkzoNobel; *For people who spit blood when they clean their teeth*: Corsodyl; *We make it nice and easy*: Carcraft; *You can make it*: Pot Noodle; *Delighting you always*: Canon; *Make more happen*: Staples; *We turn on ideas*: Seagate; *Your potential. Our passion*: Microsoft; *Imagine it. Done*: Unisys; *Passion for the road*: Mazda; *Your vision, our future*: Olympus; *Here for you*: RBS; *What Business Wants*: Abu Dhabi Global Market; *The future of awesome*: Comcast

2 It's worth pointing out that at this stage in the mid-1970s Collett Dickenson Pearce had become the kings of this style of 'long-copy' print-based advertising. This is just one example of many from the period.

3 The perfect book for more of this is *The Classic Avis Advertising Campaign of the 60s* by Peer Erikson.

4 This is an understatement: the massive growth in these alumni-focused campaigns has made the creation of anything that stands out in the global philanthropic market a huge challenge.

5 Credit to Mark Varney for this observation.

6 Thanks to Joe Barrell for bringing this to my attention and his tips and advice on this section.

7 It seems that this Henry Ford 'quote' is actually credited to him without any proof: https://hbr.org/2011/08/henry-ford-never-said-the-fast

8 As quoted by Walter Isaacson in his biography of Steve Jobs.

9 This contrasted drastically with research done in some other countries: for example, in The Netherlands over 90% of people associate Unicef with children.

10 This quote is as told directly by the current team at Lambie-Nairn and Martin Lambie-Nairn himself.

11 There's a story that the original ads, proposed by an un-named ad agency, relegated the new logo to the corner. Meanwhile, VCCP, a start-up, saw the potential of the brand idea and based the launch adverts around the oxygen theme, snaffling the account in the process.

12 The diagram is based on a brand workshop done in Tokyo with various teams at Hakuhodo.

13 The Dove team were definitely ahead of the curve with this work that started in 2004. It seems to have taken the advertising industry a decade to catch up.

14 These stats are all courtesy of the team at Red Bee.

15 The 'return to Prudence' was at the behest of their then brand advisors, Wolff Olins.

16 The eagle-eyed among you will note that 'Tomorrow's answers today' features on our list of terrible straplines on page 39.

17 It's true. A man called Hugh spent an entire two-hour journey through Switzerland trying to convince me that the symbol was based on a Roman legend.

18 You could argue that this is one of Jonathan Ive's greatest creations: he had little to do with the product's specifications and had relatively little time to 'package' purchased technology. But the thumbwheel was genius.

19 Sony co-founder Masaru Ibuka, an opera buff, pitched the idea to audio-division engineer Nobutoshi Kihara in 1978. It got to market a year later.

20 The story goes that Nike co-founder Bill Bowerman was inspired by his wife's breakfast waffles in his search for the right type of sole for his running-shoe designs.

21 Meanwhile, the Dyson story goes that it took 5,127 prototypes to develop the Dual Cyclone™ bagless cleaner.

22 Don Fisher, co-founder of Gap: 'I created Gap with a simple idea: to make it easier to find a pair of jeans. We remain committed to this basic principle.'

23 Most commentators put the problem down to distribution issues, rather than product.

24 From James Gilmore, co-author of *Authenticity: What Consumers Really Want*. See http://www.bloomberg.com/news/articles/2011-08-11/behind-five-guys-beloved-burgers

25 The *Guardian* stated that, 'The US Environmental Protection Agency discovered that 482,000 VW diesel cars on American roads were emitting up to 40 times more toxic fumes than permitted – and VW has since admitted the cheat affects 11m cars worldwide.'

26 Fannie Mae and Freddie Mac became symbols of the financial crash of 2008.

27 Northern Rock was the UK equivalent – then the UK's fifth largest mortgage lender.

Step 2

1 The graphic designer mentioned is Bob Gill. I may have paraphrased.

2 This is fair enough. It just feels like the wrong sort of language for the 21st century. And missions, by definition, end (with victory?). A 'reason to be' just keeps going.

3 Maslow first proposed his theory in a 1943 paper and subsequently in a book, *Motivation and Personality*. Maslow focused his work on what made people happy and hence placed 'self actualization' at the top of his pyramid.

4 *Positioning: The Battle for your Mind* by Al Ries.

5 *Start With Why* by Simon Sinek.

6 www.ted.com/about/our-organization

7 We chanced upon this way of working with Save the Children in 2006. It drove a very useful meeting and has formed the bedrock of how we approach this stage ever since.

8 It was also inspired by the then Chief Executive, Jasmine Whitbread, thumping the table in annoyance and saying, 'It's an outrage...' We just wrote it all down.

9 I'm especially worried about the demolishing museums bit.

10 There are various things to note about this work. First of all there's a kind of urban myth about this idea being based on Jack Kerouac – not true. There's also a tendency for the Steve Jobs camp to credit this to him – also not true. The best write-up of the 'real' story is by Rob Siltanen, who was the creative director and managing partner at TBWA\Chiat\Day and was working on the Apple pitch alongside CEO and chief creative officer Lee Clow: www.forbes.com/sites/onmarketing/2011/12/14/the-real-story-behind-apples-think-different-campaign/#399ce46755c2

11 This is useful if you're confused: asburyandasbury.typepad.com/blog/2012/06/abstract-nominalisation-never-stops.html

12 More on this in Michael Bierut's book *How to Use Graphic Design to Sell Things, Explain Things, Make Things Look Better, Make People Laugh, Make People Cry, and (Every Once in a While) Change the World*.

13 Volvo began to develop tractors in the 1940s and continued to make them for four decades.

14 In 2012, Dyson said 'There's only one word that's banned in our company: brand. We're only as good as our latest product. I don't believe in brand at all.' adage.com/article/adages/design-icon-james-dyson-i-brand/234494/

15 As quoted by Jonathan Ive in *Business Week* in 2009.

16 From Elon Musk's 2014 USC Commencement Speech: 'I'd say focus on signal over noise. A lot of companies get confused, they spend money on things that don't actually make the product better. So for example, at Tesla we've never spent any money on advertising. We put all the money into R+D, and manufacturing and design to try to make the car as good as possible. And I think that's the way to go.'

17 David Aaker writing here: www.prophet.com/thinking/view/427-muji

18 Supreme also cultivates an intriguing attitude to intellectual property, regularly placing its logo onto people (as well as images) who didn't know this was happening; also the logo is clearly derived from Barbara Kruger's work.

The names 20 brands merged into one by Nick Asbury on page 108 are: Alibaba (China), Baidu (China), Mazda (Japan), Datsun (Japan), Suzuki (Japan), Kia (South Korea), Hyundai (South Korea), Daewoo (South Korea), Lenovo (China), Shinhan (South Korea), Nissan (Japan), Acura (Japan), Daihatsu (Japan), Fujitsu (Japan), Mitsubishi (Japan), Subaru (Japan), Fuji (Japan), Samsung (South Korea), Hankook (South Korea), Yakult (Japan).

19 By 2014 there were more industrial researchers in China than in the whole of Europe and Shenzhen had overtaken Silicon Valley in California with its number of international patent applications.

20 It's true: hundreds of Luck employees daily cross-check their own personal values against company ones.

21 There is a lot of disagreement about precisely when Gen Y/Millennials/Gen Next start and stop but being born between the mid-1980s the year 2000 seems to be pretty central.

22 Here is a particularly entertaining piece on this: www.unmissablejapan.com/etcetera/superdry

23 In Busan, South Korea, 593 miles from Japan.

24 A call for puzzle entries in 1921 received 30,000 entries. The advertising department felt replies should come from a woman, so Betty was created.

25 Ernest Hemingway lived around the corner from their Cuba plant and often put Bacardi references into his novels.

26 From the Royal Enfield website: a network of 11 Brand Stores, 250 dealers in all major cities and towns, and over 200 Authorised Service Centres. Exports to 42 countries including the USA, Japan, UAE, Korea, Bahrain, UK, France, Germany, Argentina and many other countries through 40 importers and over 300 dealers across the globe.

27 and 28 Based on direct conversations with Rapha founder, Simon Mottram.

29 I'm pretty sure I first read about 'the tyranny of we' in *The Week*, the UK weekly news magazine.

30 There's more on this here: johnsonbanks.co.uk/ thoughtfortheweek/youre-my-waitrose-you- really-are/

31 Interestingly, while the final decision seems pretty obvious, in retrospect, it was a very close call with the 'emergency' route on page 129 only just getting a majority vote at the board meeting.

The great straplines are:
The future's bright: Orange; *I'm lovin' it*: McDonald's; *Beanz Meanz Heinz*: Heinz; *We try harder*: Avis; *Think small*: VW Beetle; *Think Different*: Apple; *Because I'm worth it*: L'Oréal; *A diamond is forever*: De Beers; *The world's local bank*: HSBC; *The Ultimate Driving Machine*: BMW; *Vorsprung durch Technik*: Audi; *Impossible is Nothing*: Adidas; *Have a break…*: Kit Kat; *Got Milk?*: California Milk Processor Board; *Where's the beef?*: Wendy's; *Yes we can*: Obama's 2008 presidential campaign

Step 2.5

1 The idea of 'translation' from Steps 1 and 2 into Steps 3, 4 and 5 is a concept pursued by London strategic consultancy Circus. My thanks to Dilys for her thoughts on this overall step.

2 Thanks to Mark Lee for clarifying this.

3 The initial brief was to build on a proposed core purpose of decoding science.

4 And, for at least three years or so, all departments did actually fall into line and agreed to be part of the master brand. Until they didn't.

5 This diagram is based on the one used by Martin Bishop in his post here: brandmix.blogspot. co.uk/2009/11/marriott-launches-autograph- collection.html

6 In case you doubt this story, see here: graphics. stanford.edu/~dk/google_name_origin.html

7 Co-founder Jack Dorsey explained that the definition of Twitter was 'a short burst of inconsequential information and chirps from birds'.

8 Flickr co-founder Caterina Fake recalls the naming decision: 'I'm glad we weren't able to get flicker. com. We thought it might be a problem at first, being hard to spell, but that didn't turn out to be the case. Also, I'm glad we didn't use the word "photo" or "foto" in the name. There are at least a hundred companies that have that in their name, and I can't keep track of them anymore.'

9 It also sounds mighty close to the English word for urinate – it must have been an interesting conversation in the Japanese boardroom.

10 There's more: first it was an acronym of Video Audio Integrated Operation and then Visual Audio Intelligent Organizer, and some Vaios have a start- up sound based on the V-A-I-O melody you hear when keyed into a phone.

11 There's even a video to show you how to pronounce it: www.gizmodo.com.au/2012/07/how-do-you- say-huawei/

12 Here's the Lenovo re-brand written up on Brand New: www.underconsideration.com/brandnew/ archives/new_logo_and_identity_for_lenovo_by_ saatchi_saatchi_new_york.php#.Vy-DchWDGko

13 BMP was started in 1968 by Martin Boase, Gabe Massimi and Stanley Pollitt. Massimi had left

by 1971 and Stanley Pollitt sadly died in 1979, which left Boase.

14 Thanks to Jane Wentworth for talking through the process of this project.

15 It's true. It was applied for via Project 94: 'The allocation of 94 1-2 character .ORG domain names…made available to registrants who not only reflect the core attributes of the .ORG domain but also reinforce the trust and value of the .ORG brand.'

Step 3

1 This links to the story of Carolyn Davidson, who designed the original logo in 17.5 hours at $2 per hour. To be fair, she was later given 500 shares in the company that by 2011 were worth approximately $640,000…

2 The brief shown is based on one (among others) featured here: theplanninglab.typepad.com/ theplanninglab/2009/04/a-totally-subjective- creative-brief-template-review-.html

3 The writer concerned is Siimon Reynolds, he of the late 1980s Sydney ad-scene fame.

4 It's true. It's worth reading *Where good ideas come from* by Steven Johnson for more on this.

5 The chap in question, Neil Cummings, soon became one of Wolff Olins' creative directors.

6 As advised by Peter Hale of GBH.

7 The twin-tailed brown version actually lasted from 1971 to 1987 before something closer to the modern version was introduced.

8 The original merger was in 1968.

9 As it happened, a huge furore kicked off about whether the logo symbolized body parts and genitalia, but Airbnb seemed to ride that storm pretty successfully.

The favicons featured on page 190 are (in alphabetical order):
3M, ABC, Acer, Adidas, Adobe, Airbnb, Aldi, Al Jazeera, All 4, Amazon, American Airlines, American Express, Amnesty International, Android, AOL, Apple, Argos, Asda, Asics, Ask, Asos, AT&T, B&Q, Barbican, Barcelona FC, Barclays, Basecamp, Baskin-Robbins, BBC, Beats by Dr Dre, Behance, Bestbuy, Bic, Billabong, Bing, Blackberry, Blogger, Bloomsbury, Blue Cross, BMW, Body Shop, Boeing, Boots, Bose, BP, Breitling, Bridgestone, British Gas, BT, Bupa, Burberry, Burger King, Buzzfeed, Cancer Research, Carhartt, Carrefour, Casper, Champion, Chanel, Charity: Water, Chase, Chelsea FC, Chrome, Cinelli, Citi, City Mapper, CNN, Coca-Cola, Comedy Central, Conservation International, Conservative Party, Converse, D&AD, Daily Mail, Daily Motion, DC Shoes, DEC, Deliveroo, Dell, Delta, Democrat Party, Design Boom, Dezeen, Disney, Dolby, Domino's, DreamWorks, Dr Martens, Dropbox, Dunkin' Donuts, Duolingo, Dyson, E! Entertainment, EA Games, easyJet, eBay, EDF, EE, Ellesse, E.ON, ESPN, Etnies, Etsy, Evernote, Exxon, Facebook, Ferrari, Firefox, Flickr, Foursquare, Fox, Fred Perry, Fruit of the Loom, Gap, Getty, Gillette, GitHub, Google, Google Drive, Google Mail, Google Maps, Google Play, Google Translate, Gov.uk, Greenpeace, Guardian, H&M, Habitat, Harley-Davidson, Hershey's, Hertz, Holiday Inn, Hollister, Homebase, Honda, HP, HSBC, Huffington Post, Hulu, i-D, IMDB, Innocent, Instagram, Intel, iPlayer, It's Nice That, Itsu, ITV,

Jaguar, Jeff Banks, John Lewis, Kellogg's, Kenzo, KFC, KISS FM, Kodak, Labour Party, Land Rover, lastminute, Lego, Leon, Levi's, LG, Lidl, LinkedIn, Lloyds, National Lottery, Louis Vuitton, Mack, Macmillan Cancer Support, MailChimp, Manchester United, Marmite, Marriott Hotels, Mars, Match. com, McDonald's, Medium, Mercedes, Messenger, Microsoft, Mini, Mitsubishi, Mixcloud, Monster, More Th>n, Morrisons, MOS Burger, Motorola, MSN, MTV, Myspace, *National Geographic*, National Rail, Natural History Museum, NatWest, NBC, Netflix, New Balance, Nike, Nikon, Nintendo, Nivea, NME, North Face, O₂, Obama, Oculus, Olay, Omega, Opera, Orange, Oxfam, Patagonia, Paul Smith, PayPal, Penguin, Pepsi, Persil, Petco, Peugeot, Pinterest, Pitchfork, Pixar, Playboy, PlayStation, Premier Inn, Puma, Qantas, QQ, Quiksilver, RAF, Raspberry Pi, Ray-Ban, Real Madrid, Reddit, Renault, Rolex, Royal Enfield, Ryanair, Sainsbury's, Sanpellegrino, Santander, Save the Children, Science Museum, Seagate, Sega, Selfridges, Shazam, Shell, Shelter, Sketchup, Sky, Skype, Sony, Specialized, Spotify, SquareSpace, Stack Overflow, Starbucks, Subway, Superdrug, Suzuki, Swatch, Target, TechCrunch, Ted, Telegraph, Tesco, TFL, Thames & Hudson, The Fader, The Sun, Thompson, Three, Ticketmaster, Timberland, Today, Tommy Hilfiger, Toyota, Toys R Us, TransferWise, TripAdvisor, Triumph, Tumblr, Twitter, Unicef, Unilever, Uniqlo, UPS, USA Today, Victoria & Albert Museum, Vans, Vice, Vimeo, Vine, Virgin Atlantic, Virgin Media, Visa, Vivienne Westwood, Vodafone, Vogue, Volkswagon, Wacom, Waitrose, Wallpaper, Walls, Walmart, Warner Bros., Weibo, Wella, Wendy's, Whole Foods, Wikipedia, Wildlife Trusts, Wilson, Wired, WordPress, WWE, WWF, Xbox, YouTube

10 Particularly the 'symbol as container' device that is still going strong, a decade later.

11 Initially, the idea of the 'crumpled images' was resisted by the in-house client team, but when it was shared with recovering addicts and service users, who loved it, they realized that the metaphor was both apt and appropriate.

12 It's been suggested to me that the smile is also meant to be a symbol of Jeff Bezos himself, who is apparently a very jolly chap.

13 This is a good case study of this project: www. dandad.org/en/case-study-coca-cola/

14 It's fairly clear now that this Obama campaign transformed the way political campaigns use social media to raise support.

15 See more here: creativeaction.network/ collections/design-for-obama

16 Just a quick look at Martha Stewart's activity since incarceration suggests she's going to be fine.

17 You could argue this the other way: risk analysis is becoming a critical tool across management and guides decisions constantly. My point really is that all truly 'out there' creativity involves a certain risk because, by definition, it hasn't been done before and can't be placed into any known frames of reference.

18 More here: www.qantas.com/travel/airlines/ history-kangaroo-symbol/global/en

19 This particular client revelled in 'bombing' an entire roomful of work on this particular day. As an ex- marketing director, it was clear that *he* felt he had the answer to the problem, not us…

20 Bob Gill, again. A very quotable guy.

21 My favourite version, once replaced, was the headline 'Gone-signia'.

22 Ray Wilkins, having spent time playing in Italy, seemed at that point to have a lot more style than your average 1990s football manager.

23 See here for more: www.theguardian.com/media/2010/oct/12/gap-logo-redesign

24 A very useful piece on this is here: www.aiga.org/the-uc-logo-controversy/

25 The 'TM' is used while a logo/symbol is first registered (a process that can take months). Once formally registered the TM can become an ®.

26 This Wiki page tracks the various twists and turns of this pretty well: en.wikipedia.org/wiki/Apple_Corps_v_Apple_Computer

27 Stefan Sagmeister delivered this line to my face once, looking me straight in the eye. Of course, being capable of designing something truly unique each time is trickier than it sounds… That's my defence at least.

Step 4

1 I call this a 'PowerPoint scheme', i.e., a design that looks great in the presentation but the actual, real applications never match what was originally envisaged.

2 This kind of 'art direction' involves knowing when to hand over to someone who is better at a specialized skill than you are – in this case typographer Rob Clarke.

3 The symbol was drawn by a Mr Gerry Barney while at DRU.

4 In a nice echo of the above, it was also drawn by a certain Mr Gerry Barney.

5 Looking back at this now, and at how much better the final is than the first, kudos must go the client team and our strategic partner Circus for agreeing that this development should take place. An amount of 'trust' was placed in the design team to finally get there.

6 I'm paraphrasing Erik Spiekermann here.

7 Jesse Reed and Hamish Smyth raised the cash for this on Kickstarter: www.kickstarter.com/projects/thestandardsmanual/full-size-reissue-of-the-nycta-graphics-standards/description

8 We weren't confident that it was actually readable, though, until the British Embassy in Tokyo said it was fine.

9 As reported in the *Handbook of East Asian Entrepreneurship* by Tony Fu-Lai Yu, Ho-Don Yan.

10 More detail here: www.economist.com/blogs/newsbook/2010/06/interview_uniqlos_boss

11 It's also worthwhile pointing out that while 'Ollo' may not have been rolled out exactly as Bibliotheque Design wanted, this scheme has been extremely influential on a whole host of other projects over the last few years.

12 More here: www.theverge.com/2013/5/8/4311868/the-illusion-of-simplicity-photographer-peter-belanger-on-shooting

13 The great post-war modernists of identity design, Paul Rand, Joseph Müller-Brockmann and Armin Hofmann, were the drivers of this approach. But as the market grew, their 'atelier' approach was threatened by the advent of the larger scale 'design consultancy' in the 1960s and 1970s.

14 More here: www.experimentaljetset.nl/archive/whitney-museum-identity

15 See Michael Bierut's, *How to Use Graphic Design to Sell Things, Explain Things, Make Things Look Better, Make People Laugh, Make People Cry, and (Every Once in a While) Change the World* for more on this.

16 There's a great book, *Willisau and All That Jazz*, by Niklaus Troxler and Olivier Senn that tracks this work in great detail.

17 For more: http://www.eyemagazine.com/feature/article/burger-fries-no-logo

18 Sam Taylor-Wood said she 'wanted to create an updated version of the famous Elgin marble frieze, replacing the Greek gods with cultural figures.'

19 It's true. You wouldn't believe how often, three years in, an internal team starts to change stuff, usually because of sheer boredom. This is human nature, of course, but dangerous to any long-running brand idea.

Step 5

1 Usually defined in four stages: launch, growth, maturity, decline.

2 This matches increasingly with people's desire to be more 'open' and 'agile' about the branding process.

3 Technically aired twice, once at the 1984 Superbowl, and once on 31 December 1983 in Southern Idaho (!) purely to qualify for 1983 advertising awards.

4 These were produced by Miguel Chevalier and Nicolas Gaudelet/Voxels Productions as part of the launch conception and production work carried out by Artichoke, Helen Marriage and Bill Gee.

5 There's more on this approach in Joe Barrell's book, *Make it Matter: Creating Communications Strategies in the Non-Profit Sector.*

6 *Creativity, Inc.: Overcoming the Unseen Forces That Stand in the Way of True Inspiration* by Ed Catmull is highly recommended for more on the Pixar process.

7 The Dracula/politician joke was an oblique and slightly time-locked reference to Tory politician Michael Howard, of whom Ann Widdecombe once said, 'there is something of the night about him'.

8 I'm grateful to Dan Germain, Innocent's creative director, from whom most of the insights on this page directly came.

9 As you might expect really: much as graphic designers would love to dominate posters with their logos, every time, it just isn't practical.

10 Thanks to Jane Wentworth for explaining this scheme in detail to me.

11 gizmodo.com/5485809/the-sony-timeline-birth-rise-and-decadence

12 Sony sold its Vaio PC business in 2014 to Japan Industrial Partners.

13 This is a fairly damning write-up: www.laweekly.com/news/is-myspace-destined-to-fail-again-4623363

14 This is how the Adidas blog deals with this: blog.adidas-group.com/2011/08/sport-history-jesse-owens/

15 From the Run DMC album 'Raising Hell' in 1986.

16 When you look hard you can see that Adidas is pretty protective of its three stripes – so much so that it even keeps knocking back attempts to register 'two stripe' shoes: www.williamfry.com/newsandinsights/news-article/2016/03/11/cjeu-issues-decision-in-adidas-three-stripe-case

17 'Expect More. Pay Less' was unveiled in 1994.

18 There's a great Target timeline here: /corporate.target.com/about/history/Target-through-the-years

19 www.michellebateman.com/work/Emporium_Kiehls.pdf

20 Jean-Noël Kapferer introduced the Brand Identity Prism in his book, *Strategic Brand Management,* which is highly recommended reading. The version of Kiehl's prism used here is as advised directly to us by Kiehl's themselves.

21 What's remarkable is that VCCP has managed the advertising throughout these multiple changes of view. This is testament to the power of a long-term relationship.

22 There's a very watchable film about this here: vimeo.com/162500360. Over 30,000 people registered to give blood in 10 days.

23 Here are just a few Virgin ideas that didn't really make it: Virgin Student (a sort of proto-facebook), Virgin Brides, Virgin Vie (cosmetics), Virgin Clothing, Virgin Cars, Virginware (lingerie), Virgin Megastore (from 1992 to 2009), Virgin Flowers, Virgin Pulse, Virgin Digital, Virgin Express and Virgin Charter. What very few people know is that Virgin Group is like venture capitalists: it supports an idea, shares the risk and 'lends' the brand for three years – and if it doesn't work, they're out.

24 As in 13th in the direct insurance market. There can't have been many more players than that in the entire market at the time.

25 KPI's, as they are known, could have been an entire chapter on their own. Essentially, they are the performance criteria that are deemed to be key at a project's inception and will change drastically from market sector to market sector.

BIBLIOGRAPHY

Aaker, David A. *Brand Leadership: Building Assets in the Information Society.* Simon & Schuster UK, 2009 and Free Press, New York, 2000

Aaker, David A. *Building Strong Brands.* Simon & Schuster UK, 2010 and Free Press, New York, 1996

Adams, Sean, Noreen Morioka and Terry Stone. *Logo Design Workbook.* Rockport Publishers Inc., Gloucester, Mass.; new edition, 2006

Adams, Sean. *Masters of Design: Logos & Identity: A Collection of the Most Inspiring LOGO Designers in the World (Masters of Design).* Rockport Publishers Inc., Gloucester, Mass., 2008

Atkin, Douglas. *The Culting of Brands: Turn Your Customers into True Believers.* Portfolio, New York; 4th revised edition, 2005

Barrell, Joe. *Make it Matter: Creating Communications Strategies in the Non-Profit Sector.* CharityComms, London; 1st edition, 2014

Bedbury, Scott, and Stephen Fenichell. *A New Brand World: Eight Principles for Achieving Brand Leadership in the Twenty-First Century.* Penguin, Harmondsworth and Viking, New York, 2003

Bernsen, Jens. *Design, the Problem Comes First.* Danish Design Council, Copenhagen; 3rd English/French edition, 1986

Bierut, Michael. *How to Use Graphic Design to Sell Things, Explain Things, Make Things Look Better, Make People Laugh, Make People Cry, and (Every Once in a While) Change the World.* Thames & Hudson, London and Harper Design, New York, 2015

Bierut, Michael, William Drenttel and Steven Heller. *Looking Closer: Critical Writings on Graphic Design.* Allworth Press, New York, 1994

Bierut, Michael. *Seventy-nine Short Essays on Design.* Princeton Architectural Press, New York; reprint, 2012

Boyd, Linzi. *Brand Famous: How to Get Everyone Talking About Your Business.* Capstone, Hoboken; 1st edition, 2014

British Design + Art Direction. Jeremy Myerson and Graham Vickers, *Rewind: Forty Years of Design & Advertising.* Phaidon Press, London; 1st edition, 2002

Brown, Tim. *Change by Design: How Design Thinking Transforms Organizations and Inspires Innovation.* HarperBusiness, New York, 2009

Buckminster Fuller, R., Joachim Krausse and Claude Lichtenstein. *Your Private Sky: The Art of Design Science.* Lars Müller Publishers, Baden, 1999

Catmull, Ed. *Creativity, Inc.: Overcoming the Unseen Forces That Stand in the Way of True Inspiration.* Random House, New York, 2014

Chermayeff, Ivan, Tom Geismar and Steff Geissbuhler. *Designing.* Graphis, New York, 2003

Chermayeff, Ivan, Tom Geismar and Steff Geissbuhler. *TM: Trademarks: Designed by Chermayeff and Geismar.* Lars Müller Publishers, Baden and Princeton Architectural Press, New York; 1st edition, 2000

Chipchase, Jan, and Simon Steinhardt. *Hidden in Plain Sight: How to Create Extraordinary Products for Tomorrow's Customers.* HarperBusiness, New York, 2013

Conley, Lucas. *OBD: Obsessive Branding Disorder: The Illusion of Business and the Business of Illusion.* PublicAffairs, New York, July 2009

Danchev, Alex. *100 Artists' Manifestos: From the Futurists to the Stuckists (Penguin Modern Classics).* Penguin, Harmondsworth, 2011

Della Femina, Jerry. *From Those Wonderful Folks Who Gave You Pearl Harbour: Front-line Dispatches from the Advertising War.* Canongate Books, Edinburgh, 2010

Erikson, Peer, and Henri Holmgren. *The Classic Avis Advertising Campaign of the 60s.* Dakini Books, London, 1995

Erler, Johannes. *Hello, I am Erik: Erik Spiekermann: Typographer, Designer, Entrepreneur.* Die Gestalten Verlag, Berlin; 1st edition, 2014

Evamy, Michael. *Logo: The Reference Guide to Symbols and Logotypes.* Laurence King, London; min edition, 2015

Evamy, Michael. *Logotype.* Laurence King, London, 2012

Fletcher, Alan. *The Art of Looking Sideways.* Phaidon Press, London; 1st edition, 2001

Fletcher, Alan, David Gibbs and Jeremy Myerson. *Beware Wet Paint: Designs by Alan Fletcher.* Phaidon Press, London; new edition, 2004

Gallo, Carmine. *Talk Like TED: The 9 Public Speaking Secrets of the World's Top Minds.* Macmillan, London, 2014

Gibbs, David. *The Compendium, Pentagram.* Phaidon Press, London, 1993

Gill, Bob. *Forget All the Rules You Ever Learned About Graphic Design, including the Ones in this Book.* Watson-Guptill Publications, New York, 1983

Gladwell, Malcolm. *Blink: The Power of Thinking Without Thinking.* Penguin, Harmondsworth; reprint, 2006

Gladwell, Malcolm. *Outliers: The Story of Success.* Penguin, Harmondsworth and Little Brown, New York, 2009

Gladwell, Malcolm. *The Tipping Point: How Little Things Can Make a Big Difference.* Abacus, London; new edition, 2002

Gobe, Marc. *Emotional Branding.* Allworth Press, New York; updated and revised edition, 2010

Godin, Seth. *All Marketers Are Liars: The Underground Classic that Explains How Marketing Really Works – And Why Authenticity is the Best Marketing of All.* Portfolio, New York; reprint, 2012

Hall, Peter, and Michael Bierut. *Tibor Kalman: Perverse Optimist* Hardcover. Booth-Clibborn Editions, London; 1st edition, 2002

Hara, Kenya. *Designing Design.* Lars Müller Publishers, Baden; 4th edition, 2015

Harvard Business Review. *HBR's 10 Must Reads on Strategy.* Harvard Business School Press, Boston, Mass., 2011

Heding, Tilde, Charlotte F. Knudtzen and Mogens Bjerre. *Brand Management: Research, Theory and Practice.* Routledge, London; 2nd edition, 2015

Hegarty, John. *Hegarty on Advertising: Turning Intelligence into Magic.* Thames & Hudson, London and New York, 2011

Heller, Steven. *100 Ideas that Changed Graphic Design.* Laurence King, London; 1st edition, 2012

Heller, Steven. *Paul Rand.* Phaidon Press, London; new edition, 2000

Hobsbawm, Eric. *The Invention of Tradition.* Canto Classics, Cambridge University Press, 2012

Holt, D. B. *How Brands Become Icons: The Principles of Cultural Branding.* Harvard Business Review Press, Boston, Mass., 2004

Horberry, Roger, and Gyles Lingwood. *Read Me: 10 Lessons for Writing Great Copy.* Laurence King, London; 1st edition, 2014

Hyland, Angus, and Steven Bateman. *Symbol.* Laurence King, London; 1st edition, 2011

Ingledew, John. *The A–Z of Visual Ideas: How to Solve any Creative Brief.* Laurence King, London, 2011

Ingledew, John. *How to Have Great Ideas: A Guide to Creative Thinking.* Laurence King, London; 1st edition, 2016

Isaacson, Walter. *Steve Jobs: The Exclusive Biography.* Abacus, London, 2015

Johnson, Michael. *Problem Solved: A Primer in Design, Branding and Communication.* Phaidon Press, London, 2012

Johnson, Steven. *Where Good Ideas Come From: The Seven Patterns of Innovation.* Penguin, Harmondsworth, 2011

Jones, Robert. *The Big Idea. Why Every Company Needs One.* Profile Books, London, 2011

Kahney, Leander. *Jony Ive: The Genius Behind Apple's Greatest Products.* Portfolio, London, 2014

Kapferer, Jean-Noël. *The New Strategic Brand Management: Advanced Insights and Strategic Thinking (New Strategic Brand Management: Creating & Sustaining Brand Equity).* Kogan Page, London and Philadelphia; 5th edition, 2012

Klein, Naomi. *No Logo.* Fourth Estate, London; 10th anniversary edition, 2010

Kotler, Philip, and Kevin Lane. *Marketing Management.* Pearson, Harlow, 2015

Lichtenstein, Claude, and Alfredo Haberli, Museum of Design Zurich. *Air Made Visible: A Visual Reader on Bruno Munari.* Lars Müller Publishers, Baden, 2001

Lois, George, and Bill Pits. *The Art of Advertising.* Harry N. Abrams, Inc., New York, 1977

Lovell, Sophie, and Jonathan Ive. *Dieter Rams: As Little Design As Possible.* Phaidon Press, London; 1st edition, 2011

Mau, Bruce. *Massive Change: A Manifesto for the Future Global Design Culture*. Phaidon Press, London, 2004

McAlhone, Beryl, David Stuart, Greg Quinton and Nick Asbury. *A Smile in the Mind: Witty Thinking in Graphic Design*. Revised and expanded edition. Phaidon Press, London, 2016

Meggs, Philip B., and Alston W. Purvis. *Meggs' History of Graphic Design*. John Wiley & Sons, London; 4th edition, 2006

Millman, Debbie. *Brand Thinking and Other Noble Pursuits*. Allworth Press, New York, 2011

Mollerup, Per. *The Corporate Design Programme*. Danish Design Council. 1987

Mollerup, Per. *Godt nok er ikke nok: Betragtninger om offentlig design / Good Enough is not Enough: Observations on Public Design*. Danish Design Council, 1992

Mollerup, Per. *Marks of Excellence: The History and Taxonomy of Trademarks*. Phaidon Press, London, 1997

Müller-Brockmann, Josef. *The Graphic Artist and his Design Problems*. Niggli Verlag, Zurich; 3rd edition, 2003

Munari, Bruno. *Design as Art (Penguin Modern Classics)*. Penguin, Harmondsworth, 2008

Neumeier, Marty. *The Brand Flip: Why Customers Now Run Companies and How to Profit from It*. New Riders, Berkeley, California; 1st edition, 2015

Neumeier, Marty. *The Brand Gap: How to Bridge the Distance Between Business Strategy and Design*. New Riders, Berkeley, California; 2nd edition, 2005

Neumeier, Marty. *The Designful Company: How to Build a Culture of Nonstop Innovation*. New Riders, Berkeley, California; 1st edition, 2008

Neumeier, Marty. *Zag: The Number One Strategy of High-performance Brands*. New Riders, Berkeley, California; 1st edition, 2006

Norman, Donald A. *The Design of Everyday Things*. MIT Press; 2nd revised and expanded edition, 2013

Novogratz, Jacqueline. *The Blue Sweater: Bridging the Gap Between Rich and Poor in an Interconnected World*. Rodale Books, Pennsylvania; reprint, 2010

Ogilvy, David. *Ogilvy on Advertising*. Prion Books, London, 2007

Olins, Wally. *The Brand Handbook*. Thames & Hudson, London and New York, 2008

Olins, Wally. *Brand New: The Shape of Brands to Come*. Thames & Hudson, London and New York, 2014

Olins, Wally. *Corporate Identity: Making Business Strategy Visible Through Design*. Thames & Hudson, London and New York, 1994

Olins, Wally. *The Corporate Personality: An Inquiry into the Nature of Corporate Identity*. Mayflower Books, London, 1978

Olins, Wally. *On B®and*. Thames & Hudson, London and New York, 2004

Olins, Wally. *The Wolff Olins Guide to Corporate Identity*. Design Council; new edition, 1990

Poynor, Rick. *Design Without Boundaries: Visual Communication in Transition*. Booth-Clibborn Editions, London, 2002

Poynor, Rick. *No More Rules: Graphic Design and Postmodernism*. Laurence King, London; 1st edition, 2003

Poynor, Rick. *Obey the Giant: Life in the Image World*. Birkhäuser GmbH, Basel; 2nd edition, 2007

Purcell, Kerry William. *Josef Müller-Brockmann*. Phaidon Press, London; 1st edition, 2006

Rand, Paul. *Thoughts on Design*. Chronicle Books, San Francisco; reissued edition, 2014

Ries, Al. *Positioning: The Battle for Your Mind*. McGraw-Hill Education, London and New York; 2nd edition, 2001

Roberts, Kevin. *Lovemarks: The Future Beyond Brands*. powerHouse Books, New York; revised edition, 2006

Ruder, Emil. *Typography: A Manual of Design: A Textbook of Design*. Niggli Verlag, Zurich; 4th edition, 2009

Sagmeister, Stefan. *Sagmeister: Made You Look*. Harry N. Abrams, Inc., New York; annotated edition, 2009

Sagmeister, Stefan. *Things I Have Learned in My Life So Far*. Harry N. Abrams, Inc., New York; 2008

Scher, Paula. *Make it Bigger*. Princeton Architectural Press; 1st paperback edition, 2005

Shaughnessy, Adrian. *How to be a Graphic Designer, Without Losing Your Soul*. Laurence King, London and Princeton Architectural Press, New York, 2010

Shaughnessy, Adrian. *Lubalin*. Unit Editions, London, 2012

Sinclair, Mark. *TM: The Untold Stories Behind 29 Classic Logos*. Laurence King, London; 1st edition, 2014

Sinek, Simon. *Start with Why: How Great Leaders Inspire Everyone to Take Action*. Penguin, Harmondsworth and Portfolio, New York, 2011

Slade-Brooking, Catharine. *Creating a Brand Identity: A Guide for Designers*. Laurence King, London; 1st edition, 2016

Smith, Anthony D. *National Identity*. University of Nevada Press; new edition, 1993

Steel, Jon. *Truth, Lies and Advertising: The Art of Account Planning*. John Wiley & Sons, Chichester and New York; 1st edition, 1998

Stone, Adam N. *Unbrandable. How to Succeed in The New Brand Space*. Thames & Hudson, London and New York, 2015

Sudjic, Deyan. *B is for Bauhaus: An A-Z of the Modern World*. Penguin, Harmondsworth, 2015

Thompson, Philip, and Peter Davenport. *The Dictionary of Visual Language*. Penguin, Harmondsworth, 1982

Troxler, Nicholas, Oliver Senn and John Zorn. *Willisau and All That Jazz: A Visual History 1966–2013*. Till Schaap Edition, Bern, 2014

Van der Velden, Daniel. *Uncorporate Identity*. Lars Müller Publishers, Baden, 2009

Victore, James, and Michael Bierut. *Victore or, Who Died and Left You Boss?* Harry N. Abrams, Inc., New York; 1st edition, 2010

Vignelli, Massimo. *Design*. Rizzoli International Publications, New York; reprint, 1990

Vit, Armin, and Bryony Gomez-Palacio. *Graphic Design Referenced: A Visual Guide to the Language, Applications, and History of Graphic Design*. Rockport Publishers Inc., Gloucester, Mass.; 2012

Walters, John L. *Fifty Typefaces that Changed the World: Design Museum Fifty*. Conran Octopus, London; 1st edition, 2013

Weingart, Wolfgang. *Weingart: Typography: Wege zur Typografie: My Way to Typography*. Lars Müller Publishers, Baden; bilingual edition, 2014

Wheeler, Alina. *Designing Brand Identity: An Essential Guide for the Whole Branding Team*. John Wiley & Sons, London; 4th edition, 2012

Wolfe, Tom. *From Bauhaus to Our House*. Picador USA; reprint, 2009

INDEX

FURTHER CREDITS

Every effort has been made to contact the copyright holders of the projects and images within this book. If there are omissions these can be fixed in future editions.

First published in 2016 in hardcover in the United States of America by Thames & Hudson Inc., 500 Fifth Avenue, New York, New York 10110

thamesandhudsonusa.com

Library of Congress Catalog Card Number
2016931255

ISBN 978-0-500-51896-0

Printed and bound in India by Replika Press Pvt. Ltd.

Acknowledgments

At one level, this book should fill a simple gap: there are very few books that truly cover the entire branding process from start to finish.

Yet the book's gestation was far from simple: I worked on the synopsis for at least a year before sharing it with anyone. And that certain someone was Jamie Camplin, whom I met at Wally Olins' memorial service in the autumn of 2014. As we bemoaned the sad loss of the branding world's pre-eminent thinker, I had no idea that Jamie was his publisher. Eventually the conversation turned to books and I admitted that I was grappling with a synopsis. Jamie graciously offered to read it.

Two years, and a lot of hard thinking later, here we are. *Now* I know why there are so few books that attempt to look at the entire process – it's pretty tough to cover coherently in 300-odd pages. Even though johnson banks' focus has been branding for much of the last 15 years, and even though I've been running branding workshops for much of that time, distilling this down still hasn't been easy.

I'm indebted to a whole team of individuals who have helped. Years ago, a colleague suggested the first thing to do when starting a book was to 'find a good researcher' and I've been very lucky – I've had several. First of all, Emily Penny, a brand consultant in her own right, agreed to do some key early research that fed directly into the initial drafts (and then returned as a reader to supply some incisive feedback). Tilda Ruck provided some invaluable help in the summer of 2015, followed by Clare King, who came to work with us for a few weeks and stayed for months. Lizzie Schoon has been key to an image research task so labyrinthine we could almost write another book about just that. Image research then morphed into editing and collecting credits – she's worn several hats throughout this process and has excelled in all of them.

At Thames & Hudson, Andrew Sanigar and Ilona de Nemethy Sanigar and their team have expertly guided the book through production. At johnson banks, I'm indebted to Kat Heaton for taking on some very specific permissions and research, Julia Woollams for finding time to chip in, Leanne Bentley for her stoic favicon research, Esther Shelley and Rhys George for their research and photos, Tom Hutton for his car drawings and, of course, Kath Tudball for taking my chaotic files and turning them into a viable book design that seems to have survived all of my attempts to destroy it.

Other contributions were invaluable: Dilys Maltby, Jane Wentworth and Robert Jones kindly lent their time, thoughts and examples to the thinking process and Joe Barrell did likewise. Nick Asbury happily mashed Asian brand names together very nicely. Jane Rankin read the first half and was encouraging at just the right time, Mark Lee bravely read an entire draft and offered detailed critiques at critical stages that went well beyond the call of duty. And a special mention must go to johnson banks' clients over the last two decades: many of the projects we have done together have informed the ideas in this book, and a few dozen have even illustrated it. Without their support on this branding journey, this book would probably never have happened.

Thanks once again to Lizzie, Joe and Molly for putting up with my long hours at the kitchen table, the disappearing to the spare room or that punishing stretch of 5.30 starts. I might wait a bit to start book three.

And as a final dedication, this book is in memory of the man who gave me my first job, introduced me to the branding world, and, indirectly, to his publisher. To Wally.

About the author

Michael Johnson is the founder and creative and strategy director of johnson banks, London.

He trained in marketing and design, worked at Wolff Olins, and then in Sydney, Melbourne and Tokyo, before setting up johnson banks in 1992.

Johnson banks works for NGOs and non-profits, impact investors and philanthropists, cultural and educational institutions, and the occasional blue-chip (as long as they are polite). The work is increasingly international: it began with a re-brand of Parc de la Villette in Paris in the late 1990s, continued with work in Japan, China and the Middle East, and now encompasses projects in North America and across the globe.

The company is known for its synthesis of both the strategic and creative sides of the branding process and has demonstrated this with key projects for clients such as Shelter, Acumen, the Science Museum in London and the University of Cambridge.

Johnson and his company have established an award-winning reputation, receiving seven yellow 'pencils' and one black 'pencil' from D&AD, among many others. Johnson is the author of *Problem Solved: A Primer in Design and Communications* (published by Phaidon) and was initiator, co-curator and contributor to *Rewind*, the 40 years retrospective of D&AD held at the Victoria & Albert Museum in London. He has been cited as one of the most notable British designers by both the *Guardian* and *Independent*, he lectures around the world and has featured in *Design Week*'s 'Hot 50' list of influential figures in design three times.

He lives and works in South London and dreams of being a better husband, a better dad, *and* a better guitar player.